my revision notes

WJEC EDUQAS GCSE (9–1)

HISTORY

R. Paul Evans
Rob Quinn

HODDER
EDUCATION
AN HACHETTE UK COMPANY

The Publishers would like to thank the following for permission to reproduce copyright material.

Photo credits

p.3 © Photo12/UIG via Getty Images, **p.13** © Photo12/UIG via Getty Images, **p.21** © Chronicle / Alamy Stock Photo, **p.48** © Heritage Image Partnership Ltd / Alamy Stock Photo, **p.52** © Solo Syndication/Associated Newspapers Ltd (British Cartoon Archive, University of Kent), **p.68** © ullsteinbild / TopFoto, **p.122** © World History Archive / Alamy Stock Photo, **p.123** *t* © Granger Historical Picture Archive / Alamy Stock Photo, **p.123** *b* © Pictorial Press Ltd / Alamy Stock Photo, **p.140** *t* © The Art Archive / Alamy Stock Photo, **p.140** *b* © Davies/Keystone/Hulton Archive/Getty Images, **p.141** © Media Minds / Alamy Stock Photo, **p.144** © Wellcome Images (available under Creative Commons Attribution only licence CC BY 4.0)

Although every effort has been made to ensure that website addresses are correct at time of going to press, Hodder Education cannot be held responsible for the content of any website mentioned in this book. It is sometimes possible to find a relocated web page by typing in the address of the home page for a website in the URL window of your browser.

Hachette UK's policy is to use papers that are natural, renewable and recyclable products and made from wood grown in sustainable forests. The logging and manufacturing processes are expected to conform to the environmental regulations of the country of origin.

Orders: please contact Bookpoint Ltd, 130 Park Drive, Milton Park, Abingdon, Oxon OX14 4SE. Telephone: (44) 01235 827720. Fax: (44) 01235 400401. Email education@bookpoint.co.uk Lines are open from 9 a.m. to 5 p.m., Monday to Saturday, with a 24-hour message answering service. You can also order through our website: www.hoddereducation.co.uk.

ISBN: 9781510403826

First published in 2018 by
Hodder Education,
An Hachette UK Company
Carmelite House
50 Victoria Embankment
London EC4Y 0DZ

www.hoddereducation.co.uk

Impression number   10 9 8 7 6 5 4 3 2

Year   2022 2021 2020 2019 2018

Cover photo © The Trustees of the British Museum. All rights reserved.

Typeset by Integra Software Services, Pvt, Ltd, Pondicherrry, India

Printed in India

A catalogue record for this title is available from the British Library.

Get the most from this book

This book will help you revise for the WJEC Eduqas GCSE History specification, which can be downloaded from the WJEC Eduqas website www.eduqas.co.uk/qualifications/history/.

This book covers the following options:

Component 1: Studies in depth

- British study in depth: 1B The Elizabethan Age, 1558–1603
- Non-British study in depth: 1G Germany in transition, 1919–1939

Component 2: Studies in breadth

- Period Study: 2A The Development of the USA, 1929–2000

- Thematic Study: 2E Changes in crime and punishment in Britain, c.500 to the present day
- Thematic Study: 2F Changes in health and medicine in Britain, c.500 to the present day

You can use the revision planner on pages 4 and 5 to plan your revision, topic by topic. Tick each box when you have:

1 revised and understood a topic
2 answered the exam practice questions
3 checked your answers online.

You can also keep track of your revision by ticking off each topic heading throughout the book. Be a scribbler, make notes as you learn. You will need an exercise book for most of the revision tasks, but you can also write in this book.

Tick to track your progress

Key terms

Key terms are highlighted the first time they appear, with an explanation nearby in the margin.

Exam practice

Sample exam questions are provided for each topic. Use them to consolidate your revision and practise your exam skills.

Revision tasks

Use these tasks to make sure that you have understood every topic and to help you think about what you are revising. If you do the tasks you will have to use the information in the book. If you use the information you will remember it better. The more you use it the better you will remember it.

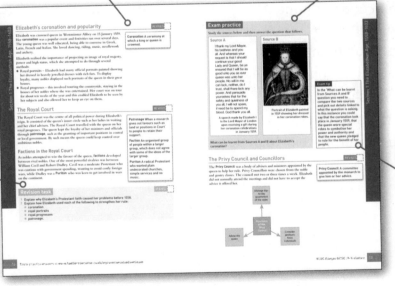

Exam tips

Throughout the book there are tips that explain how you can boost your final grade.

My revision planner

Section 4 Changes in crime and punishment

Section 5 Changes in health and medicine

REVISED

Introduction

How to revise

There is no single way to revise, but here are some good ideas.

1 Make a revision timetable

For a subject like history, which involves learning large amounts of factual detail, it is essential that you construct a revision plan.

- Start early – you should start by looking at the dates of your exams and work backwards to the first date you intend to start revising, probably six to eight weeks before your exam.
- Be realistic – work out a realistic revision plan to complete your revision; don't try to do too much. Remember that you have to fit in your history revision alongside your other GCSE subjects. Plan to include breaks to give yourself a rest.

- Revise regularly – regular, short spells of 40 minutes are better than panicky six-hour slogs until 2 a.m.
- Plan your time carefully – give more revision time to topic areas you find difficult and spend longer on the sections you feel less confident about.
- Track your progress – keep to your timetable and use the revision planner on pages 4 and 5 to tick off each topic as you complete it. Give yourself targets and reward yourself when you have achieved them.

2 Revise actively

Different people revise in different ways and you will have to find the methods which best suit your learning style. Here are some techniques which students have used to help them revise:

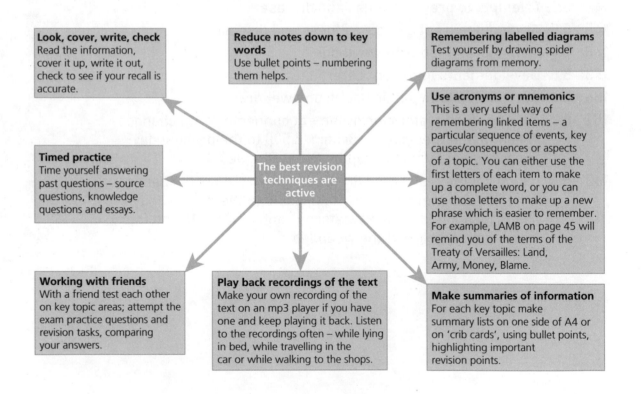

Look, cover, write, check
Read the information, cover it up, write it out, check to see if your recall is accurate.

Reduce notes down to key words
Use bullet points – numbering them helps.

Remembering labelled diagrams
Test yourself by drawing spider diagrams from memory.

Use acronyms or mnemonics
This is a very useful way of remembering linked items – a particular sequence of events, key causes/consequences or aspects of a topic. You can either use the first letters of each item to make up a complete word, or you can use those letters to make up a new phrase which is easier to remember. For example, LAMB on page 45 will remind you of the terms of the Treaty of Versailles: Land, Army, Money, Blame.

Timed practice
Time yourself answering past questions – source questions, knowledge questions and essays.

The best revision techniques are active

Working with friends
With a friend test each other on key topic areas; attempt the exam practice questions and revision tasks, comparing your answers.

Play back recordings of the text
Make your own recording of the text on an mp3 player if you have one and keep playing it back. Listen to the recordings often – while lying in bed, while travelling in the car or while walking to the shops.

Make summaries of information
For each key topic make summary lists on one side of A4 or on 'crib cards', using bullet points, highlighting important revision points.

How to prepare for the exam

1 Decode the exam question – look for the 'command' words

To perform well in the exam, you will have to answer the questions correctly. The key to success is understanding what the question is asking – look for the key command words which will tell you the type of answer you should write.

Common command words and what they mean

Command word	What it means
Explain	Provide a number of reasons, showing how or why each contributed to the event named in the question.
Describe Outline	Provide specific factual detail upon the key issue named in the question.
How important ...? How successful ...? How far ...? To what extent ...?	Provide a judgement about the importance of a named event/person supported by reasons, explanations and evidence.
Do the interpretations support the view that ...? Which of the sources is more useful to a historian studying ...?	Provide a judgement about how useful or accurate historical sources and interpretations are for historians.

2 Look at how the mark schemes work

All your answers on the exam paper will be marked by using a level of response mark scheme. In the low tariff questions (4–6 marks) there will normally be two levels, for the medium tariff questions (8–10 marks) there will be three levels and for the higher tariff questions (11–16 marks) there will be four levels. The more detailed, informed and well-reasoned your answer is, the higher up the level of responses you will advance.

A typical level of response mark scheme will look like this:

Band 1: Generalised points, not fully focused upon the topic area being examined; the general points will not be supported by accurate or relevant factual details or examples.

Answers at this level will be very simplistic and contain little factual support.

Band 2: A number of relevant points with some focus upon the question; these points will be supported by accurate factual detail, although the range might be narrow or some points might not be fully developed.

Answers will display good focus, will be supported with relevant detail and demonstrate an argument which goes some way to answering the question.

Band 3: A range of relevant points which clearly address the question and show understanding of the most important factors involved; a clear explanation which is well structured and supported by detailed and accurate factual information.

Answers at this level will be thorough and detailed; they will clearly engage with the question and provide a balanced and reasoned argument that reaches a well-supported judgement.

Band 4: A full range of relevant points that clearly focus on the thrust of the question with a clear and balanced judgement supported by detailed, accurate and fully relevant factual information.

Answers at this level will fully answer the question supported by detailed factual information which is put into the correct historical context.

Guide to the WJEC Eduqas GCSE History examination

About the course

REVISED

You are required to study two components. Each component has a weighting of 50 per cent towards your final GCSE grade.

Component 1: Studies in depth focusing on the evaluation of historical sources and interpretations.

This is in two parts and consists of:
- A British depth study (1B The Elizabethan Age, 1558–1603)
- A non-British depth study (1G Germany in transition 1919–1939)

Component 2: Studies in breadth focusing on assessing continuity, change, cause, consequence, significance, similarity and difference.

This is in two parts and consists of:
- A period study (2A The development of the USA, 1929–2000)
- A thematic study, which includes the study of a historical site (2E Changes in crime and punishment in Britain, c.500 to the present day, OR 2F Changes in health and medicine in Britain, c.500 to the present day)

Components 1 and 2 are assessed through two written examinations (Component 1 being two hours, made up of one hour per study, and Component 2 being two hours, made up of 45 minutes for the period study and 1 hour 15 minutes for the thematic study).

Component 1

This examination tests your knowledge and understanding through the analysis and evaluation of historical sources and interpretations. You will have to answer all of the questions in these examinations.

British study in depth

Time allowed: 1 hour

Question 1 is worth 4 marks and asks you to say what can be learnt from Sources A and B.

1 What can be learnt from Sources A and B about…?

- You will need to put several points for Source A, linking them to the question.
- Repeat this for Source B.
- You should aim to write equal amounts from both sources.

Question 2 is worth 8 marks and asks you to analyse and evaluate the accuracy of the source.

2 To what extent does this source accurately reflect…?
- You need to test the source's accuracy against your knowledge.
- Consider:
  - who wrote it
  - when it was written
  - why was it written
  - how this affects the accuracy of the source.
- Make a judgement about the accuracy of the source.

Question 3 is worth 12 marks and asks you to provide a well-supported explanation of the significance of the identified issue or individual.

3 Why was [name/issue] significant…?
- You will need to show what the background situation to this was.
- Include specific details to show why this was significant.
- Finish with a well-supported judgement about the significance of this.

Question 4 is worth 10 marks and asks you to identify and explain the connections between two features of a historical topic.

4 Explain the connections between TWO of the following…
- Clearly identify the connections between the two features you have chosen.
- Explain these connections using detail historical knowledge of the topic.

Question 5 is worth 16 marks and asks you to reach a substantiated judgement about the accuracy of the interpretation.

5 How far do you agree with this interpretation of...?
- You will need to outline the view in the interpretation and link it to your knowledge.
- Consider what the attribution tells us about how and why the author formed the interpretation.
- Suggest why other historians might have different views.
- Make a judgement on why there are different interpretations of this issue.

Non-British study in depth

Time allowed: 1 hour

Question 1 is worth 5 marks and asks you to use the source and your own knowledge to describe a historical issue.

1 Use Source A and your own knowledge to describe...
- Describe what you can see or read in the source.
- Link this information to your knowledge of this subject.
- Aim to make at least two developed points.

Question 2 is worth 8 marks and asks you to analyse and evaluate the purpose of the source in order to reach a substantiated judgement.

2 What was the purpose of Source B?
- You need to use your knowledge of this period of time to describe the message of this source.
- Use the details of the caption/attribution of the source to explain who the source was aimed at and why it would give this particular message at this particular time.

Question 3 is worth 10 marks and asks you to reach a substantiated judgement about the extent to which the interpretations support a particular view.

3 Do the interpretations support the view that...?
- Describe the message of Interpretation 1.
- Does the message of the interpretation support or contradict the main focus of the question?
- Use the interpretation attribution to consider why the interpretation was produced.
- Repeat for Interpretation 2.
- Give your judgement on how much the interpretations support the view in the question, considering why they support or differ from this view.

Question 4 is worth 11 marks and asks you to analyse and evaluate the relative usefulness of the source material to a historian studying the issue.

4 Which of the sources is more useful to a historian studying... ?
- For each source consider:
  ○ what the source tells you about the topic
  ○ who said it
  ○ why was the source produced
  ○ how the source fits into what was happening at that time.
- Remember to give a judgement on which source is the most useful and why.

Question 5 is worth 16 marks and asks you to reach a substantiated judgement about the extent to which you agree with the interpretation.

5 To what extent do you agree with this interpretation?
- Use your knowledge to build up a case to support the interpretation.
- Suggest other interpretations and use your knowledge to build up a case for them.
- Conclude with a judgement on how far you agree with the interpretation.
- Check your spelling, punctuation and grammar for accuracy.

Component 2

This examination tests your knowledge and understanding of continuity, change, cause, consequence, significance, similarity and difference. You will have to answer all the questions on these examinations.

Period study

Time allowed: 45 minutes

Question 1 is worth 5 marks and asks you to describe a historical issue.

1 Describe...
- Include specific factual detail such as dates, events or names of key people.
- Aim to write at least three key features/points.

Question 2 is worth 6 marks and asks you to give a well-supported judgement on how much change there has been.

2 How far did... change... between... and...?
- Identify important changes in the topic across the period of time in the question.
- Use specific factual details to back up the points you make.
- End with a concluding sentence which shows how far you think there was change in this topic.

Question 3 is worth 9 marks and asks you to give a well-supported explanation about the relative importance of three developments.

3 Arrange the developments in order of their significance to... Explain your choices.
- Choose three factors and put them in order of their importance in your judgement.
- Explain the importance of each factor using detailed knowledge to support your points.

Question 4 is worth 8 marks and asks you to provide a focused and well-supported explanation.

4 Explain why...
- You need to give several reasons to explain this event.
- Each reason needs to be supported with relevant factual specific detail.

Question 5 is worth 12 marks and asks you to analyse and evaluate the importance of one issue compared to others.

5 How important was...?
- Explain the importance of the factor named in the question.
- You need to support your argument with specific factual detail.
- Consider the importance or significance of other factors as well.
- Finish with a well-supported judgement whether or not the factor in the question was the most important factor.

Thematic study

Time allowed: 1 hour 15 minutes

Question 1 is worth 4 marks and asks you to identify one similarity and one difference between the sources.

1 Use Sources A, B and C to identify one similarity and one difference in...
- Pick out a similarity between the sources.
- Pick out a difference between the sources.

Question 2 is worth 6 marks and asks you to evaluate the relative reliability of two historical sources to a historian studying a particular issue.

2 Which of the two sources is the more reliable to a historian studying...?
- Use your knowledge to decide how accurate you think the content of Source D is.
- Repeat this for Source E.
- Finish with a clear judgement about which of the two sources you think is the most reliable and why.

Question 3 is worth 5 marks and asks you to describe a historical issue.

3 Describe...
- Include specific factual detail such as dates, events or names of key people.
- Aim to write at least three key features/points.

Question 4 is worth 9 marks and asks you to give a focused and well-supported explanation of an issue.

4 Explain why...
- You need to give several reasons to explain this event.
- Each reason needs to be supported with relevant factual detail.

Question 5 is worth 16 marks (plus 4 marks for spelling punctuation and grammar) and asks you to write an extended piece of writing about an issue, covering the three historical eras.

5 Outline how... changed from c.500 to the present day.
- Describe the main changes in this topic using specific factual details.
- Cover all three historical time periods – medieval, early modern and modern.
- Finish your paragraph on each time period with a judgement about how much change there had been.
- Check your spelling, punctuation and grammar for accuracy.

Question 6a is worth 8 marks and asks you to describe two features of a historic site.

6 a Describe two main features of...
- You need to describe two key features using specific details.

Question 6b is worth 12 marks and asks you to provide a well-supported explanation of the way in which the historic site demonstrates continuity or change over time.

b Explain why the environment of... was significant in showing changes in...
- Identify a number of reasons which illustrate change/improvement.
- Consider each reason using specific factual detail, explaining how and why the environment studied brought about such changes.
- Finish with a judgement that clearly answers the question.

Section 1 The Elizabethan Age, 1558–1603

1 Elizabethan government

Key question

How successful was the government of Elizabeth I?

Elizabeth's path to power

REVISED

The Tudor monarchs ruled England and Wales from 1485 to 1603.
Elizabeth was the fifth and the last of the Tudor rulers.

- The Tudor dynasty comprised:
  - Henry VII (1485–1509)
  - Henry VIII (1509–1547)
  - Edward VI (1547–1553)
  - Mary I (1553–1558)
  - Elizabeth I (1558–1603).
- Elizabeth's father was Henry VIII who married six times:
  - by his first wife, Catherine of Aragon, he had a daughter – Mary
  - by his second wife, Anne Boleyn, he had a daughter – Elizabeth
  - by his third wife, Jane Seymour, he had a son – Edward.
- In 1527, Henry VIII fell in love with a noblewoman, Anne Boleyn. To marry her once she became pregnant, Henry had to obtain a divorce from Catherine. The **Pope** refused this request, causing Henry to break away from the **Roman Catholic Church** and create a new Church of England with himself as head.
- In 1533, Anne gave birth to Elizabeth, who was brought up in the **Protestant** faith of her mother. In 1536, Anne was accused of having an affair and was executed and Elizabeth, aged just 2, was declared illegitimate.
- When Henry died in 1547 he was succeeded by his 9-year-old son who became King Edward VI. He was brought up by Protestant advisers who also attempted to make the Church of England more Protestant.
- In 1553, Edward died at the age of 15. He was succeeded by his elder sister Mary, a strict Roman Catholic. She undid the Protestant reforms and made the Catholic religion the new faith of the land. Protestants who refused to change faith were put to death by being burnt at the stake.
- Mary's reign was a difficult time for Elizabeth, especially after she was accused of being involved in the Wyatt Rebellion (a Protestant plot), for which she was arrested and imprisoned in the Tower of London. It was only Mary's death in 1558 that saved Elizabeth.
- On 17 November 1558, Elizabeth became queen of England and Wales at the age of 25.

> **Pope** The head of the Roman Catholic Church.
>
> **Roman Catholic Church** The Christian church headed by the Pope.
>
> **Protestant** Member of Christian church which separated from the Roman Catholic Church in the sixteenth Century.

Elizabeth's coronation and popularity

Elizabeth was crowned queen in Westminster Abbey on 15 January 1559. Her **coronation** was a popular event and festivities ran over several days. The young queen was well educated, being able to converse in Greek, Latin, French and Italian. She loved dancing, riding, music, needlework and archery.

> **Coronation** A ceremony at which a king or queen is crowned.

Elizabeth realised the importance of projecting an image of royal majesty, power and high status, which she attempted to do through several methods:

- Royal portraits – Elizabeth had many official portraits painted showing her dressed in heavily jewelled dresses with rich furs. To display loyalty, many nobles displayed such portraits of the queen in their great houses.
- Royal progresses – this involved touring the countryside, staying in the houses of her nobles where she was entertained. Her court was on tour for about ten weeks of the year and this enabled Elizabeth to be seen by her subjects and also allowed her to keep an eye on them.

The Royal Court

The Royal Court was the centre of all political power during Elizabeth's reign. It consisted of the queen's inner circle such as her ladies in waiting and her chief advisers. The Royal Court travelled with the queen on her royal progresses. The queen kept the loyalty of her ministers and officials through **patronage**, such as the granting of important positions in central or local government. By such means the queen could keep control over ambitious nobles.

> **Patronage** When a monarch gives out favours such as land or positions in Court to people to retain their support.
>
> **Faction** An organised group of people within a larger group, which does not agree with some of the ideas of the larger group.
>
> **Puritan** A radical Protestant who wanted plain undecorated churches, simple services and no music.

Factions in the Royal Court

As nobles attempted to win the favour of the queen, **factions** developed between rival nobles. One of the most powerful rivalries was between William Cecil and Robert Dudley. Cecil was a moderate Protestant who was cautious with government spending, wanting to avoid costly foreign wars, while Dudley was a **Puritan** who was keen to get involved in wars on the continent.

Revision task

1 Explain why Elizabeth's Protestant faith caused her problems before 1558.
2 Explain how Elizabeth used each of the following to strengthen her rule:
   - coronation
   - royal portraits
   - royal progresses
   - patronage.

Exam practice

Study the sources below and then answer the question that follows.

Source A

I thank my Lord Mayor, his brethren and you all. And whereas your request is that I should continue your good Lady and Queen, be ye ensured that I will be as good unto you as ever queen was unto her people. No will in me can lack, neither, do I trust, shall there lack any power. And persuade yourselves that for the safety and quietness of you all, I will not spare, if need be to spend my blood. God thank you all.

A speech made by Elizabeth I to the Lord Mayor of London upon receiving a gift during her coronation celebrations in January 1559.

Source B

Portrait of Elizabeth painted in 1559 showing her dressed in her coronation robes.

What can be learnt from Sources A and B about Elizabeth's coronation?

Exam tip

In the 'What can be learnt from Sources A and B' question you need to compare the two sources and pick out details linked to what the question is asking. In this instance you could say that the coronation took place in January 1559, that the queen wore special robes to symbolise her power and authority and that the new queen pledged to rule for the benefit of her people.

The Privy Council and Councillors

REVISED

The **Privy Council** was a body of advisers and ministers appointed by the queen to help her rule. Privy Councillors were chosen from the noble and gentry classes. The council met two or three times a week. Elizabeth did not normally attend the meetings and did not have to accept the advice it offered her.

Privy Council A committee appointed by the monarch to give him or her advice.

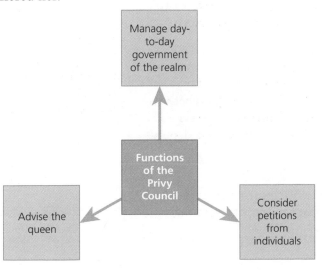

Manage day-to-day government of the realm

Functions of the Privy Council

Advise the queen

Consider petitions from individuals

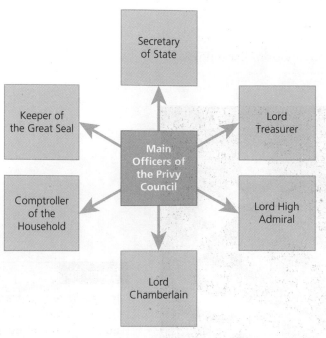

Important Privy Councillors

- Sir William Cecil (created Lord Burghley in 1571) – served as Secretary of State and later Lord Treasurer; was adviser to Elizabeth for over 40 years.
- Robert Dudley (created Earl of Leicester in 1564) – his close friendship with Elizabeth gave rise to rumours of an affair between them; in 1585 he was made commander of the army sent to the Netherlands.
- Sir Christopher Hatton – responsible for organising the queen's progresses, and in 1587 became Lord Chancellor.
- Sir Francis Walsingham – he headed Elizabeth's secret service, controlling a network of spies in an effort to uncover plots against the queen.
- Robert Devereux (Earl of Essex) – put in charge of organising attacks on Spain and Ireland; he was executed in 1601 for his involvement in a plot against some of the queen's councillors.
- Robert Cecil – son of William Cecil, he took over Walsingham's duties after his death in 1591.

> **Revision task**
>
> 1 Describe the main function of the Privy Council and its councillors.
>
> TESTED ☐

Local government

REVISED ☐

Elizabeth came to rely upon a trusted body of officials to ensure that her rule was respected and that law and order was maintained across the country.

The Lord Lieutenant

Operating as the chief officer at the local level, this post was held by a wealthy noble landowner. They kept the queen informed about what was happening in their area, they controlled the local militia and supervised the **Justices of the Peace (JP)**. They were sometimes helped by a deputy.

> **Justice of the Peace (JP)**
> An official appointed by the government to keep law and order and try minor court cases.

The sheriff

Each county had a sheriff who was concerned with legal affairs such as appointing juries, delivering prisoners to court and supervising the collecting of taxes.

Exam practice answers at **www.hoddereducation.co.uk/myrevisionnotesdownloads**

Justice of the Peace

JPs numbered between 30 and 60 in each county and were wealthy gentlemen. They became the chief officer responsible for ensuring that law and order was maintained at the local level. Their tasks included:
- sitting as a magistrate in the Quarter Session courts
- organising the parish constable
- fixing prices and wages, checking weights and measures
- giving out licences to enable the poor to beg
- administering the Poor Law
- overseeing the maintenance of the highways.

Parish constable

This unpaid post was held by tradesmen or husbandsmen (farmers) for one year. They were expected to carry out a range of tasks under the close supervision of the JP.
- General policing duties such as keeping an eye on taverns/inns; watching out for **vagabonds**.
- Administering punishments such as placing criminals in the stocks or pillory.
- In towns they also served as night watchmen, patrolling the streets looking out for wrongdoers.

Overseer of the Poor Rate

They organised and collected the Poor Rate (local tax) and distributed the money to those most in need.

Without this body of unpaid officers, local government would not have been able to operate effectively.

The role of Parliament

Parliament only met when the queen called it and closed down when she commanded it to. Elizabeth called just ten parliaments and for 26 years of her reign there were no parliamentary sessions.

Parliament was made up of two bodies:
- House of Lords – a non-elected body of about 100 lords, bishops and judges.
- House of Commons – made up of about 450 MPs elected by wealthy landowners. There were two MPs from each county and two from each important town within the county.

Elizabeth called Parliament only when she needed to, usually because:
- she needed money and only Parliament had the power to raise money through taxes
- she needed to pass an Act of Parliament
- she desired support and advice from her MPs on important issues.

Vagabond A homeless unemployed person.

Revision task

1 Explain how each of the following officers helped to maintain law and order:
- Lord Lieutenant
- Justice of the Peace
- Parish Constable.

TESTED ☐

REVISED ☐

Freedom of speech

REVISED

The queen appointed the speaker of the House of Commons and decided what topics were to be debated. In theory MPs had freedom to discuss whatever they wanted, but in practice the queen made it clear that some topics such as her possible marriage were not to be discussed.

Taxation and finance

REVISED

- Tudor monarchs were expected to use their own finances, raised from rents and customs duties, to pay the costs of running the country.
- On occasions, when they ran short of money, monarchs had to ask Parliament to grant funds from taxes.
- Elizabeth's reign was a time of high **inflation**, causing prices to rise. The queen also had to pay for costly foreign wars against Spain. This meant she needed more money.
- Chief Minister William Cecil began a programme of cutting costs but Parliament still had to be recalled periodically to release funds.
- Local taxes rose sharply to help pay for increased **poor relief**.

> **Inflation** An increase of a wide range of prices and services.
>
> **Poor relief** Action taken by the government, the church or private individuals to help the poor.

Conclusion: How successful was the government of Elizabeth I?

REVISED

- Elizabeth was a strong monarch which resulted in strong government, especially during the 1570s and 1580s.
- Her strong, forceful and volatile character helped her to keep her powerful nobles under control.
- Elizabeth was served by an able body of Privy Councillors.
- Central government – the queen used the power of patronage to ensure loyalty and efficient service.
- Local government – this worked well under the management of a body of unpaid amateur officers such as the lord lieutenant, JPs, parish constables, overseers of the poor.

> **Revision task**
>
> 1 Describe the role and function of Parliament.
> 2 Explain why Elizabeth was sometimes forced to ask Parliament to meet.
>
> TESTED

2 Lifestyles of the rich and poor

> **Key question**
>
> How did life differ for the rich and poor in Elizabethan times?

Contrasting lifestyles of the rich and poor

REVISED

Elizabethan society was based upon a very structured class system that kept everybody in their place. There was an enormous difference in the standards of living among those groups at the top of the social order and those at the bottom.

Exam practice answers at **www.hoddereducation.co.uk/myrevisionnotesdownloads**

The monarch – Queen Elizabeth I

Nobles and Lords – great landowners (about 50 families) with an income of up to £6,000 per year

Gentry – lesser landowners (about 10,000 families) with an income of up to £200 per year

Wealthy merchants – successful in the business of buying and selling goods (about 30,000 families)
Professionals – the emerging middle class; e.g. lawyers, physicians, apothecaries, clergy, schoolmasters

Yeomen – owned their own property, had a few servants, and farmed some land
Tenant farmers – they rented between 10 and 30 acres from a landowner (about 100,000 families)

Cottagers – had small gardens to farm and also carried out some small-scale industry in the home such as spinning
Skilled artisans – men with a trade; craftsmen

Landless unskilled labourers – seasonal workers; unemployed during certain times of the year
The poor and unemployed

The social structure in Elizabethan England and Wales

Between 20 per cent and 30 per cent of the population lived on the edge of starvation – bad harvests, rising prices and changes in employment often helped to tip people into poverty.

Lifestyle of the rich

REVISED

During Elizabeth's reign, many of the rich landowning class increased their wealth through various means, including:
- agricultural change and the adoption of profitable sheep farming rather than labour-intensive cultivation of the land
- exploitation of the mineral resources on their estate such as the mining of coal, lead or iron ore
- advantageous marriages.

Homes

This was the age of the 'Great rebuilding' when many rich landowners used their increased wealth to build new homes which they filled with the latest fashions in furniture and fittings.
- The old medieval style defensive dwellings designed for defence were replaced with Elizabethan mansions.
- Houses were symmetrical in design, often in the shape of the letter E or H.
- They included large glass windows, brick or stone walls, large fireplaces and chimney stacks, finely plastered ceilings and wood panelled walls on which to hang fine tapestries.
- Many houses had a long gallery lined on one side with a wall of large windows; this gallery was used for recreation and socialising and for

the display of family portraits/tapestries. The family and servant wings were now separate; the house had a series of rooms such at the parlour (sitting room) and bedrooms.

- Noted Elizabethan houses include Burghley House, Lincolnshire (built by William Cecil); Longleat House, Wiltshire (built by Sir John Thynne); Hardwick Hall, Derbyshire (built by Elizabeth or 'Bess' Hardwick).

Fashion

An Elizabethan noblemen and his lady wife wore the latest fashions made out of the finest materials (silk, linen, velvet) and laden with fine jewels.

Education

The sons of nobles were home tutored in the classics and languages (French, Latin and Greek). Daughters of nobles were taught how to run a large house and its staff.

Household

The wife of a nobleman supervised the day-to-day running of the household.

Lifestyle of the gentry

REVISED

The gentry attempted to copy the lifestyle of the nobles, though not on such a grand scale.

Homes

The gentry modernised and re-fashioned their homes. They built new houses made of stone, brick or half-timbered. Such houses had fireplaces, brick-built chimneys, panelled or plastered walls and large windows.

Fashion

The gentry generally wore modern, stylish outfits, but without the expense of fine threads and jewels seen in noble clothes.

Education

The sons of gentry often attended grammar schools and some went to university in Oxford or Cambridge. After university some began careers as lawyers, clerics or entered royal service.

Lifestyle of the lower classes

REVISED

The lower classes led very different lives to those of their social superiors.

Homes

The lower classes lived in much smaller homes. Their cottages were little more than one room, sometimes shared with animals, with an earth floor, timber-framed walls with **wattle and daub** infill and a thatched roof.

> **Wattle and daub** The infill between timber beams in the wall of a house, formed from a mesh of poles and twigs woven together and coated with a layer of clay or plaster.

Fashion

Owing to poverty, the lower classes possessed few changes of clothes. These were usually made of rough twilled cloth.

Exam practice answers at **www.hoddereducation.co.uk/myrevisionnotesdownloads**

Education and leisure

They received very little, if any, education. They had little time to socialise but when they did so, they often went to the local inn where they sometimes watched and gambled upon cock fighting or bear baiting.

Revision task

1 Use your knowledge of this section to complete the following table which compares the lifestyles of the rich and poor during Elizabeth's reign.

	Description of type of house	Fashion	Education
Rich Nobles			
The Gentry			
The Lower Classes			

2 Explain what the 'Great rebuilding' phase was during Elizabeth's reign.

Poverty in Elizabethan times

Tudor governments classified the poor into two categories:
- impotent poor – those genuinely unable to work and in need of poor relief
- able-bodied poor – those capable of work but who were either unable or unwilling to find employment.

Causes of poverty

There was a sharp rise in poverty during Elizabethan times. This was due to a number of reasons.

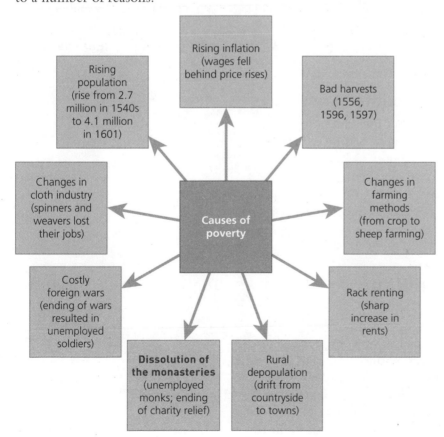

Rising inflation (wages fell behind price rises)

Rising population (rise from 2.7 million in 1540s to 4.1 million in 1601)

Bad harvests (1556, 1596, 1597)

Changes in cloth industry (spinners and weavers lost their jobs)

Causes of poverty

Changes in farming methods (from crop to sheep farming)

Costly foreign wars (ending of wars resulted in unemployed soldiers)

Rack renting (sharp increase in rents)

Dissolution of the monasteries (unemployed monks; ending of charity relief)

Rural depopulation (drift from countryside to towns)

Dissolution of the monasteries The official closure of all monasteries between 1536 and 1539 on the order of Henry VIII.

The issue of unemployment and vagrancy

The increase in wandering homeless 'sturdy beggars' was seen as a threat to society. They were blamed for an increase in crime. In 1566, Thomas Harman wrote a book, *A Caveat or Warning for Common Cursitors, vulgarly called Vagabonds*, in which he named the different types of vagabonds according to the method they used to seek out a living.

- Hooker or Angler – used a hooked stick to reach through windows to steal clothes or valuables.
- Clapper dudgeon – tied arsenic to their skin to attract sympathy when begging.
- Doxy – female vagabond who stole items and hid them in her bag.
- Abraham man – pretended to be mad to attract sympathy and charity.
- Ruffler – ex-soldiers who stole and threatened.
- Drumerer – pretended to be dumb in order to beg for charity.
- Counterfeit crank – sucked soap to foam at the mouth and pretended to have epilepsy.

Government legislation

During Elizabeth's reign a number of Acts were passed to deal with the increasing problem of poverty:

Year	Act	Key features of the Act
1563	Statute of Artificers	Compulsory seven-year apprenticeship
1572	Vagrancy Act	Severe punishments for vagrants; local people had to pay a poor rate
1576	Act for Relief of the Poor	Houses of Correction to be built in each county
1598	Act for Relief of the Poor	Overseers appointed to supervise issue of poor relief
1598	Act for Punishment of Rogues	Houses of Correction to be set up for rogues and vagabonds; begging was forbidden
1601	Act for Relief of the Poor	Set up a legal framework to tackle poverty – the Elizabethan Poor Law

How successful were the Elizabethan Poor Laws?

Elizabeth's Poor Laws did not end poverty but they did introduce a system to manage poor relief. Overall the impact was mixed.

- Laws did help many people in need of support.
- Helped to reduce threat of rebellion and social unrest.
- Government now began to take action to look after the poor.
- System of poor relief established by Elizabeth's government remained for over 200 years.
- But poverty continued to rise.

Conclusion: How did life differ for rich and poor in Elizabethan times?

- Noble and gentry classes experienced considerable improvements in their lifestyles – built fashionable houses, with rich interior decoration, fine tapestries, portraits and furniture, landscaped gardens.
- Lifestyle of lower classes changed little – due to inflation many struggled to make ends meet; changes in agriculture from crop farming to sheep farming caused unemployment and migration of labourers to the towns.

- Sharp increase in number of wandering beggars some of whom turned to crime; government responded by building houses of correction and issuing poor relief.

Revision task

TESTED

1 Identify and explain FOUR main causes of poverty during Elizabethan times.
2 Describe the crimes each of the following vagabonds specialised in:
   - The Angler
   - Clapper dudgeon
   - Doxy
   - Counterfeit crank.
3 Explain how each of the following Acts of Parliament helped to deal with the problem of vagrancy:
   - The Vagrancy Act, 1572
   - Act for the Relief of the Poor, 1576
   - Act for the Punishment of Rogues, 1598.

Exam practice

Study the sources below and then answer the question that follows.

Source A

A sixteenth century illustration showing a vagabond being whipped.

Exam tip

In the 'What can be learnt from Sources A and B' question you need to compare the two sources and pick out details linked to what the question is asking. In this instance you could say that those accused of being a vagabond were given a physical punishment. This usually involved being whipped in public but it could also include having a hot iron burnt through the right ear. Such punishments were meant to be cruel to deter people from begging.

Source B

Where all the parts of the realm of England and Wales be presently exceedingly pestered with rogues, vagabonds and sturdy beggars, by means whereof daily happeneth horrible murders, thefts and other outrages, be it enacted that all persons above the age of fourteen years, being rogues, vagabonds or sturdy beggars, shall be grievously whipped and burnt through the gristle of the right ear with a hot iron.

A section from the Vagabonds Act of 1572

What can be learnt from Sources A and B about the treatment of vagabonds during Elizabeth's reign?

3 Popular entertainment

Key question

What were the most popular types of entertainment in Elizabethan times?

The importance of popular entertainment

REVISED

For many, the only time for relaxation was a Sunday, the day of worship, together with the few days of religious festival and special days such as May Day, New Year and Shrove Tuesday. Entertainment was important during Elizabethan times and took many forms.

Cruel sports

A popular pastime enjoyed by all sections of society was the watching of blood sports.

● Bear and bull-baiting – bears were chained to a wooden stake and attacked by dogs, the spectators betting how long the dogs would survive. The 'Bear Garden' arena in Southwark, London, could accommodate 1,000 people. Bulls were tied by the horns and set upon by dogs, the audience betting on the outcome.
● Cockfighting – this took place in cockfighting pits, the spectators betting on which of a pair of birds would win the fight.

Entertainment enjoyed by the rich

The rich had the wealth and leisure time to allow them to engage in a number of pastimes.

● Hunting – many wealthy nobles had their own deer parks allowing them to hunt.
● Hawking – the use of a trained falcon or hawk for hunting was a popular pastime.
● Archery – this was popular throughout the Tudor period.
● Dancing, music and singing – wealthy nobles employed musicians to entertain them with music and singing; they were able to dance to popular dances such as the Volta.
● Ball games – tennis became popular during Elizabeth's reign, as did bowls and skittles. Football was popular among the lower classes, but the wealthy also played (often on horseback).

Revision task

1 Describe the main types of cruel sports popular during Elizabeth's reign.
2 How did the rich entertain themselves during Elizabethan times?

TESTED

The development of the Elizabethan theatre

REVISED

The English theatre developed during Elizabeth's reign, passing through several developmental stages.

Bands of strolling players

During the reigns of the early Tudor monarchs, wandering bands of players (actors) toured the countryside, performing in towns or village squares on portable stages. They were a popular form of entertainment, especially among the lower classes.

Exam practice answers at **www.hoddereducation.co.uk/myrevisionnotesdownloads**

Formation of theatre companies

Fearing possible civil disobedience following the performance of plays which could encourage ideas of rebellion and disobedience, a law of 1572 banned strolling players from touring the country unless they had a licence to enable them to perform. This led to the formation of the first theatre companies:

- Earl of Leicester's players, formed in 1574
- The Queen's Men, formed in 1583
- Lord Admiral Howard's Company, formed in 1583
- Lord Chamberlain's Men, formed in 1594.

Building of the first theatres

A number of theatres had opened in the Shoreditch area of London by the end of Elizabeth's reign:

- 1576 The Theatre – the first purpose-built theatre in London since Roman times, financed by James Burbage
- 1577 The Curtain
- 1587 The Rose
- 1596 The Swan
- 1599 The Globe.

The theatres quickly proved to be a popular form of entertainment, attracting large audiences.

Design of the theatre

Copying the design of earlier bear and bull baiting pits, the first theatres were round or octagonal in shape, with staged seating surrounding an open central and raised stage. It was timber-framed building with lime-washed walls and a straw roof. There was only a limited amount of scenery.

Plays were performed in the afternoons, during daylight hours. A flag was flown or a cannon sounded to announce the starting time. Prices were low to encourage all social classes to attend.

The actors

All parts were played by men, each actor taking on a number of roles. Some of the most popular actors included:

- Richard Burbage – son of James Burbage; often played a tragic actor; went on to co-own The Globe theatre
- Edward Alleyn – tragic actor who played the leading role in many of Marlowe's plays; went on to co-own The Fortune theatre
- Will Kempe – comic actor; played leading roles in Shakespeare's comedies
- Thomas Pope – best known as a comic actor and acrobat.

Playwrights

Elizabeth's reign witnessed the 'Golden Age' of English drama, owing to the writings of a number of important playwrights.

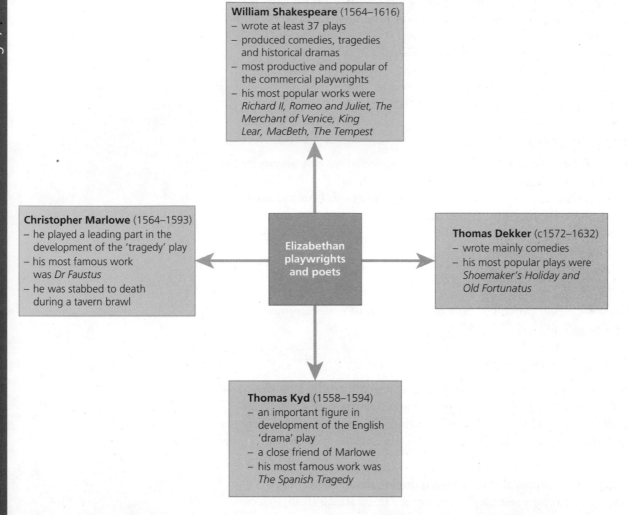

William Shakespeare (1564–1616)
- wrote at least 37 plays
- produced comedies, tragedies and historical dramas
- most productive and popular of the commercial playwrights
- his most popular works were *Richard II, Romeo and Juliet, The Merchant of Venice, King Lear, MacBeth, The Tempest*

Christopher Marlowe (1564–1593)
- he played a leading part in the development of the 'tragedy' play
- his most famous work was *Dr Faustus*
- he was stabbed to death during a tavern brawl

Elizabethan playwrights and poets

Thomas Dekker (c1572–1632)
- wrote mainly comedies
- his most popular plays were *Shoemaker's Holiday* and *Old Fortunatus*

Thomas Kyd (1558–1594)
- an important figure in development of the English 'drama' play
- a close friend of Marlowe
- his most famous work was *The Spanish Tragedy*

Revision task

TESTED ☐

Construct your own mind map using the heading 'The Golden Age of the Theatre'. You need to make sure you mention the changes from strolling players to the building of theatres, celebrated actors, noted playwrights and the popularity of the theatre.

Exam practice

Explain the connections between **TWO** of the following that are to do with the development of the Elizabethan theatre:
- Theatre companies
- Will Kempe, actor
- The Globe theatre
- William Shakespeare, playwright.

Exam tip

In the 'Explain the connections' question you need to select two out of the four choices and use your knowledge of this topic area to identify links between them. In this instance all four choices are connected to the Elizabethan theatre. One connection could be that the actor performed a lead role in the plays written by the playwright, or that such plays were performed in the new theatres such as The Globe in London.

Attitudes towards the theatre

REVISED

Elizabethan society became bitterly divided in its attitude towards the theatre.

Support for the theatre

- Popular form of cheap entertainment, attracting large audiences.
- Playwrights produced plays with gripping storylines and colourful characters.
- Plays served to deliver the message that obedience and loyalty to the monarch was essential to ensure that law and order was maintained.

Opposition to the theatre

- The authorities saw the theatre and its large audiences as a threat to law and order, arguing that it encouraged the gathering of beggars, pickpockets and other petty criminals in one place.
- Religious groups, especially the Puritans, believed the theatre to be the work of the devil, encouraging people to be sinful. They believed the plays lacked decency and morals, encouraging a sinful lifestyle.

Conclusion: What were the most popular types of entertainment in Elizabethan times?

REVISED

- Entertainment was important in the lives of people of all classes during Elizabethan times.
- Sports such as bear and bull-baiting, cockfighting and gambling were popular pastimes.
- Richer folk enjoyed hunting, hawking, archery and dancing as popular pastimes.
- The theatre developed during Elizabeth's reign, resulting in the building of new theatres in London and other large towns.
- Theatre companies developed, the crowds wishing to see their favourite actors perform.
- Playwrights supplied the theatre with a steady stream of new plays covering comedies, tragedies and historical drama.
- Opinions towards the new theatre were split – those who welcomed and enjoyed the new theatre productions and those who bitterly opposed such developments, often on religious grounds (the Puritans).

Revision task

1 What were the main arguments (a) in support of, and (b) against, the growth of the theatre during Elizabethan times?
2 What information would you put forward to support the argument that entertainment played an important role in the lives of Elizabethans?

TESTED

4 The problem of religion

Key question

How successfully did Elizabeth deal with the problem of religion?

Religious problems in 1559

REVISED

A major problem facing the new queen upon her accession was issue of religion. The previous three reigns had seen a succession of changes in religious focus:

- Henry VIII – he replaced the Pope as head of the Church in England and Wales; he introduced an English Bible but he did not change church services; many people turned Protestant during his reign.

- Edward VI – he was influenced by Protestant advisers (the Duke of Somerset and the Duke of Northumberland); his reign saw the introduction of a new Protestant **Prayer Book** and **Communion** service; church services were now in English not Latin; decorations and images were torn down; priests were allowed to marry.
- Mary I – she restored the Pope as head of the church; restored Latin Mass and Catholic doctrines; priests had to be single; persecuted Protestants.

> **Prayer Book** A book containing prayers used in church services.
>
> **Communion** Religious service which involved the offering of bread and wine to the congregation.

Differing attitudes towards Elizabeth in 1559 `REVISED`

Catholic view

Catholics viewed Elizabeth as being illegitimate and therefore she had no right to be queen; many Catholic rulers of Europe saw Mary Stuart, Queen of Scotland, as the rightful ruler of England and Wales; Catholic extremists wanted to get rid of Elizabeth as their monarch.

Protestant view

Radical Protestants known as Puritans posed a possible threat to Elizabeth; they wanted to wipe out all traces of the Catholic faith.

Reaching a compromise

Elizabeth faced the difficult task of attempting to satisfy contrasting religious groups, each of whom had a view on how the church should be run.

Catholic beliefs	Protestant beliefs	Extreme Protestant (Puritan) beliefs
- Pope is head of church - Cardinals, archbishops, bishops help run the church - Church services and Bible to be in Latin - Churches should be highly decorated - Priests must not marry - When bread and wine is given during Mass a miracle takes place and it becomes the actual body and blood of Christ	- Monarch is head of church - Archbishops and bishops help run the church - Church services and Bible to be in English - Little decoration in churches - Priests should be able to marry - Bread and wine given during Holy Communion remains bread and wine but were also the body and blood of Jesus	- Should be no head of church - No bishops - Churchgoers should elect committees to run their church - No decoration in churches - Bread and wine remained bread and wine during Communion, as Jesus was spiritually but not physically present during the service

Revision task `TESTED`

Explain how Catholics, Protestants and Puritans differed in their views on each of the following religious issues:

a head of the church
b organisation of the church
c decoration within the church
d attitudes towards communion service.

Aims of the religious settlement

Elizabeth had to proceed carefully, attempting to reach a compromise that would satisfy the different rival religious groups.

Factors to consider:
- France – Mary Stuart, Elizabeth's cousin, was married to King Francis II of France; France might press the claim for Mary to become queen of England.
- Spain – King Philip II of Spain had been the husband of Mary I and he did not want to see France and Scotland gaining influence over England.
- Scotland – the country was ruled by a French regent, Mary of Guise, who was the Catholic widow of King James V and the mother of Mary, Queen of Scots; many of the Scottish nobles were firm Protestants and disliked her rule.
- The Pope – if he chose to **excommunicate** Elizabeth this would free her subjects to rebel against her rule.
- Lords and MPs – most of Elizabeth's MPs in the House of Commons were Protestants but many of the Lords in the House of Lords were Catholics.
- Protestant exiles – many returned exiles had become influenced by the Puritan ideas of John Calvin and hoped that Elizabeth's settlement would reflect these views.

> **Excommunicate** To expel from the Roman Catholic Church and denying the individual the right to enter heaven.
>
> **Vestments** The official clothes worn by church clergy.

Elizabeth's own religious beliefs

- She had received a Protestant upbringing, being influenced by her chaplain and tutor Matthew Parker (who later became her Archbishop of Canterbury).
- Her life had been put at risk during Mary's reign due to her Protestant beliefs and she had spent time under house arrest and in confinement in the Tower of London.
- She was a moderate Protestant and was in favour of certain aspects of the Catholic faith – priests should wear **vestments**, she liked ornaments and decorations in churches such as candles; she opposed the idea that bishops and clergymen should be allowed to marry.

The 'middle way'

Elizabeth wanted to avoid the strict religious policy adopted during the reigns of Edward and Mary. She wanted a church which displayed tolerance and one which belonged to everyone. In an attempt to achieve this she adopted a '**via media**' (middle way) – a church which reflected both Protestant and Catholic attitudes.

> **Via media** The 'middle way' between Catholicism and Protestantism.

- Protestantism was to be the official religion.
- The settlement introduced a new Prayer Book, a Bible in English, simpler churches and allowed priests to marry.
- She refused to give way to extreme Protestant beliefs.
- She kept some aspects of the Catholic faith – the church kept its archbishops, bishops and cathedrals; priests could wear vestments; it kept crosses and candles.
- She fined Catholics for not attending church, rather than persecuting them.

Acts of Supremacy and Uniformity

REVISED

Two important Acts of Parliament were passed in 1559 which together formed the Elizabethan Church Settlement, making England and Wales a Protestant country again.

- Act of Supremacy – established the monarch's authority over the church.
- Act of Uniformity – this spelled out the form of service which was to be followed.

Act of Supremacy, 1559	Act of Uniformity, 1559
• Elizabeth, not the Pope, is head of the church • She had the title 'Supreme Governor of the Church of England' • All important officials in all levels of government had to swear an oath of loyalty; those who refused could be fined or imprisoned • Bishops were to help run the church • A church High Commission was set up to check that the religious changes were being followed in the parishes	• Protestant Book of Common Prayer was to be used in all churches • Services to be in English • Compromise on the issue of real presence during Communion service • Ornaments and decorations allowed in churches • Clergy to wear vestments • Everyone to attend service on a Sunday and holy days • **Recusants** were to pay a fine for non-attendance

Revision task

TESTED

1 Give THREE reasons why Elizabeth felt it necessary to reach a compromise in her religious settlement.
2 Complete the table below to illustrate how the Religious Settlement of 1559 can be seen as a 'middle way'.

Areas of the Settlement which reflect Protestant views	Areas of the Settlement which reflect Catholic views

Measures to enforce the Acts

REVISED

A number of measures were introduced to enforce Elizabeth's religious settlement.

Royal Injunctions, 1559

These were a set of instructions drawn up to ensure uniformity of worship and behaviour. They ordered clergy to:

- condemn Catholic practices and denounce Papal authority (the authority of the Pope)
- report recusants to local JPs
- fine recusants for not attending church services
- obtain a licence to preach from the bishop
- use an English Bible and wear clerical dress
- obtain the permission of the bishop and two JPs to marry.

Visitations

A force of 125 Commissioners was set up to tour the countryside to check that the regulations were being followed and make sure the clergy had taken the **Oath of Supremacy**.

> **Recusant** A person who refused to attend the services of the Church of England.

> **Oath of Supremacy** The oath sworn by priests to say that they accept and will follow the Religious Settlement of 1559 and that they acknowledge Elizabeth as head of the Church of England.

Exam practice answers at **www.hoddereducation.co.uk/myrevisionnotesdownloads**

Act of Exchange, 1559

This allowed Elizabeth to take land and buildings from the church and force bishops to rent land to the monarch. It enabled the queen to exercise royal control over the church.

The episcopacy

The episcope (the bishop) was responsible for the day-to-day running of the church.

Thirty-Nine Articles, 1563

These laid down the beliefs of the Church of England, confirming the key elements of the Protestant belief.

Reactions to the settlement

REVISED

Elizabeth had not intended her settlement to be too strict in the hope that people of all religions would support it.

Reactions at home

By the mid-1560s most people had come to accept the new church:
- the new Archbishop of Canterbury, Matthew Parker, was a moderate Protestant who commanded respect
- only 250 of the 7,000 priests refused to take the Oath of Supremacy
- the majority of devout Catholic bishops resigned and were replaced by Protestants
- fines for recusancy were not strictly enforced
- opposition emerged later in Elizabeth's reign.

Reactions abroad

To begin with the reaction abroad was limited:
- France was drifting towards civil war
- King Philip II of Spain hoped the changes would not be permanent
- the Pope hoped the changes could be overturned with time.

By the 1570s and 1580s, attitudes had hardened; both Spain and the papacy had become actively involved in plots to overthrow Elizabeth and the Protestant faith.

Revision task

1 Create your own spider diagram to show how Elizabeth put measures in place to enforce her Religious Settlement.
2 How much opposition was there (a) at home and (b) abroad to the Religious Settlement?

TESTED

Conclusion: How successfully did Elizabeth deal with the problem of religion?

REVISED

Elizabeth had the difficult task of achieving a settlement between two competing religious faiths – Catholicism and Protestantism.
- To a large extent her 'middle way' proved successful and the Religious Settlement of 1559 was accepted by the majority.
- It brought an end to the period of religious upheaval and persecution of previous reigns.
- However, there was still opposition from the extremes – devout Catholics and radical Protestants, the Puritans.

Exam practice

Study the interpretation below and then answer the question that follows.

> The Settlement of 1559 has been described as a Via Media, that is a middle way, between Catholicism and Protestantism, but it clearly was far from establishing a Catholic Church. It was a Protestant Settlement, but not an extreme one and the 'wolves coming out of Geneva', against whom one of the Catholic bishops had warned Elizabeth, were dissatisfied with some of the content. They expected further revisions in a more Calvinist direction. But Elizabeth had made her Settlement with some difficulties and sacrifices and she had no intention of re-visiting or revising her decisions.
>
> > The view of writers Nicholas Fellows and Mary Dicken who were commissioned to write a school history textbook called *England 1485–1603*, published in 2015.

How far do you agree with this interpretation that the Religious Settlement of 1559 was a Protestant Settlement?

[In your answer you should refer to how and why interpretations of this issue differ. Use your knowledge and understanding of the wider historical debate over this issue to reach a well-supported judgement.]

Exam tip

In the interpretation question you need to demonstrate knowledge and understanding of a key issue by reasoning how and why interpretations can differ. You also need to provide a judgement upon the accuracy of the given interpretation. Consider how the author arrived at their view and the reason why they are writing. Then outline how other authors, with different reasons for writing, might present different interpretations.

5 The Catholic threat

Key question

Why were the Catholics such a serious threat to Elizabeth?

Early toleration

REVISED

During the 1560s, Elizabeth adopted an attitude of toleration towards Catholics and did not vigorously impose her Protestant ideas. However, events of the late 1560s and early 1570s caused her to adopt a harsher policy towards some Catholics.

Recusancy

Recusants posed a direct challenge and in 1581 Elizabeth increased the fines to £20 and made it a treasonable offence to attempt to convert people to Catholicism. She desired to stem the tide of **seminary priests** being smuggled into England and Wales from northern France after 1574.

- In 1568, William Allen set up a training college for Catholic priests at Douai in Flanders.
- Once trained, these new seminary priests were sent to England to re-establish the Catholic faith.
- 438 seminary priests were sent over.
- In 1585, Parliament ordered all such priests to leave the country or be put to death.
- 98 priests were sentenced to death.

Seminary priests Priests trained in Roman Catholic colleges.

Jesuits

Jesuits belonged to the 'Society of Jesus' which had been founded in 1540 with the aim of destroying Protestantism. They began to arrive in England in disguise in 1580. Swearing an oath of loyalty to the Pope, these priests were seen as a threat to national security.

Government response to recusancy

The government passed several acts in an attempt to curb recusancy.

- 1581 – two Acts which (a) increased fines against recusants and (b) made attempts to convert people to the Catholic faith a treasonable offence.
- 1585 – an Act ordered all Jesuit and seminary priests to leave the country or be killed; anybody found hiding a priest could be given a death sentence.
- 1593 – an Act banned large gatherings of Catholics and confined Catholics to a radius of five miles from their home.

Case of Edmund Campion

- Born in London, he crossed to Flanders to train as a seminary priest at Douai.
- He then joined the Jesuits.
- 1580 – he arrived in secret in southern England and preached in the homes of wealthy Catholic families in London.
- 1581 – he was arrested at Lyford, Berkshire and tortured in the Tower of London before being hanged for treason.

The arrival of Mary, Queen of Scots, in England in 1568

REVISED

In May 1568, Mary, Queen of Scots, cousin to Elizabeth I, was forced to flee from Scotland across the border into northern England. She had experienced an eventful past.

Mary sent to France

- Born in 1542, daughter of James V of Scotland and his Catholic French wife, Mary of Guise.
- Her father died when she was a baby and her mother then acted as regent.
- 1548 – at age of 6, Mary was sent to be educated in Catholic France.
- Age of 15 – she married Prince Francis, eldest son of Henry II of France.
- 1559 – Francis became king of France, only to die in 1560.

Mary returns to Scotland

- 1561 – Mary married Henry Stuart, Lord Darnley.
- 1566 – Mary gave birth to a son, the future James VI of Scotland.
- March 1566 – Darnley, believing Mary to be too familiar with her Italian secretary, David Rizzio, stabbed him to death.

> **Jesuit** Member of the Society of Jesus founded in 1540 to support the Pope in the fight against Protestants and to carry out missionary work.

Revision task

Construct a timeline for the period 1560 to 1600. Above the date line, mark on events which show a threat to the Religious Settlement from Catholics, and below the date line the government response to deal with the Catholic threat.

TESTED

Mary and Bothwell

- Mary then became friendly with James Hepburn, Earl of Bothwell.
- In 1567, Darnley became ill with smallpox and Mary brought him to Kirk O'Field, a large house in Edinburgh.
- On night of 9 February 1567, the house was blown up (Mary was at a wedding); Darnley's body was found strangled in the garden.
- Bothwell was accused of the murder but was found not guilty at his trial.
- Mary soon afterwards married Bothwell.
- The Protestant Lords now rebelled against Mary; she was imprisoned in Loch Leven castle.
- July 1567 – she was forced to abdicate in favour of her Protestant son.

Mary arrives in England

In May 1568, Mary escaped and fled across the border into England. Elizabeth had several choices open to her and decided to hold Mary captive. Over the next two decades Mary remained a problem for Elizabeth, becoming the centre of Catholic plots to unset the Protestant queen.

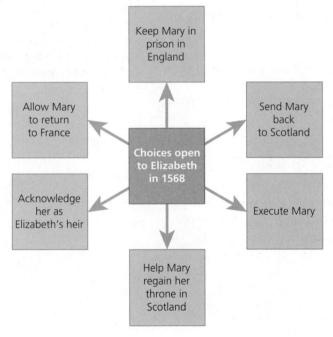

Revision task

Explain how each of the following factors shaped the life of Mary, Queen of Scots:
- France
- Lord Darnley
- Earl of Bothwell
- escape to England.

TESTED

Rebellion of the Northern Earls, 1569

REVISED

This was the first in a series of Catholic plots to replace Elizabeth as queen with Mary.

Causes

- The arrival of Mary in 1568 gave hope to many English Catholics.
- Two powerful Catholic lords, Charles Neville, Earl of Westmoreland and Thomas Percy, Earl of Northumberland, planned to depose Elizabeth and marry Mary to Northumberland's brother-in-law, Thomas Howard, Duke of Norfolk.
- Elizabeth's spies found out about the marriage and Norfolk was sent to the Tower; the other two earls avoided capture and started a rebellion.

Exam practice answers at **www.hoddereducation.co.uk/myrevisionnotesdownloads**

Events

- In November 1569, a force of 4,600 men marched south through Durham to Bramham Moor.
- Plans to besiege York were abandoned and the forces retreated north.
- The two earls fled across the border into Scotland.

Reasons for the failure

- Poor planning and leadership.
- Lack of foreign support.
- Popularity of Elizabeth.

Aftermath

- Northumberland was captured and handed over to Elizabeth, tried for treason and beheaded.
- Westmoreland managed to escape to Flanders where he soon after died in poverty.
- The Duke of Norfolk was released from prison.
- Over 800 rebels, mostly commoners living in the north, were executed.

> **Revision task**
>
> 'The rebellion of the Northern Earls had little chance of ever being successful.'
>
> Use your knowledge of this event to identify evidence to support this statement.
>
> TESTED ☐

Excommunication of Elizabeth, 1570

REVISED ☐

In February 1570, Pope Pius V issued a **Papal Bull** *Regnans in Excelsis* which excommunicated Elizabeth. It called upon all Catholics to remove Elizabeth from the throne and it released them from their oath of allegiance to the crown. It was a serious threat to Elizabeth.

Parliament responded by issuing a new Treason Act in 1571 which:
- made it treasonable to declare that Elizabeth was not the lawful queen
- made it treasonable to publish any Papal Bull
- confiscated the property of Catholics who had fled abroad and did not return within twelve months.

> **Papal Bull** A document containing the Pope's instructions which all Catholics were instructed to obey.

Exam practice

Study the source below and then answer the question that follows.

Source A

Elizabeth ... the pretended queen of England ... having seized on the kingdom, and monstrously usurped the place of Supreme Head of the Church in all England, and the chief authority and jurisdiction thereof, hath again reduced the said kingdom into a miserable and ruinous condition, which was so lately reclaimed to the Catholic faith and a thriving condition [during reign of Mary I] ... declare Elizabeth as being an heretic and favourer of heretics ... to have incurred the sentence of excommunication and to be cut off from the unity of the body of Christ. And moreover we do declare her to be deprived of her pretended title to the kingdom aforesaid and we do command and charge all and every noblemen, subjects, people and others aforesaid, that they presume not to obey her or her orders and laws.

> An extract from the Papal Bull issued by Pope Pius V in February 1570 which excommunicated Elizabeth.

To what extent does this source accurately reflect the threat to Elizabeth posed by the Catholics?

> **Exam tip**
>
> In the 'To what extent' question you need to pass judgement upon the accuracy of what is said in the written source. You need to use your knowledge of this topic area to identify the strengths and weaknesses of the source as a piece of historical evidence. In this instance the source is an official document issued by the Pope and its content is very anti-Elizabeth in its tone, instructing Catholics not to obey the queen. The source is very one-sided but it does help to demonstrate the seriousness of the Catholic threat to Elizabeth.

Catholic plots

The 1570s and 1580s witnessed several Catholic plots to overthrow Elizabeth.

The Ridolfi Plot, 1571

- The plot was organised by Roberto Ridolfi, a Florentine merchant and banker.
- It involved Mary, the Duke of Norfolk, Philip II of Spain, De Spes the Spanish ambassador and the Pope.
- The plan was for a Spanish army to land, help English Catholics overthrow Elizabeth and put Mary on the throne.
- The plot was discovered by William Cecil and Francis Walsingham, who organised the arrests.
- Norfolk was found guilty of treason and sentenced to death; Ridolfi and De Spes were expelled from the country; Elizabeth refused to execute Mary.

Throckmorton Plot, 1583–84

- In 1583, Francis Throckmorton, an English Catholic, organised a plot to overthrow Elizabeth.
- The plan was for French Catholic forces, backed by Spanish and Papal money, to invade England and free Mary from captivity.
- Throckmorton acted as the go-between contacting the various sides.
- The plot was discovered, Throckmorton was arrested, tortured and then executed.
- Mary was moved to Tutbury castle in Staffordshire; she was banned from receiving any visitors and her mail was checked.

Increasing Catholic threat, 1584–85

In 1583, John Summerville, an English Catholic, attempted to assassinate Elizabeth with a pistol. He was sentenced to death but committed suicide in his cell before his execution. In 1584, William of Orange, leader of the Dutch Protestants, was shot dead by a Catholic assassin. Concerned for the queen's safety, Parliament issued the Bond of Association which stated that if Elizabeth was murdered Parliament would ensure the murderers were punished.

In 1585, Spain declared war on England and Philip gave orders for the building of a large invasion fleet – the **Armada**. In response, Parliament ordered all Jesuit and seminary priests to leave the country within 40 days.

The Babington Plot, 1586

- Anthony Babington, a young Catholic nobleman, was at the centre of a plot to overthrow Elizabeth and place Mary on the throne.
- Letters written in code between Babington and Mary were intercepted by Walsingham's spy network.
- In June 1585, Babington wrote to Mary outlining the plan, a plan accepted by Mary.
- In August 1586, Walsingham struck – Babington was arrested and confessed.
- In September 1586, Babington and six other plotters were executed.
- Through the letters, Walsingham now had absolute proof that Mary was involved in the plot.

Revision task

Which of the following Catholic Plots posed the greatest threat to Elizabeth:
- The Ridolfi Plot
- The Throckmorton Plot
- The Babington Plot?

Provide evidence to justify your main choice and say why you thought the other two plots posed a less serious threat.

TESTED

Trial of Mary, Queen of Scots, 1586

After much pressure, Elizabeth agreed to allow Mary to be put on trial for **treason**. The trial took place at Fotheringhay Castle in Northamptonshire in October 1586. Mary was found guilty and sentenced to death, but Elizabeth repeatedly refused to sign her death warrant. It was not until 1 February 1587 that she finally agreed. Mary was executed on 8 February 1587 at Fotheringhay.

Treason Plotting against the monarch or government.

Consequences of the death of Mary

Mary's execution had only a limited impact.
- There were no further Catholic plots during the rest of Elizabeth's reign.
- King James VI of Scotland protested at his mother's death but took no action.
- King Henry III of France did nothing, wanting to keep England friendly against the growing power of Spain.
- King Philip II of Spain was already planning an invasion.

Conclusion: Why were the Catholics such a serious threat to Elizabeth?

REVISED

- Devout Catholics did not accept the Religious Settlement of 1559; they refused to attend Church of England services and were fined. They celebrated Catholic Mass in secret, administered by seminary priests who entered England after 1574. They were later joined by Jesuit priests.
- There were a number of Catholic plots during the 1570s and 1580s which aimed to overthrow Elizabeth, thereby posing a significant threat. Mary posed a threat as she was a central focus of these plots.
- There was fear that these plots might secure foreign support. While this did not happen, Mary's execution did cause Philip II to push ahead with his plans for an Armada.
- However, the majority of Catholics remained loyal to Elizabeth; the propaganda issued by Walsingham and Cecil made the support for such plots appear larger than it actually was.

Revision task

What made Elizabeth finally decide to sign the death warrant to execute Mary, Queen of Scots?

TESTED

6 The Spanish Armada

Key question

How much of a threat was the Spanish Armada?

Reasons for the Spanish Armada

REVISED

As early as 1586, King Philip II of Spain had drawn up plans for an invasion of England. The execution of Mary, Queen of Scots, made Philip even more determined to launch an armada.

Armada Spanish word for a fleet of warships.

Ambitions of King Philip II of Spain

- 1554 – Philip married Mary Tudor; both were devout Catholics.
- 1555 – Philip became king of Spain, the Netherlands and Spanish lands in Italy and America.
- Philip was now ruler of the most powerful and wealthiest empire in the world.
- He was determined to use this power to attack the growth of Protestantism across Europe.

- 1556 – Philip became co-ruler of England with his wife, Mary I.
- 1558 – Mary's death ended Philip's rights to the English throne.
- 1559 – Elizabeth's Religious Settlement, which created a Protestant church, alarmed Philip.
- Philip planned a 'holy crusade' to re-establish the Roman Catholic faith in England; his crusade took the form of an armada.

War in the Netherlands

REVISED

A revolt by Dutch Protestants in August 1566 against Spanish rule had caused relations between England and Spain to become less friendly. Philip sent an army of 10,000 troops to the Netherlands under the command of the Duke of Alba. The rebellion was put down ruthlessly, with over 1,000 rebels being burnt to death. Elizabeth had supplied the Dutch rebels with money and weapons.

In 1575, a second rebellion started which, by 1579, had split the Netherlands into two:
- the southern provinces formed the Union of Arras and made peace with Spain
- the northern provinces, led by William the Silent (William of Orange), formed the Union of Utrecht and rejected Spanish rule.

Philip appointed a new commander, the Duke of Parma, to deal with the rebels. Following the assassination of William the Silent in 1584, Elizabeth signed the Treaty of Nonsuch with the Dutch rebels in 1585. She promised to protect the Dutch Protestants and sent an army of 5,000 troops under the Earl of Leicester to support rebel activity. England and Spain were now in a state of undeclared war.

Actions of English privateers in the Spanish Main

- During the 1570s and 1580s, Elizabeth encouraged English **privateers** or 'sea dogs' to attack Spanish treasure ships in the **Spanish Main**.
- One of the most active and successful of the sea dogs was Francis Drake.
- Between 1577 and 1580, Drake sailed around the world in the *Golden Hind*, during which he attacked Spanish treasure ships and returned to England with gold, silver and jewels worth over £140,000 (£200 million today).
- King Philip ordered that Drake be executed; Elizabeth knighted him in 1581.
- When war with Spain broke out, Drake was sent to the West Indies to disrupt trade routes.

> **Privateer** A privately owned ship commissioned for war service by a government.
>
> **Spanish Main** Those parts of central and southern America ruled by Spain and the seas around them which they controlled.

> **Revision task**
>
> Explain how each of the following factors made war between England and Spain more and more likely from the mid-1580s onwards:
> - events in England after 1558
> - actions of the Dutch Protestants
> - actions of English privateers.
>
> TESTED

Philip's preparation of the Armada

REVISED

To invade England, Philip needed to transport his army in the Netherlands across the English Channel and to do this he began the construction of a large fleet – the Armada.

Philip's plan

- First planned in 1586, Philip ordered the construction of an armada.
- It was to sail north from Lisbon and destroy the English fleet in the Channel, then anchor off Calais.
- It would then protect the Duke of Parma's army of 17,000 soldiers as it crossed the Channel in flat bottomed barges from Dunkirk to Margate on the English coast.
- Parma's army would then march on London and overthrow Elizabeth, turning England Catholic again.

Exam practice answers at **www.hoddereducation.co.uk/myrevisionnotesdownloads**

Drake's attack on Cadiz

- On 20 April 1587, Drake led a group of English warships in an attack on the Spanish fleet which was gathering in Cadiz harbor.
- Drake also destroyed important timber supplies which were to be used for the construction of storage barrels; this later had a serious impact on the Armada's food supplies.
- Drake's attack 'singed the King of Spain's beard' and delayed the Armada for a year.

Changes to the plan

Philip's plan had serious weaknesses:

- Philip ignored the advice of his ministers and military commanders to delay the launch.
- February 1588, the admiral in charge died and Philip replaced him with the Duke of Medina Sidonia; he was reluctant to undertake the task, fearing he was not sufficiently qualified for the job.
- Soon after setting out in April 1588, the Armada ran into a dreadful storm and was forced to seek refuge in Corunna for repairs.

Threat posed by the Armada

The Armada posed a serious threat:

- English land forces were weak and not knowing where the Spanish might land made it difficult to plan where to place the army.
- English soldiers were untrained and poorly equipped compared to Parma's army which was one of the best in Europe.
- The English navy was the country's main line of defence; it was commanded by Lord Charles Howard, Duke of Effingham and his two vice-admirals, Francis Drake and John Hawkins. However, the Spanish fleet was much bigger, consisting of 130 **galleons** and supply ships and 30,000 experienced sailors and well-trained troops, compared to England's 54 battleships. Despite being heavily outnumbered, the English ships had the advantage of being light, fast moving and had superior firepower.

Elizabeth's government was forced to make hasty preparations:

- A line of warning beacons was set up along the coast – these would be lit when the Armada was spotted and church bells rung.
- Elizabeth gave a rousing speech to her army at Tilbury on 9 August, urging them to fight to the last.

> **Galleon** A large sailing ship or warship with many decks and three or more masts.

> **Revision task**
>
> Identify and explain THREE weaknesses in Philip's plan to invade England.
>
> TESTED ☐
>
> REVISED ☐

The arrival of the Armada

The threat of invasion hung over England during the summer and autumn of 1588.

- 29 July – the Armada was sighted off Lizard Point, Cornwall, and warning beacons were lit along the south coast.
- The Armada sailed through the English Channel in a crescent formation, making it difficult for the English to attack.
- 6 August – the Armada anchored off Calais, having lost just two ships.

Calais and the fireships

Parma's army had been delayed by Dutch attacks and was not ready to meet the Armada. Drake took advantage of the delay and on 7 August eight unmanned ships filled with tar, gunpowder and loaded cannons, were set alight and allowed to drift into the anchored Spanish fleet in Calais harbour. The Spanish ships were forced to cut their anchor chains in a hasty escape, breaking their formation.

Battle of Gravelines, 8 August

The English attacked the scattered Armada off Dunkirk. Known as the Battle of Gravelines, it proved to be a key turning point. The plan to join with Parma's army was now in ruins and a change in the wind forced the Armada to sail north.

Pursuing the Armada north

A change in wind direction prevented the Armada returning to Spain through the English Channel. It would have to sail around the coasts of Scotland and Ireland. Lacking accurate sea charts, the Spanish ships sailed into severe storms. Two ships were wrecked off Scotland and 25 off the Irish coast. Only 67 of the original 130 ships made it back to Spain.

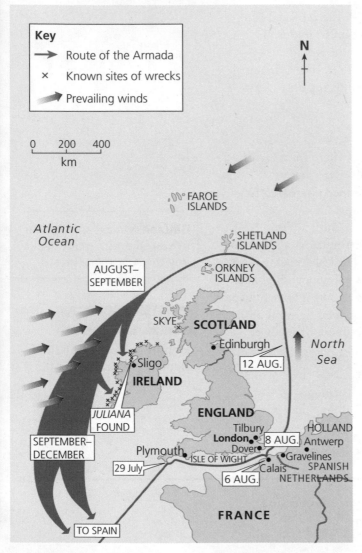

The route of the Spanish Armada in 1588

Reasons for the failure of the Armada

A combination of factors contributed to the failure of the Armada:

- English strengths – smaller, faster, more manoeuvrable ships, fitted with heavier firepower.
- Spanish weaknesses – Spanish cannons proved ineffective; the shot was of poor quality and many cannons exploded when fired; the Duke of Medina Sidonia was not an experienced commander, in contrast to Drake and Hawkins; the Duke of Parma was not ready.

Exam practice answers at **www.hoddereducation.co.uk/myrevisionnotesdownloads**

- Tactics – the crescent formation made it difficult for the English to attack but following the Calais attack the Spanish ships were out-gunned and easy targets for attack; the use of fireships proved decisive.
- Weather – following the Battle of Gravelines the wind changed and forced the scattered Spanish fleet northwards; the fleet experienced severe storms off the Scottish and Irish coasts.

Results of the Armada

REVISED

While the country rejoiced at the defeat of the Armada, Spain still posed a threat.

- War with Spain dragged on for a further decade.
- There was still a Spanish army under Parma's control waiting across the Channel in the Netherlands.
- Philip planned a second armada and on two occasions it was sent to invade England but was driven back by storms.
- England continued to support Dutch Protestants in the Netherlands.
- English sea dogs continued to attack Spanish treasure ships in the Spanish Main.

Exam practice

Why was the Spanish Armada seen as a significant threat to the rule of Elizabeth?

Exam tip

In the 'Why' question you have to display good knowledge and understanding of an identified issue, providing a range of reasons to explain why something happened or was important. You are also required to make a reasoned judgement. In this instance you could comment on how England was threatened by invasion and that threat was a very real one. The Armada sailed up the English Channel and had Drake not attacked it as it anchored off Calais, it might well have transported Philip's Spanish army from the Netherlands to the English coast. Elizabeth's position as queen would then have been seriously threatened.

Revision task

Rank the following events in order of importance in helping to explain the reasons for the defeat of the Spanish Armada. In each case, provide a reason for your decision to award a higher or lower ranking of importance.

- use of fire ships
- Battle of Gravelines
- change in wind direction
- Duke of Parma's army not ready.

TESTED

Conclusion: How much of a threat was the Spanish Armada?

REVISED

The Armada posed a serious threat and had it been successful in transporting Parma's army across the Channel the consequences could have been severe for Elizabeth. England did not have a strong army. However, poor leadership, large slow galleons and inferior fire power weakened the effectiveness of the Spanish fleet. Superior leadership by Drake and Hawkins, together with smaller more manoeuvrable ships, enabled the English to outperform the Spanish. The use of the fire ships proved decisive as did the Battle of Gravelines, serving to end the near threat of a Spanish invasion. The weather also played its part.

7 The Puritan threat

Key question

Why did the Puritans become an increasing threat during Elizabeth's reign?

Who were the Puritans?

Puritans were radical Protestants.
- They wanted to rid the church of all Catholic associations and follow a simpler or 'purer' form of worship.
- During Mary's reign, Puritans had been forced to flee abroad to escape persecution. Many went to Geneva, Zurich, Frankfurt and Strasbourg where they came into contact with the beliefs of the Swiss preacher, John Calvin.
- When Elizabeth became queen many returned to England, calling for the Settlement to be more radical.

The role of bishops

Puritans opposed the role of bishops, believing them to be an invention by the Pope to maintain his power over the church. Some English bishops held Puritan beliefs and hoped to reform the church from within. They included:
- John Jewel, Bishop of Salisbury
- Edwin Sandys, Bishop of Worcester
- Edmund Grindal, Bishop of London
- Richard Cox, Bishop of Ely.

Puritan beliefs and practices

Puritans were against practices not referenced in the Bible. They opposed:
- bowing when the name of Jesus was said
- kneeling to receive Communion
- using a ring to formalise marriage
- making the sign of the cross during baptism
- the celebration of saints days
- playing organ music during church services
- the display of ornaments, paintings and stained glass in churches.

They strongly believed that Sunday was the Lord's Day and should be devoted to religious study. They wore plain clothes (black and white colours). They opposed gambling, visits to the theatre and alehouse, drunkenness and swearing, believing such behaviour to be sinful and immoral.

Different types of Puritans

There were different types of Puritans:
- Moderate Puritans – they accepted the Religious Settlement of 1559 but hoped for further reform to purify the church.
- **Presbyterians** – they wanted reform and called for the abolition of bishops, each church to be run by a committee of presbyters (elders or teachers) elected by the congregation.
- **Separatists** – they wanted to break away from the national church and for each church to be independent and self-controlling.

> **Presbyterian** A Puritan who sought further reform of the church and for the abolition of bishops.
>
> **Separatist** A member of the most radical Puritan group, wanted to break away from a national church and for each church to be independent and run on a parish-by-parish basis by committees chosen from the congregation.

Revision task

1 Construct a mind map to show the main beliefs and practices of the Puritans.
2 Explain the main difference between moderate Puritans, Presbyterians and Separatists.

Exam practice answers at **www.hoddereducation.co.uk/myrevisionnotesdownloads**

Puritan challenges to the Religious Settlement

REVISED

Many Puritans continued to push for further reform of the church.

The vestments controversy, 1566

In 1566, Matthew Parker, Archbishop of Canterbury, published his Book of Advertisements which laid down rules for conducting services and for the wearing of vestments. 37 Puritan priests in London were dismissed from their posts for refusing to wear vestments. It was seen as a challenge to Elizabeth's authority as Supreme Governor of the church.

Proposals by Thomas Cartwright, 1570

In 1570, Thomas Cartwright, Professor of Divinity at Cambridge University, argued for the introduction of a presbyterian system of church government. He wanted to abolish the posts of archbishop and bishop and called for churches to be run locally by their congregations. His views were opposed by the government and he was forced to flee to Geneva.

Pamphlet of John Stubbs, 1579

In 1579, John Stubbs, a Puritan, wrote a pamphlet which criticised Elizabeth for entering into marriage talks with the Duke of Anjou, who was a Roman Catholic. He was arrested, put on trial and charged with 'seditious writing'. He had his right hand cut off and was imprisoned for 18 months.

The Marprelate Tracts, 1588–89

During 1588–89 anonymous pamphlets known as the *Marprelate Tracts* were published. They criticised the church and its bishops. Their publication lost Puritans support.

Puritan opposition in Parliament and the Privy Council

REVISED

Within the Privy Council Elizabeth faced calls for further religious reforms from moderate Puritans such as the Earl of Leicester and Sir Francis Walsingham. Within Parliament there were Puritan MPs who also supported calls for reform.

Individuals within Parliament

- Walter Strickland, 1571 – Puritan MP for Yorkshire, he proposed a bill calling for the introduction of a new Book of Common Prayer, the banning of vestments, the use of a ring in marriage and kneeling to receive communion. He was prevented from attending the House of Commons, causing his bill to be dropped.
- John Field and Thomas Wilcox, 1572 – they published books which argued the structure of the Presbyterian church was the one laid down in the Bible. It was an attack on the Elizabethan church. Both men were arrested and imprisoned for a year.
- Peter Wentworth, 1576 – Puritan MP for Barnstable, he complained that MPs did not have the freedom to discuss what they wanted to in Parliament. Elizabeth responded by closing Parliament down and ordering that it should not discuss religious matters without her permission. Wentworth was imprisoned in the Tower for a month.

- Peter Turner, 1584 – Puritan MP for Bridport, he failed to get a bill passed that would have introduced a system of church government based on Calvin's model in Geneva.
- Anthony Cope, 1586–87 – Puritan MP for Banbury, he introduced a bill calling for the abolition of bishops and the replacement of the Book of Common Prayer with the Geneva Prayer Book of John Calvin. Wentworth supported the bill but it failed to win support. Cope and Wentworth were both confined in the Tower during 1587.

Revision task

Explain the part played by each of the following in the Puritan challenge to the Religious Settlement:
- vestments Controversy
- *Marprelate Tracts*
- Bills proposed by Puritan MPs.

TESTED ☐

Measures taken to deal with the Puritan challenge

REVISED ☐

From the 1570s onwards, Elizabeth and her ministers became concerned with two developments within the Puritan movement – **prophesyings** and separatists. Measures were introduced aimed at tackling these developments.

Prophesyings Meetings of ministers and other interested parties in which ministers practised their preaching skills.

Archbishop Grindal and prophesyings

The growth of prophesying meetings came to be seen as a threat by Elizabeth. In 1576 she ordered Archbishop Grindal to ban such meetings. Grindal was sympathetic to Puritan ideas and refused to carry out the queen's instructions. He was suspended from his duties and confined to his house at Lambeth Palace. Elizabeth herself now banned prophesyings.

John Whitgift's attack on presbyteriansim

When Grindal died in 1583 he was replaced as Archbishop by John Whitgift. He had little sympathy for Puritan ideas and in 1583 he issued his Three Articles. This demanded uniformity from all clergy, including the acceptance of bishops. Between 300 and 400 ministers refused to swear acceptance and were removed from office. Whitgift continued in his quest to end all prophesyings and to demand conformity.

Development of the Separatist movement, 1580s

Whitgift's efforts caused strict Puritans to operate underground. Some, known as Separatists, decided to leave the established church and set up their own church. One of their leaders, Robert Brown and his followers, became known as 'Brownists'. He set up a separatist congregation in Norwich, believing that the Protestant church lacked moral discipline. He was imprisoned for his beliefs and upon release he emigrated to Holland.

Act against Seditious Sectaries, 1593

Government propaganda linked Puritanism to Separatism and Separatism to treason. The Act against Seditious Sectaries of 1593 gave authorities the power to execute those suspected of being separatists. Other penalties of imprisonment and banishment were given out to those who held unauthorised meetings or who refused to go to Anglican Church services. The arrests and executions which followed ended the separatist movement.

Revision task

Describe the measures introduced to limit the Puritan development of prophesyings and separatist meetings.

TESTED ☐

Conclusion: Why did the Puritans become an increasing threat during Elizabeth's reign?

- Elizabeth refused to allow any changes to the Religious Settlement and this led to developments within the Puritan movement.
- The Presbyterians desired a change to the structure of the church such as the removal of archbishops and bishops and this was seen as a threat to Elizabeth.
- Some Puritans set up prophesying movements in the hope of purifying the church. The actions of Archbishop Whitgift to suppress such meetings led to the development of a more radical separatist movement.
- The separatists posed the greatest threat to the church structure but government legislation helped to remove this threat.

Exam practice

Explain the connections between **TWO** of the following that are to do with Puritan beliefs and practices:
- Prophesyings
- Presbyterians
- Separatist movement
- Archbishop John Whitgift.

Exam tip

In the 'Explain the connections' question you need to select two out of the four choices and use your knowledge of this topic area to identify links between them. In this instance, all four choices are connected to Puritan beliefs and practices. One connection could be that the Puritans wanted to purify the Protestant faith and reduce its leadership structure (Presbyterian ideas) and if this could not be achieved they were prepared to go their separate way (Separatist movement). Archbishop John Whitgift was determined to stop this from happening.

1 The impact of the First World War

> **Key question**
>
> What challenges were faced by the Weimar Republic from 1919 to 1923?

The Weimar Republic

REVISED

The First World War broke out in 1914 with the Triple Entente (Britain, France and Russia) fighting against the Triple Alliance (Germany, Austria-Hungary and Italy). By the autumn of 1918 the German army was on the point of collapse. On 9 November the **Kaiser** abdicated and fled to the Netherlands. Germany became a **republic** and on 11 November the provisional government agreed to an **armistice** which brought Germany's fighting in the First World War to an end. Not all Germans welcomed the new republic and Berlin faced armed unrest from both left-wing and right-wing extremist groups. For this reason the newly elected Constituent Assembly, which met for the first time in January 1919, did so in the town of Weimar in southern Germany. This town gave its name to the **Weimar Republic**.

The Weimar Republic lasted from 1919 to 1933. During that time it was ruled by two presidents – Friedrich Ebert (1918–25) and Paul von Hindenburg (1925–34). They often battled to keep weak and unstable governments in office.

> **Kaiser** The hereditary emperor of Germany.
>
> **Republic** A government in which supreme power is exercised by representatives elected by the people.
>
> **Armistice** An agreement to end hostilities in a war.
>
> **Weimar Republic** Following the abdication of the Kaiser in November 1918, Germany became a republic. It is named after the town of Weimar where the temporary government met to write a new constitution.

The weaknesses of the Weimar Constitution

REVISED

The Republic faced many weaknesses.

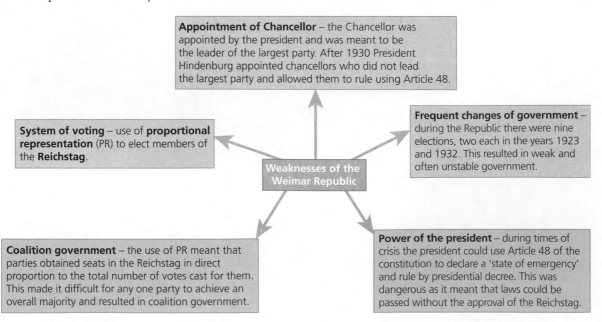

Appointment of Chancellor – the Chancellor was appointed by the president and was meant to be the leader of the largest party. After 1930 President Hindenburg appointed chancellors who did not lead the largest party and allowed them to rule using Article 48.

System of voting – use of **proportional representation** (PR) to elect members of the **Reichstag**.

Frequent changes of government – during the Republic there were nine elections, two each in the years 1923 and 1932. This resulted in weak and often unstable government.

Weaknesses of the Weimar Republic

Coalition government – the use of PR meant that parties obtained seats in the Reichstag in direct proportion to the total number of votes cast for them. This made it difficult for any one party to achieve an overall majority and resulted in coalition government.

Power of the president – during times of crisis the president could use Article 48 of the constitution to declare a 'state of emergency' and rule by presidential decree. This was dangerous as it meant that laws could be passed without the approval of the Reichstag.

Until the appointment of Hitler, most Chancellors came from moderate parties, yet they ruled over **Reichstags** which included extreme parties such as the Communists and Nazis, both of whom wanted to destroy the Republic.

Revision task

TESTED ☐

Copy and complete the following table to show how each factor helped to weaken the Weimar Republic.

Factor	How this factor helped to weaken the Weimar Republic
Proportional representation	
Coalition government	
Article 48	

Reichstag The German parliament.

Proportional representation System where the number of votes won in an election directly determines the number of seats in parliament.

Coalition government A government made up of two or more political parties.

The impact of the Treaty of Versailles on Germany

REVISED ☐

The new German government had no choice but to sign the Treaty of Versailles on 28 June 1919 which formally punished Germany for its involvement in the First World War. The majority of Germans were horrified by the terms and viewed the treaty as a great humiliation.

The treaty contained 440 clauses. The main terms were:
- territorial terms – Germany lost 13 per cent of its land, 6 million citizens and all her colonial possessions; Germany was forbidden to unite with Austria; Alsace-Lorraine was given to France; East Prussia was to be cut off from the rest of Germany by the Polish corridor; the Saarland was to be administered by the League of Nations
- military terms – the German army was limited to 100,000 men; it was forbidden to possess any tanks, heavy guns, aircraft or submarines; its navy was limited to ships of less than 10,000 tons; the Rhineland was to be demilitarised
- financial terms – under Clause 231 (War Guilt) Germany had to accept full responsibility for having caused the war and agree to pay money as **reparations** for the damage caused (a figure of £6,600 million was fixed in 1921)
- political terms – Germany was forbidden to join the newly created League of Nations. Germany also had to accept blame for causing the war.

Reparations War damages to be paid by Germany.

Revision task

TESTED ☐

For your exam you need to remember the key terms in the treaty. To remember these, use the acronym LAMB.

L = LAND

A = ARMY

M = MONEY

B = BLAME

Write down one specific example to go with each letter of this acronym.

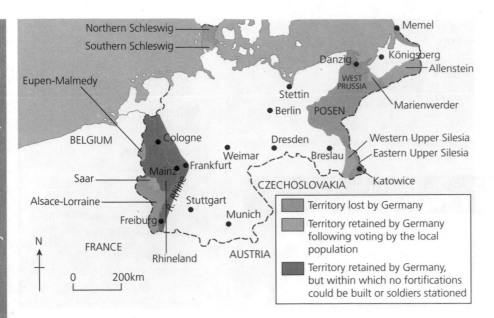

Territorial terms of the Treaty of Versailles

The shame and humiliation of the Treaty and the fact that the Germans were not allowed any role in negotiating the terms, gave ammunition to the opponents of Weimar, especially the extreme parties.

Political instability – the Spartacist, Kapp and Munich Putsches

REVISED

The Weimar government was initially unpopular among many Germans because it had surrendered, established a weak constitution and failed to end food shortages. Weimar was hated by communists, **socialists**, **nationalists**, army leaders and those who had run Germany before 1918. It faced constant threats from the left and right and there were several uprisings across Germany that threatened the government's existence.

> **Socialist** A person who believes in state ownership.
>
> **Nationalist** A person who has a passionate devotion to his or her country.

The Spartacist uprising

The Spartacist League, led by Karl Liebknecht and Rosa Luxemburg, wanted to establish a state based on communist ideals. In December 1918, the Spartacists' demonstrations against the government led to clashes with the army. The Spartacists formed the German Communist Party (KPD – Kommunistische Partei Deutschlands). On 6 January 1919, the Spartacists began their attempt to overthrow Ebert and the Weimar government in order to create a communist state. The government used the **Reichswehr** and the **Freikorps** to put down the rebellion. They succeeded. Spartacist leaders were captured and executed.

The Kapp Putsch

The Weimar government tried to reduce the size of the army and disband the Freikorps in March 1920. The Berlin Freikorps refused to comply. They worked with leading Berlin politician, Wolfgang Kapp, to seize Berlin and form a new right-wing government with Kapp as the **Chancellor**. The Reichswehr in Berlin supported Kapp. The Weimar government moved to Dresden and then Stuttgart. The new regular army refused to fire on Kapp's supporters. Ebert called on the people of Berlin to go on strike. Trade unionists and civil servants supported the government so the **Putsch** collapsed.

> **Reichswehr** The regular German army.
>
> **Freikorps** Paramilitary groups formed from demobilised soldiers at the end of the war.
>
> **Chancellor** The head of the German government, chosen by the president.
>
> **Putsch** A political uprising.

The Munich Putsch

On 8 November 1923, Hitler and 600 Nazis burst into a public meeting held in a beer hall in Munich. At gunpoint, the Bavarian chief minister von Kahr and the army chief von Lossow agreed to help in the planned takeover of the German government in Berlin. They later informed the police and authorities of Hitler's plan. Next morning they were met by the police. Sixteen Nazis and four policemen were killed. Hitler was put on trial and the Nazi Party was banned.

Revision task

TESTED

Use the information on pages 46–47 and your knowledge to complete the table below.

Revolt	Brief description of revolt	How revolt was stopped
Spartacist Uprising		
Kapp Putsch		
Munich Putsch		

The hyperinflation crisis and events in the Ruhr, 1923

REVISED

The currency had been devalued by **inflation** since 1914. The Weimar government claimed that it could not pay reparations. The loss of industrial areas after Versailles made this even more difficult. As inflation continued, the Weimar government began to print more money to pay France and Belgium, as well as its own workers. The value of the German currency started to fall rapidly.

French and Belgium troops invaded the industrial district of the Ruhr in the Rhineland in 1921 and then again in January 1923 when Germany failed to pay reparations. The French were angry because they needed the money to help to pay off their war debts to the USA.

The occupation was met with **passive resistance** and industrial sabotage. German workers went on strike in protest. A number of strikers were shot by French troops and their funerals led to demonstrations against the invasion. It reminded people of the war. The strikers became German heroes and the government printed more money to pay them even though fewer goods were being produced. The extra strike money plus the collapse in production turned inflation into **hyperinflation**.

People with savings or on a fixed income like pensions found themselves with nothing. They blamed Weimar politicians. However, inflation did benefit certain people:

- businessmen who had borrowed money from the banks were able to pay off these debts
- serious food shortages led to a rise in prices which helped farmers
- foreigners who were in Germany suddenly found that they could afford things that ordinary people couldn't.

> **Inflation** When the value of a currency is reduced; the same amount of money buys you fewer things.
>
> **Passive resistance** Opposition that does not involve violence.
>
> **Hyperinflation** A very extreme form of inflation where money becomes almost worthless.

> **Hyperinflation**
>
> July 1914
> £1 = 20 marks
>
> July 1923
> £1 = 1,413,648 marks
>
> November 1923
> £1 = 1,680,800,000,000,000 marks

Exam practice

Study the source below and then answer the question that follows.

Source A

Photograph of Freikorps in front of the Vorwärts newspaper building, which they had captured from the Spartacists in January 1919. The Vorwärts newspaper was a socialist newspaper

Use Source A and your own knowledge to describe the political situation in Germany in the early 1920s.

Exam tip

Underline key words in the question. This will enable you to focus upon what the examiner wants you to write about. Describe what you can see or read in the source, remembering to make use of the information provided in the caption of a visual source. Link this information to your knowledge of this period. Aim to make at least two developed points.

2 The recovery of Weimar

Key question

Why were the Stresemann years considered a 'golden age'?

Recovery from hyperinflation

REVISED

German economic recovery was largely due to the work of Gustav Stresemann who worked successfully with Britain, France and the USA to improve Germany's economic position by organising the Dawes Plan, the Rentenmark and the Young Plan.

The Dawes Plan

Stresemann persuaded the French, British and Americans to change the reparation payment terms in August 1924. The main points of the plan were:
- reparations payments were reduced to a more sensible and manageable payments and were based upon Germany's capacity to pay
- the Ruhr area was to be evacuated by Allied occupation troops. This was carried out in 1925
- the USA would give loans to Germany to help its economic recovery – $3,000 million over six years.

The Rentenmark

In November 1923, Stresemann introduced a temporary currency called the Rentenmark. This was issued in limited amounts based on property values. In 1924 the Rentenmark was converted into the Reichsmark, a new currency now backed by gold reserves.

The Young Plan

In 1929, the Allied Reparations Committee asked an American banker, Owen Young, to come up with a new plan for payments. The reparations figure was reduced from £6,600 million to £1,850 million, while the length of time Germany had to pay was extended to 59 years. Right-wing politicians objected to any further payment of reparations.

The extent of economic recovery

Compared to the years of inflation and hyperinflation there was an economic recovery. The economy seemed to grow as money came to Germany from the USA:
- public works provided new stadiums, apartment blocks and opera houses
- big business had paid many of its debts and benefited from a period of industrial growth
- there were fewer strikes between 1924 and 1929
- unemployment, which had risen to 9 million by 1926, fell to the 6 million mark.

However, for all the good that had been done, the Weimar economy was over-dependent on American loans. The economic recovery did not affect everyone equally:

- factory workers' hours stayed the same while their wages rose, but not as fast as living costs
- the lower middle-class did not fully recover from the savings they lost to hyperinflation in 1923
- farmers struggled as prices fell and they did not have the money to modernise their farms and food production was not recovering as fast as industrial production.

Revision task

TESTED ☐

Use the information on pages 49–50 and your knowledge to complete the table below.

Action	How this helped economic recovery
Dawes Plan	
Rentenmark	
Young Plan	

Improvement in relations between Germany and other countries

REVISED ☐

Stresemann, who was Foreign Secretary from 1923 to 1929, had several achievements abroad.

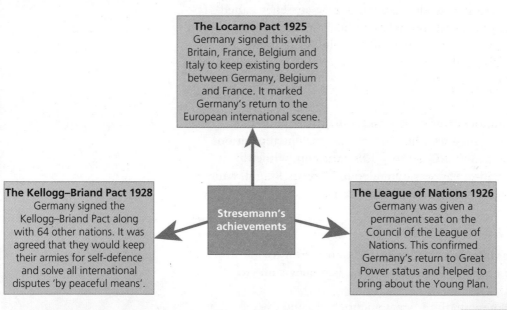

The Locarno Pact 1925
Germany signed this with Britain, France, Belgium and Italy to keep existing borders between Germany, Belgium and France. It marked Germany's return to the European international scene.

The Kellogg–Briand Pact 1928
Germany signed the Kellogg–Briand Pact along with 64 other nations. It was agreed that they would keep their armies for self-defence and solve all international disputes 'by peaceful means'.

Stresemann's achievements

The League of Nations 1926
Germany was given a permanent seat on the Council of the League of Nations. This confirmed Germany's return to Great Power status and helped to bring about the Young Plan.

As a result of Stresemann's foreign policies:

- in 1925, France withdrew from the Ruhr
- the Allies agreed to the Dawes Plan and the Young Plan
- in 1927, Allied troops withdrew from the west bank of the Rhine, five years before the original schedule of 1933.

Overall, Stresemann had played a crucial role in the recovery of the Republic, particularly through the Dawes Plan and American loans as well his successes abroad, which re-established the international position of Germany and brought closer relations with Britain and France.

Revision task

For each of these international agreements write a sentence to explain why it was good for Germany:
- Locarno Pact, 1925
- League of Nations, 1926
- Kellogg-Briand Pact, 1928.

TESTED ☐

The main political developments in Germany, 1924–29

The period 1924 to 1929 saw greater support for the parties like the moderate **Social Democrats** that supported the Weimar Republic and generally less support for extremist groups such as the Nazis, because of the economic recovery and successes abroad. This political stability was also due to two key personalities – Stresemann and Hindenburg. Stresemann's successes abroad made him the most popular political leader of the Weimar Republic. Hindenburg, one of Germany's war leaders, was elected president in 1925 which showed that the old conservative order now accepted the Republic.

> **Social Democrats** The moderate political party that had set up the Weimar Republic.

The main social developments in Germany, 1924–29

The period 1924–29 is described as a 'golden age' in the Weimar Republic due to significant changes.

Improvement in the standard of living

There were improvements in wages, housing and unemployment insurance. By 1928, Germany had some of the best paid workers in Europe, but many of the middle class did not share in this increased prosperity as they had been bankrupted by inflation and found it hard to get suitable jobs

Housing

The government employed architects and planners to devise ways of reducing housing shortages. Government investment, tax breaks, land grants and low-interest loans were also used to stimulate the building of new houses and apartments. Between 1924 and 1931 more than 2 million new homes were built.

Unemployment insurance

The Unemployment Insurance Law in 1927 required workers and employees to make contributions to a national scheme for unemployment welfare. There were also benefits for war veterans, wives and dependents of the war dead, single mothers and the disabled.

The position of women

Women over 20 were given the vote and took an increasing interest in politics and guaranteed equality in education, equal opportunity in civil service appointments and equal pay in the professions. There were growing numbers of women in new areas of employment, for example the civil service, teaching or social work, as well as in shops or on the assembly line. Women also enjoyed much more freedom, socially. They went out unescorted, drank and smoked in public and were fashion conscious, often wearing relatively short skirts and make-up.

> **Revision task**
>
> Explain how each of these developments show that life in Germany improved between 1924 and 1929:
> - political stability
> - standard of Living
> - housing
> - unemployment insurance
> - the position of women.
>
> TESTED

Exam practice

Study the source below and then answer the question that follows.

Source A

THE CLASP OF FRIENDSHIP (FRENCH VERSION).

A British cartoon showing the foreign ministers of Britain, France and Germany joining hands following the signing of the Locarno Pact in 1925. Briand, the French politician, is wearing a boxing glove, suggesting he might use force against Germany

What was the purpose of Source A?

[Use Source A and your own knowledge and understanding of the historical context to answer the question.]

Exam tip

You need to spell out why this source was produced. Use your knowledge of this topic area when considering the content of the source and what it shows. Make use of the information provided in the caption/attribution of the source. This can supply important information such as publication date, the name of the newspaper, book or magazine. Use this information to help identify the motive – who was the intended audience? What did the source aim to do?

3 The Nazi rise to power and the end of the Weimar Republic

Key question

How and why did the Weimar Republic collapse between 1929 and 1934?

The early development of the Nazi party

REVISED

In 1919, Anton Drexler founded the German Workers Party (Deutsche Arbeiter Partei, DAP) in Munich, Bavaria. It was a right–wing, nationalistic party which stressed the ideal of a pure German people. Adolf Hitler joined in September 1919. In 1920, he was put in charge of the party's propaganda machine. In February 1920, Hitler and Drexler wrote the party's 'Twenty-Five Point Programme', which became its political manifesto. In July 1921, Hitler replaced Drexler as leader and he changed the name of the party to National Socialist German Workers Party (NSDAP). He adopted the title Führer (leader), developed a party symbol, the swastika, and introduced the raised arm salute. Party membership increased from 1,100 members in June 1920 to 55,000 in November 1923.

In 1921, Hitler set up the Sturmabteilung (SA) which was led by Ernst Röhm. Often referred to as the 'Brownshirts' because of the colour of their uniform or the 'Stormtroopers', this armed group of mostly ex-military men were charged with protecting Nazi speakers from attacks by rival political groups.

The Munich Putsch

REVISED

The political atmosphere in the early years of Weimar was one of chaos and disruption. In this atmosphere, Hitler thought the time was right for the Nazi Party to seize power, first in the Bavarian state capital in Munich, followed by a march on Berlin. This became known as the Munich Putsch.

The Putsch failed and its leaders were arrested. The Nazi Party was banned. Hitler's trial started in February 1924 and lasted one month. It gave him national publicity. He criticised the '**November Criminals**', the Treaty of Versailles and the 'Jewish **Bolshevists**' who had betrayed Germany. While Ludendorff was let off, Hitler was found guilty of treason and sentenced to five years in Landsberg prison. He served only nine months.

> **November Criminals**
> Those politicians who had agreed to the signing of the Armistice in November 1918.
>
> **Bolshevists or Bolsheviks**
> Followers of Lenin who carried out a Communist Revolution in Russia in February 1917.

The importance of the Munich Putsch

REVISED

While in prison Hitler had time to reflect. He realised that in order to win power the Nazi Party would have to change its strategy. Instead of an armed rising, the party would have to build upon recent publicity and work towards achieving a majority in the polls and be elected into office through the ballot box. He also used the time to complete his autobiography, *Mein Kampf* (My Struggle), which contained his political views.

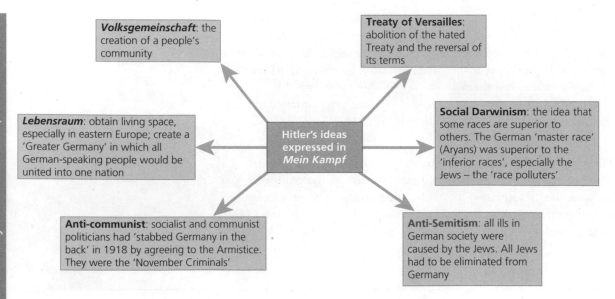

Boxes connected to central node **Hitler's ideas expressed in *Mein Kampf***:

Volksgemeinschaft: the creation of a people's community

Treaty of Versailles: abolition of the hated Treaty and the reversal of its terms

Lebensraum: obtain living space, especially in eastern Europe; create a 'Greater Germany' in which all German-speaking people would be united into one nation

Social Darwinism: the idea that some races are superior to others. The German 'master race' (Aryans) was superior to the 'inferior races', especially the Jews – the 'race polluters'

Anti-communist: socialist and communist politicians had 'stabbed Germany in the back' in 1918 by agreeing to the Armistice. They were the 'November Criminals'

Anti-Semitism: all ills in German society were caused by the Jews. All Jews had to be eliminated from Germany

Further development of the Nazi Party

REVISED

Upon his release from prison, Hitler managed to have the ban on the Nazi Party lifted and he quickly set about reorganising and re-establishing his leadership.

- He created his own bodyguard, the **Schutzstaffel** (SS).
- He introduced the **Hitler Jugend** (Hitler Youth) to attract younger members.
- He used every opportunity to attack the weaknesses of Weimar, and the Nazi Party began to attract support from all classes.
- In 1925 the Party had 27,000 members and by 1928 this had increased to over 100,000.

Despite these changes, the Nazis won only 12 seats in the Reichstag in the 1928 general election, having held 32 in 1924. The lack of success was largely due to the economic recovery brought about between 1924 and 1929 by the Chancellor and later Foreign Minister, Gustav Stresemann, whose policies dissuaded people from voting for the extreme parties.

Anti-Semitism Hatred and persecution of the Jews.

Schutzstaffel The SS, which originally started as Hitler's private bodyguard but which grew into a powerful organisation with wide powers; they wore black uniforms.

Hitler Jugend The Hitler Youth organisation set up in 1925 to convert young Germans to Nazi ideas.

Revision task

TESTED

1 Construct a timeline to show the key events in the history of the Nazi Party between January 1919 and November 1923.
2 Identify three ways in which the Nazi Party developed into a more powerful political force between 1924 and 1929.

The social and political impact of the Depression on the Weimar Republic

Much of the economic recovery in Germany in the late 1920s was heavily reliant upon American loans. Following the **Wall Street Crash** in October 1929, US banks recalled their loans. Depression hit the German economy.

> **Wall Street Crash** The collapse of the American stock market in October 1929 that resulted in a world-wide economic depression.

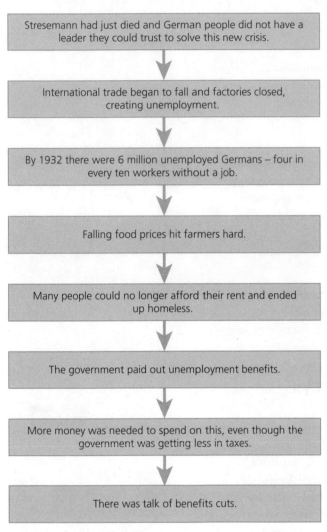

Stresemann had just died and German people did not have a leader they could trust to solve this new crisis.

↓

International trade began to fall and factories closed, creating unemployment.

↓

By 1932 there were 6 million unemployed Germans – four in every ten workers without a job.

↓

Falling food prices hit farmers hard.

↓

Many people could no longer afford their rent and ended up homeless.

↓

The government paid out unemployment benefits.

↓

More money was needed to spend on this, even though the government was getting less in taxes.

↓

There was talk of benefits cuts.

Weimar politicians appeared to be doing too little too late and in desperation people increasingly began to turn to the extremist parties for solutions. Support for the communists and Nazis rose sharply in the general election of September 1930. Middle-class voters feared a communist uprising if the problems of the Depression could not be solved.

Increasing support for the Nazis

By 1932, the Nazi Party was the largest party in the Reichstag and had attracted electoral support from all sections of German society. There were many reasons for this electoral success.

Impact of the Depression

The onset of the Depression created the political and economic conditions that caused millions of Germans to switch their voting habits and vote for the extreme parties. The moderate parties which had formed the coalitions appeared unable to tackle the worsening economic conditions. What was needed was radical action and the Nazi Party seemed to offer this.

The appeal of Hitler

Hitler was a gifted public speaker who captivated his audiences. He projected the image of being the messiah, the saviour who would solve the problems facing Germany. Using his private plane he toured the country delivering speeches to mass audiences, offering something to all sections of society. He kept his message simple, blaming scapegoats for Germany's problems, especially the Jews and communists.

The use of propaganda

Dr Josef Goebbels was in charge of the party propaganda machine. Through staging mass rallies, huge poster campaigns, using the radio and cinema, he ensured that the Nazi message was hammered home.

Financial support

The Nazi Party could not have financed its electoral campaigns without large-scale financial backing from big industrialists like Thyssen, Krupp and Bosch. These industrialists feared a communist takeover and were concerned at the growth of trade union power. Hitler promised to deal with both fears.

The use of the SA

The SA played a vital role in protecting Nazi speakers during election meetings and also in disrupting the meetings of their political rivals, especially the communists. These 'bully boy thugs' of the party engaged in street fights with the political opposition.

The end of parliamentary democracy: the coalition of Brüning

REVISED

The harsh economic climate created severe problems for the weak coalition governments of Weimar and they soon collapsed, resulting in three general elections between 1930 and 1932. In March 1930, President Hindenburg appointed Heinrich Brüning of the Centre Party as Chancellor. Brüning lacked a majority and had to rely on President Hindenburg and Article 48 to allow him to rule using presidential Decrees. From this point on, the Reichstag was used less frequently and the use of Article 48 marked the end of parliamentary democracy in Germany.

As the Depression deepened, Brüning's government became more and more unpopular. It was forced to cut unemployment benefits and Brüning became known as the 'hunger chancellor'. In May 1932 he resigned and in the general election which followed in July the Nazis polled their highest ever vote, securing 230 seats (37 per cent) making them the largest party in the Reichstag.

> **Revision task**
>
> Write down how these developments explain why support for the Nazis grew between 1929 and 1933:
> - the Depression
> - the appeal of Hitler
> - propaganda
> - financial support
> - the SA
>
> TESTED

	Elections to the Reichstag						
Party	May 1924	Dec 1924	May 1928	Sept 1930	July 1932	Nov 1932	March 1933
Social Democrats	100	131	152	143	133	121	120
Centre Party	65	69	61	68	75	70	73
People's Party	44	51	45	30	7	11	2
Democrats	28	32	25	14	4	2	5
Communists	62	45	54	77	89	100	81
Nationalists	106	103	79	41	40	51	53
Nazis	32	14	12	107	230	196	288

The coalitions of von Papen and von Schleicher

REVISED

In March 1932, Hitler stood against Hindenburg in the presidential elections. He polled 13.4 million votes against 19.3 million cast for Hindenburg. Hitler was becoming a well-known figure in German politics and following the Nazi Party success in the July election he should have been appointed Chancellor. Hindenburg, however, despised him and instead appointed the Nationalist leader Franz von Papen as his Chancellor.

Unable to obtain a working majority, von Papen was forced to call another election in November when the Nazi vote fell and they obtained 196 seats, 34 less than July. As the Nazi Party was still the largest party in the Reichstag, Hitler again demanded the post of Chancellor and again he was denied it. This time Hindenburg turned to General von Schleicher, the Minister of Defence, and appointed him Chancellor. His attempts to form a working majority failed and in January 1933 von Papen managed to persuade Hindenburg to appoint a **Nazi-Nationalist government** with Hitler as Chancellor and von Papen as vice-Chancellor. Von Papen believed he could control Hitler as only three of the eleven cabinet seats would be held by Nazis.

On 30 January 1933, Adolf Hitler became Chancellor of Germany – he had attained power by legal and democratic means.

Nazi-Nationalist government Coalition of NSDAP (Nazi Party) and DNVP (German National People's Party) after January 1933.

German chancellors and their governments, 1930–33	
Bruning	March 1930 – May 1932
Von Papen	May 1932 – December 1932
Von Schleicher	December 1932 – January 1933
Hitler – Von Papen	January 1933 – March 1933

Revision task

TESTED

Construct a timeline showing political developments in Germany between March 1930 and March 1933. Mark on unemployment figures, the presidential election, chancellors and governments.

Exam practice

Study the interpretations below and then answer the question that follows.

Interpretation 1

Perhaps the miracle of Weimar is that the Republic survived as long as it did. The Republic had already been heading for the crossroads before the immediate crisis of 1929–30 occurred. Everything had been pointing towards a possible crash.

The German historian Detlev Peukert, writing in his book *The Weimar Republic*, published in 1987

Interpretation 2

The personality of the Fuhrer became a significant historical factor. He had a combination of good public speaking skills and political instinct … Luck was also with him, mainly because all other players in the field turned out to be so inadequate and mistaken in their judgements.

The German historian Edgar Feuchtwanger, writing in his book *From Weimar to Hitler: Germany 1918–33*, which was published in 1993

Do the interpretations support the view that the collapse of the Weimar Republic was inevitable?

[In your answer you should refer to how and why the interpretations differ. Use your own knowledge and understanding of the wider historical debate over this issue to reach a well-supported judgement.]

> **Exam tip**
>
> Look at Interpretation 1 - What is its main message? Does that message support or contradict the main focus of the question? Explain and develop the content of Interpretation 1, bringing in knowledge of this topic. Consider the attribution - who is the author of the interpretation? What is the type of publication? When and why was it produced?
>
> Repeat the above process for Interpretation 2.
>
> Remember to provide a reasoned judgement on how and why the interpretations differ, making reference to the content, authorship and intended audience.

4 Consolidation of power, 1933–34

Key question

How did the Nazis consolidate their power between 1933 and 1934?

Between January 1933 and August 1934, Hitler turned Germany into a one-party **dictatorship**. By August 1934, the posts of Chancellor and president had been merged into a new post – Führer (leader). For the next twelve years Germany was ruled by a **totalitarian** regime known as the **Third Reich**.

> **Dictatorship** A regime in which the leader has total power and does not tolerate any opposition.
>
> **Totalitarian** A state that has a one-party political system which holds total power.
>
> **Third Reich** The period of Nazi government, 1933–45.

The importance of the Reichstag fire

REVISED

When Hitler became Chancellor there were only two other Nazis in the cabinet – Wilhelm Frick and Hermann Goering. Hitler's position was not strong as the Nazi–Nationalist alliance did not have a majority in the Reichstag. Hitler therefore persuaded Hindenburg to dissolve the Reichstag and call a general election for 5 March in which he hoped to increase the support for the Nazi Party. The Nazi propaganda machine helped deliver the party's message and the SA took to the streets to harass left-wing groups.

On 27 February, one week before the election, the Reichstag building was set on fire. A young Dutch communist, Marinus van der Lubbe, was arrested and charged with starting the fire. Hitler used this event to his advantage.

- He argued that the communists were planning a revolution.
- He persuaded Hindenburg to sign the 'Decree for the Protection of the People and State'.
- This gave Hitler the power to restrict free speech, limit the freedom of the press and imprison enemies of the state without trial.
- Communist and socialist newspapers were banned.

> **Revision task**
>
> Make a list of reasons why the Reichstag Fire was important in the Nazi's consolidation of power.
>
> TESTED

The 1933 election and the Enabling Act

REVISED

In the election on 5 March 1933, the Nazis won 288 seats but they still lacked an overall majority. A coalition was formed with the National Party. Hitler was disappointed as he needed two-thirds of the seats to be able to change the constitution, which was necessary to secure the passing of his Enabling bill.

On the day the Enabling bill was discussed in the Kroll Opera House (the temporary home of the Reichstag), Hitler banned the communists from attending and encircled the building with SA men who prevented known opponents from entering. Absentees were counted as present and therefore in favour of the proposed bill. Promises were made by Hitler to the Catholic Centre Party to secure their votes. As a result the bill was passed, by 444 votes in favour to 94 against. Its passing marked the end of the Weimar Constitution. The Enabling Act became the 'foundation stone' of the Third Reich and it was used by Hitler to establish his dictatorship.

Through the use of the Enabling Act, Hitler was able to establish his dictatorship and impose his policy of **gleichschaltung** (forcing into line).

> **Gleichschaltung** Nazi policy of forced co-ordination, bringing all social, economic and political activities under state control.

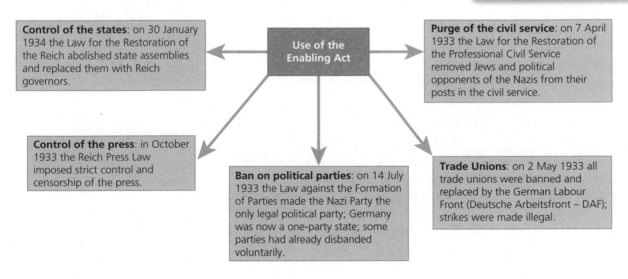

Control of the states: on 30 January 1934 the Law for the Restoration of the Reich abolished state assemblies and replaced them with Reich governors.

Use of the Enabling Act

Purge of the civil service: on 7 April 1933 the Law for the Restoration of the Professional Civil Service removed Jews and political opponents of the Nazis from their posts in the civil service.

Control of the press: in October 1933 the Reich Press Law imposed strict control and censorship of the press.

Ban on political parties: on 14 July 1933 the Law against the Formation of Parties made the Nazi Party the only legal political party; Germany was now a one-party state; some parties had already disbanded voluntarily.

Trade Unions: on 2 May 1933 all trade unions were banned and replaced by the German Labour Front (Deutsche Arbeitsfront – DAF); strikes were made illegal.

The removal of Hitler's political opponents

With the new Enabling Act, Hitler wanted Gleichschaltung – to create a truly National Socialist state by bringing every aspect of life in Germany under Nazi control. To achieve this he got rid of any organisations who could resist this.

- Trade unions – on 2 May 1933, all trade unions were banned. The Labour Front (Deutsche Arbeitsfront – DAF) was set up to replace them. The DAF decided wages and workers could not get work without their DAF work book. Strikes were made illegal.
- Political parties – the Communist Party (KPD) had been banned after the Reichstag fire in March 1933. The Social Democratic Party had its headquarters, property and newspapers seized in May. The remaining political parties disbanded themselves voluntarily by July. On 14 July 1933 the Law Against the Formation of Parties was passed.
- State government – Germany was made up of eighteen Länder, each with its own parliament. Sometimes they refused to accept decisions made in the Reichstag. Hitler decided that the Länder were to be run by Reich governors and their parliaments were abolished in January 1934.

The Night of the Long Knives, 30 June 1934

The SA had played a key part in the growth of the Nazi Party and as a reward their leader, Ernst Röhm, now wanted to incorporate the army into the SA. Röhm also wanted more government interference in the running of the country and he began pushing for a social revolution which would do away with Germany's class structure.

Hitler now saw the SA and its leadership as an increasing threat to his power. He needed the support of the army but the generals would never agree to Röhm's demands for the SA to control them. Hitler had to make a choice between the SA and the army. He decided upon the latter and on the night of 30 June 1934 he used the SS to carry out a purge. Codenamed 'Operation Hummingbird' and known as the 'Night of the Long Knives', over 400 'enemies of the state' were arrested and shot by the SS. They included Röhm, former Chancellor von Schleicher and Bavarian Chief Minister von Kahr.

The importance of the Night of the Long Knives

The Night of the Long Knives is seen as a turning point in establishing Hitler's dictatorship:
- it eradicated would-be opponents to Hitler's rule
- it secured the support of the army
- it relegated the SA to a minor role
- it provided Himmler with the opportunity to expand the SS.

The death of Hindenburg: Hitler becomes Führer

On 2 August 1934, President Hindenburg died. Hitler seized the opportunity to combine the two posts of president and Chancellor and gave himself the new title of Führer (leader). He was now Head of State and Commander-in-Chief of the Armed Forces.

Exam practice answers at **www.hoddereducation.co.uk/myrevisionnotesdownloads**

That same day the officers and men of the German army were made to swear an oath of loyalty to the Führer. In a **referendum** on 19 August more than 90 per cent of votes agreed with his action. Hitler was now absolute dictator of Germany.

> **Referendum** When people are asked to vote on important decisions about their country.

Revision task

TESTED ☐

1 How did each of the factors below help to increase Hitler's power and control over Germany:
   ● Reichstag Fire
   ● Night of the Long Knives
   ● Decree for Protection of the People and State
   ● Death of Hindenburg
   ● Enabling Act?
2 Which of these events were the most important in making Hitler dictator of Germany? Rank them in order of their importance, giving reasons for your choice.

Exam practice

Study the sources below and then answer the question that follows.

Source A

I was a member of the Communist Party until 1929 … In Holland, I read that the Nazis had come to power in Germany. In my opinion, something had to be done in protest against this system … Since the workers would do nothing, I had to do something myself. I thought arson a suitable method. I did not wish to harm ordinary people, but something belonging to the system itself. I decided on the Reichstag. As to the question whether I acted alone, I declare emphatically that this was the case. No one at all helped me.

Part of Marinus van der Lubbe's statement to the police, 3 March 1933

Source B

At a luncheon on the birthday of the Fuhrer in 1942 the conversation turned to the topic of the Reichstag building. I heard with my own ears when Goering interrupted the conversation and shouted: 'The only one who really knows about the building is I, because I set in on fire.'

General Halder, Chief of the German General Staff, speaking at the Nuremberg War Crimes trial in 1945

Which of the sources is more useful to a historian studying who was responsible for the Reichstag Fire in February 1933?

[You should refer to both sources in your answer and use your knowledge and understanding of the historical context.]

> **Exam tip**
>
> In your answer you have to evaluate the usefulness of two sources to the historian studying the key issue named in the question. For each source you must determine usefulness in terms of: content value (what the source tells you about the key issue); authorship (who said it and when); the intended audience (why was the source produced and what was its purpose) and the context (link the source content to the bigger picture of what was happening at that time). Remember to provide a reasoned judgement upon which source is the most useful and why.

5 Nazi economic, social and racial policies

Key question

How did Nazi economic, social and racial policy affect life in Germany?

The impact of Nazi policies on German workers

REVISED

When Hitler became Chancellor in January 1933, Germany had experienced more than three years of economic depression. Hitler immediately introduced a number of measures designed to reduce unemployment, which stood at 6 million.

Creation of the National Labour Service Corps (RAD)

From 1935 it was compulsory for all males aged 18–25 to serve in the RAD for six months undertaking manual labour jobs. Workers lived in camps, wore uniforms and carried out military drill as well as work.

Public works programme

Men were put to work on public works schemes which included the building of 7,000 km of autobahns (motorways), tree planting and the construction of hospitals, schools and houses.

Rearmament

Hitler's decision to re-arm transformed German industry and created jobs. Heavy industry expanded. Coal and chemical usage doubled between 1933 and 1939, while oil, iron and steel usage trebled.

Control of the economy

In 1934, Hjalmar Schacht, president of the Reichsbank, was made Economic Minister. He believed in **deficit spending** to create jobs and used **Mefo bills** (credit notes) to finance public spending. In 1936, Schacht was replaced by Hermann Goering as Economic Minister and he introduced the **Four-Year Plan** (1936–40). This was designed to speed up rearmament, prepare the country for war and establish the policy of **autarky** which was designed to make Germany self-sufficient, e.g. extracting oil from coal.

Invisible unemployment

Unemployment fell dramatically, from 6 million in 1933 to 350,000 by 1939. However, these figures hid the true picture as they did not include Jews or women dismissed from their jobs, or opponents of the Nazi regime held in concentration camps.

Deficit spending When the government spends more money than it receives in order to expand the economy.

Mefo bills Credit notes issued by the Reichsbank and guaranteed by the government. They were used to fund rearmament.

Four-Year Plan A plan which aimed to make Germany ready for war within four years, giving priority to rearmament and autarky.

Autarky A Nazi government policy of making Germany self-sufficient with no foreign imports.

Control of the workforce

Hitler viewed trade unions as the breeding ground for socialism and communism. To avoid strikes and industrial unrest he banned the unions and in May 1933 replaced them with the German Labour Front (DAF). It had complete control over the discipline of workers, regulating pay and hours of work.

Rewarding the workforce

To reward loyal workers, the Strength through Joy (Kraft durch Freude – KdF) organisation was set up. It aimed to improve leisure time by sponsoring subsidised leisure activities and cultural events. These included concerts, theatre visits, sporting events, weekend trips, holidays and cruises. The Beauty of Work organisation aimed to improve working conditions through the building of canteens and sports facilities. In 1938 the Volkswagen (People's Car) Scheme was introduced, allowing workers to save five marks a week to buy their own car.

> **Revision task**
>
> Identify five factors which drove forward Germany's economic recovery after 1933. Rank them in order of importance.
>
> TESTED ☐

The Nazi's policies toward women

REVISED ☐

Progress made by women during the Weimar period

During the Weimar period, women made substantial advances in German society. They had achieved equal voting rights with men; they had been encouraged to obtain a good education and had taken up careers in the professions, especially in the civil service, law, medicine and teaching. German women (who chose to) could go out unescorted, follow fashion, wear make-up, smoke and drink in public.

Nazi attitudes towards women

Nazi attitudes were very traditional and they introduced policies which reversed many of the gains made by women during the 1920s. The Nazis viewed men as the decision makers and political activists, while women were relegated to being responsible for the home and for bringing up children. They discouraged women from wearing make-up, trousers, high heels and from dyeing their hair.

> **Aryan** Nazi term for a non-Jewish German; someone of supposedly 'pure' German stock.
>
> **Indoctrinating** Making someone accept a system of thought without question.

Nazi policies aimed at women

The Three Ks	Law for the Encouragement of Marriage (1933)	Lebensborn (Life Springs) Programme (1936)
Instead of going to work women were encouraged to stick to the Three Ks (Kinder, Kuche, Kirche – Children, Kitchen, Church). They were expected to give up their jobs, to get married and start a family.	This provided loans to encourage couples to marry, provided the wife left her job. Couples were allowed to keep one-quarter of the loan for each child born, up to four children. The Motherhood Cross medal was introduced to reward women with large families.	In an effort to boost the population, unmarried **Aryan** women were encouraged to 'denote a baby to the Führer' by becoming pregnant by 'racially pure' SS men.

Nazi control of education

REVISED ☐

Hitler realised the importance of **indoctrinating** young people in Nazi beliefs. His aim was to turn them into loyal and enthusiastic supporters of the Third Reich. This was to be achieved through the control of education.

- Teachers had to belong to the Nazi Teachers' League; they had to promote Nazi ideas in the classroom and swear an oath of loyalty to Hitler.
- The curriculum was strictly controlled: 15 per cent of the timetable was devoted to physical education; for the boys the emphasis was upon preparation for the military; for the girls it was needlework and cookery to enable them to become good homemakers and mothers.
- Lessons started with pupils saluting and saying 'Heil Hitler'. Every subject was taught through the Nazi point of view – biology lessons were used to study racial theory and the importance of the 'master race'; geography lessons were used to show how Germany was surrounded by hostile neighbours.
- Textbooks were rewritten to reflect Nazi views – history textbooks contained a heavy emphasis upon German military glory and the evils of communism and the Jews who were blamed for the problems of the Depression.

Nazi control of the German youth

REVISED

The Nazis wanted to influence young people in school but also out of school. This was achieved through the Hitler Youth Movement which had existed since 1925. The Hitler Youth Law of 1936 made it difficult to avoid joining, blocking the promotion of parents who refused to allow their children to join. The Second Hitler Youth Law of 1939 made membership compulsory. By 1939 there were 7 million members. Baldur von Schirach was Reich Youth Leader.

There were several divisions of the Youth Movement, according to age.

Age	Boys	Girls
6–10	Pimpfen (Little Fellows)	
10–14	Jungvolk (Young Folk)	Jungmädel (Young Girls)
14–18	Hitler Jugend (Hitler Youth)	Bund Deutsche Mädchen (German Girls League)

- Boys were instructed in military skills such as shooting, map reading and drill; they took part in athletics, hiking and camping.
- Girls received physical training and learned domestic skills in preparation for motherhood and marriage; their groups had less emphasis upon military training.

> **Revision task**
>
> Describe how the Nazis tried to control young people through:
> - education
> - the Hitler Youth.
>
> TESTED

The treatment of the Jews

REVISED

In *Mein Kampf*, Hitler had spelled out his ideas on race. He argued that pure Germans – Aryans – formed the 'master race' and they were characterised by being tall, having fair hair and blue eyes. However, over time this race had been contaminated by 'subhumans' – the Untermenshen. In order to rebuild the 'master race' as a pure line, it would be necessary to introduce selective breeding, preventing anyone who did not conform to the Aryan type from having children and, in extreme cases, eliminating them. Measures were introduced to sterilise the mentally ill, the physically disabled, homosexuals, black people and gypsies. Among those groups who received widespread persecution were the Jews.

Exam practice answers at **www.hoddereducation.co.uk/myrevisionnotesdownloads**

The Nazi policy of anti-Semitism

Anti-Semitism goes back to the Middle Ages and attacks upon Jews were common in Europe in the early twentieth century, particularly in Russia. The Nazis played upon existing hatred and found a scapegoat in the Jews, blaming them for Germany's defeat in the First World War, the hyperinflation of 1923 and the economic depression of 1929. Hitler had no master plan to eliminate Germany of its Jews and until 1939 most of the measures introduced against the Jews were unco-ordinated.

To begin with, Jews were encouraged to leave the country – in 1933 there were 550,000 Jews living in Germany, by 1939 280,000 had emigrated (including Albert Einstein who left for America in 1933). Life for German Jews got harsher as the 1930s progressed, starting with acts of public humiliation, until the Nazis eventually took away their human rights.

The persecution of German Jews, 1933–39

April 1933	Boycott of Jewish shops and businesses
April 1933	Jews banned from working in the civil service and holding positions such as teachers, doctors, dentists, judges
October 1933	Jews banned from working as journalists
May 1935	Jews banned from entering the armed forces
September 1935	The Nuremberg Laws: the Reich Law on Citizenship took away from Jews the right of German citizenship; the Law for the Protection of German Blood and Honour made it illegal for them to marry or to have sexual relations with Aryans
November 1936	Jews banned from using the German greeting 'Heil Hitler'
July 1938	Jews issued with identity cards; Jewish doctors, dentists and lawyers were forbidden to treat Aryans
August 1938	Jews forced to adopt the Jewish forenames of 'Israel' for a man and 'Sarah' for a woman
October 1938	Jewish passports had to be stamped with the large red letter 'J'
November 1938	Kristallnacht (Night of Broken Glass): the murder of a Nazi official in Paris by a young Polish Jew, resulted in the events of 9–10 November. In reprisal for the murder, Goebbels organised attacks on Jewish property in cities across Germany; so many windows were smashed that the event became known as the 'Night of Broken Glass'; over 7,500 Jewish shops were destroyed, 400 synagogues burnt down and about 100 Jews were killed; over 30,000 Jews were arrested and taken to concentration camps; Jews were fined one billion Reichsmarks as compensation for the damage caused
December 1938	Forced sale of Jewish businesses
February 1939	Jews forced to hand over precious metals and jewellery
April 1939	Jews evicted from their homes and forced into **ghettos**

Revision task

Give five examples of how life for Jews living in Germany became more difficult after 1933.

> **Ghetto** Part of a city inhabited by a minority because of social and economic pressure.

Exam practice

Study the interpretation below and then answer the question that follows.

> The Nazis brought prosperity and improved living conditions after the harsh years of the depression. The German people benefited from these changes.
>
> G. Lacey & K. Shephard, two historians, writing in a school history textbook, *Germany 1918–1945*, published in 1999

To what extent do you agree with this interpretation?

[In your answer you should refer to how and why interpretations of this issue differ. Use your own knowledge and understanding of the wider historical debate over this issue to reach a well-supported judgement.]

Marks for spelling, punctuation and the accurate use of grammar and specialist terms are allocated to this question.

Exam tip

Make an initial judgement about the accuracy of the interpretation. Use your knowledge to build up a case to support the interpretation. Suggest other interpretations and use your knowledge to build up a case to support other interpretations. Conclude with a reasoned judgement upon the interpretation.

6 Terror and persuasion

Key question

What methods did the Nazis use to control Germany?

The Nazi police state

REVISED

By 1934 Germany was a police state. The key organs for ensuring conformity were the SS and the Gestapo.

The SS (Schutzstaffel)

Formed in 1925 as a bodyguard for Hitler, they were part of the SA. They wore black uniforms and after 1929 they were led by Heinrich Himmler. After the Night of the Long Knives (see page 60), the SS replaced the SA as the main security force, responsible for the removal of all opposition to the Nazis within Germany. SS officers had to be pure Aryans. By 1934 the SS numbered 50,000.

The Gestapo (Secret State Police)

Set up by Goering in 1933, in 1936 they came under the control of the SS and were led by Himmler's deputy, Reinhard Heydrich. The Gestapo became feared as they could arrest and imprison suspected 'enemies of the state' without trial. Many of those arrested ended up in **concentration camps**. By 1939, 160,000 people were under arrest for political crimes.

Revision task

What role did the following groups play in Nazi Germany?
- the SS
- the Gestapo

TESTED

Concentration camp A prison camp for opponents of the Nazi regime.

Control of the legal system

REVISED

The Nazis also aimed to control the courts and the legal system.
- Judges and lawyers had to belong to the National Socialist League for the Maintenance of Law and Order which forced them to accept Nazi policy. Those who refused were sacked.

- In October 1933, the German Lawyers Front was established and its 10,000 members swore an oath of loyalty to the Führer.
- In 1934 a new People's Court was set up to try enemies of the state. By 1939 it had sentenced over 500 people to death. The number of crimes punishable by death rose from three in 1933 to 46 in 1943. They included such crimes as listening to a foreign radio station.

Goebbels and propaganda   REVISED

In March 1934, the Ministry for Popular Enlightenment and Propaganda was set up under Dr Josef Goebbels. The aim of the organisation was to control the thoughts, beliefs and opinions of the German people. It attempted to brainwash them through a variety of methods.

- Cinema – all films had to be given pro-Nazi story lines, for example, *Hitlerjunge Quex,* about a boy who runs away from a communist family to join the Hitler Youth; film plots had to be shown to Goebbels before going into production; official newsreels which glorified Hitler and Nazi achievements were shown with every film.
- Rallies – an annual mass rally of over 100,000 was staged in September at Nuremberg to showcase the Nazi regime; floodlights, stirring music, flags, banners and marching columns, followed by a speech by Hitler, created an atmosphere of frenzy; spectacular parades were held on other special occasions such as Hitler's birthday in April.
- Radio – all radio stations were placed under Nazi control; cheap mass-produced radios were sold; radio sets were placed in cafés and factories and loudspeakers broadcast programmes in the streets; by 1939, 70 per cent of German families owned a radio.
- Posters – great use was made of posters to put across the Nazi message, for example 'Ein Reich, Ein Volk, Ein Führer' – 'One State, One People, One Leader' about Hitler's leadership.

> **Revision task**
>
> Explain the purpose of propaganda in Nazi Germany.
>
> TESTED

Censorship of newspapers and the arts   REVISED

Goebbels set up the Reich Chamber of Culture. All musicians, writers and actors had to be members.

- Newspapers – all newspapers were subject to strict censorship and editors were told what they could print; the German people only read what the Nazis wanted them to know; by 1935 the Nazis had closed down thousands of magazines and newspapers; the German Press Agency told editors what foreign stories to print.
- Books – all books were censored and those published had to put across the Nazi message; over 2,500 writers were banned; in May 1933 Goebbels organised the burning of banned books through mass bonfires; authors like Bertolt Brecht and Thomas Mann went into exile.
- Music – Hitler hated modern music, jazz in particular; he preferred German folk music and the classical music of German composers Bach, Beethoven and Wagner.
- Theatre – this was meant to focus on German history and political drama; cheap tickets encouraged people to see Nazi-inspired plays.
- Architecture – Hitler favoured the 'monumental' style of architecture and liked the ideas of the ancient Greeks and Romans as they had not been influenced by the Jews.
- Art – Hitler hated modern art and preferred more heroic imagery that promoted Nazi ideals, for example, women as housewives and mothers.

> **Revision task**
>
> Use the information in this section to explain how each of the following factors helped the Nazis gain control over the German people:
> - use of the SS and Gestapo
> - control of the legal system
> - control over central government
> - propaganda
> - censorship.
>
> TESTED

Exam practice

Study the source below and then answer the question that follows.

Source A

German citizens searched in the street by the Gestapo and armed uniformed police

Use Source A and your own knowledge to describe the role of the Gestapo.

Exam tip

Underline key words in the question. This will enable you to focus upon what the examiner wants you to write about. Describe what you can see or read in the source, remembering to make use of the information provided in the caption of a visual source. Link this information to your knowledge of this period. Aim to make at least two developed points.

7 Hitler's foreign policy

Key question

What factors led to the outbreak of war in 1939?

Hitler's foreign policy aims

REVISED

Part of Hitler's popularity was down to his promise to make Germany great again after the humiliation of the Treaty of Versailles. He wrote ideas about how to achieve this in *Mein Kampf* (1924).

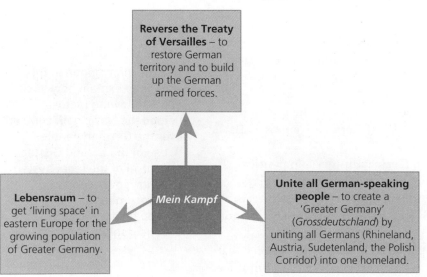

Reverse the Treaty of Versailles – to restore German territory and to build up the German armed forces.

Mein Kampf

Lebensraum – to get 'living space' in eastern Europe for the growing population of Greater Germany.

Unite all German-speaking people – to create a 'Greater Germany' (*Grossdeutschland*) by uniting all Germans (Rhineland, Austria, Sudetenland, the Polish Corridor) into one homeland.

Exam practice answers at **www.hoddereducation.co.uk/myrevisionnotesdownloads**

How did Hitler plan to achieve this? In November 1937 Hitler told his military chief in Berlin that, 'Germany's problem could only be solved by the use of force' – in other words, by war.

Rearmament and conscription

REVISED

When Hitler became Chancellor in 1933, there were a number of circumstances that made it easier for him to break the Treaty of Versailles and begin building up Germany's armed forces.

- After the recent world economic depression, countries were more concerned about focusing on their internal problems than issues abroad.
- The **League of Nations** was seen as weak after its failure to stop the Japanese in Manchuria.
- The British people and politicians felt that Germany had been harshly dealt with by the Treaty of Versailles.

> **League of Nations**
> International body established after the First World War in order to maintain peace.

The Disarmament Conference

REVISED

At the Disarmament Conference in 1932, countries met to discuss ways in which they might disarm to prevent war in future. The Conference failed because of differences between France and Germany. When they argued about all countries disarming equally, Hitler withdrew from the Conference. Hitler could now say he wanted to re-arm to make Germany equal with other countries, for self-defence against the growing armies of France and the Soviet Union. In October 1933, he withdrew Germany's membership of the League of Nations.

Hitler said he would set up a new Air Ministry to train pilots and build 1,000 aircraft. Nothing was done to stop Germany. In March 1935, Hitler announced that he was breaking the terms of the Treaty of Versailles which dealt with **disarmament**. The army, navy and airforce were all built up openly. **Conscription** was introduced. The army was increased from 100,000 in 1933 to 1,400,000 in 1939. In 1933, 3.5 billion marks was spent on producing tanks, aircraft and ships. By 1939 this figure had increased to 26 billion marks.

Rearmament and conscription made Hitler popular within Germany. Jobs were created and people could see that Germany was beginning to be seen as a strong nation once again.

> **Disarmament** When countries reduce the number of weapons they have.
>
> **Conscription** Compulsory military service.
>
> **Rearmament** When countries build up the number of weapons they have.

Stresa Front, April 1935

REVISED

German rearmament alarmed the other European powers. To restrict German rearmament, France, Italy and Britain met at Stresa, a town in Italy. They formally protested about Hitler's plans. This show of unity, known as the Stresa Front, did not last long because of:

- the Anglo-German Naval Treaty of June 1935, which said Germany was allowed to build a fleet up to 35 per cent of the size of Britain's. This encouraged Hitler to break the Treaty of Versailles further
- Anglo-French reactions to the Italian invasion of Abyssinia in October 1935. This destroyed co-operation between France, Italy and Britain.

Revision task

TESTED

What steps did Hitler take to re-arm Germany in the 1930s?

Hitler's attempts to unify German-speaking peoples

REVISED

STEP 1: Return of the Saarland, January 1935
- In 1935 the Saar, which had been taken from Germany in the Treaty of Versailles and run by the League of Nations since 1920, voted by 477,000 to 48,000 to rejoin Germany.

STEP 2: Re-militarising the Rhineland, 1936
- The Rhineland had been demilitarised under the Treaty of Versailles. Allied troops were withdrawn from the Rhineland in 1935 and in the following March Hitler re-occupied it. This was a risk.
- Hitler was convinced that neither Britain nor France would stop him. It convinced Hitler that Britain and France were unlikely to act against further aggression.
- A referendum was held asking the German people to approve the re-occupation and 98.8 per cent voted in favour.

STEP 3: Anschluss, 1938
- In 1934, there was a failed attempt to bring about Anschluss with Austria. The Austrian Nazi Party killed the Austrian chancellor, Dollfuss, after he banned the Nazi Party. Hitler did not support them because he was afraid that Mussolini would use the Italian Army to stop him.
- Hitler was in a much stronger position in 1938 after re-armament. Mussolini was now on his side. Hitler encouraged the Nazi Party in Austria to protest, demanding union with Germany.
- Austrian Chancellor Schuschnigg decided to allow the Austrians to vote on this; 99.75 per cent of Austrians voted in favour of Anschluss.
- Mussolini did not protest.
- Britain, France and the League did protest but took no further action as they did not have the armed forces to stop the Nazis. No one in Europe wanted a repeat of the First World War.

STEP 4: The Sudetenland Crisis, 1938
- The Sudetenland was a part of Czechoslovakia and contained 3 million German speaking people, as well as three-quarters of Czechoslovakia's industry and important armament factories.
- Hitler ordered the Sudeten Nazi Party to stir up trouble in the area. German newspapers published reports of atrocities committed against Sudeten Germans by Czech officials.
- Because of the 'crisis' Hitler said he would support the Sudeten Germans with military force. It would leave Czechoslovakia defenceless against a German attack.
- Four leaders met at Munich in Germany in September 1938 – Chamberlain, Hitler, Mussolini and the French Prime Minister, Daladier. Czechoslovakia and the USSR were not invited.
- They agreed that the Sudetenland would be transferred to Germany. Czechoslovakia's new frontiers would be guaranteed by the four powers.
- Chamberlain also met Hitler alone and they agreed an Anglo-German Declaration, promising never to go to war with each other again. They would settle all disputes between the two countries by talks.
- Britain and France were relieved that war had been avoided but Hitler was convinced that no one would now stop him when he moved on Czechoslovakia and Poland.

STEP 5: The takeover of Czechoslovakia, 1939
- In March 1939, Hitler put pressure on the Czech leader, Hacha, threatening invasion.
- German troops were invited in to restore order, even though there was no disorder. Hitler claimed he had not broken any international laws by securing control of Czechoslovakia even though the Czechs were not Germans.
- The Czech provinces of Bohemia and Moravia became German provinces. Slovakia became a republic but was controlled by Germany.
- Britain and France ended their policy of appeasement and agreed that they had to stop further German aggression.

STEP 6: Danzig and the Polish Corridor, 1939
- Danzig and the Polish Corridor had been taken from Germany at the end of the First World War.
- The Polish Corridor was created to allow Poland access to the Baltic Sea and Danzig was controlled by the League of Nations. Britain had guaranteed Poland's borders.
- Hitler began to make preparations for the invasion of Poland.
- The date for the invasion was set for 1 September 1939.

Revision task

TESTED

Put these steps in Hitler's attempts to unify German-speaking peoples in order of their importance to Hitler's foreign policy and explain your choice:
- re-militarising the Rhineland
- Anschluss with Austria
- Sudetenland Crisis
- invasion of Poland.

Anschluss Union between Germany and Austria.

Appeasement Trying to avoid conflict, in this case allowing Hitler to take over other countries to avoid a future war.

Exam practice answers at **www.hoddereducation.co.uk/myrevisionnotesdownloads**

Alliances and agreements between Germany and other countries

Non-aggression pact with Poland, 1934

In the **non-aggression** pact with Poland in January 1934, Hitler promised to accept the borders of Poland and encouraged trade. The pact was to last ten years and meant Hitler no longer feared an attack from Poland.

Rome–Berlin Axis, 1936

In October 1936, Italy and Germany signed the Rome–Berlin Axis. They agreed to follow a common foreign policy and stop the spread of communism in Europe. Mussolini was keen on closer relations with Germany after Anglo-French opposition to the Italian invasion of Abyssinia.

Anti-Comintern Pact, 1936

In November 1936, Hitler signed a treaty with Japan, called the Anti-**Comintern** Pact. Mussolini joined in November 1937. Their aim was to limit communist influence around the world. It resulted in closer relations between Germany, Japan and Italy.

Pact of Steel, 1939

In May 1939, Hitler and Mussolini formed the Pact of Steel, a full military alliance. They agreed to assist each other in the event of war and would plan operations together. There would be closer economic co-operation between them.

Nazi–Soviet Pact, 1939

Hitler wanted to destroy Poland, not just take back Germany's lost land. He needed the co-operation of the Soviet Union. Ribbentrop, the Nazi Foreign Minister, and Molotov, the Soviet Foreign Minister, signed the Nazi–Soviet Pact in August 1939. The public terms of the pact included promising not to support attacks on each other. In secret they agreed to divide Poland and the Soviet Union was to be allowed to occupy the Baltic states of Estonia, Latvia and Lithuania. It meant Hitler could easily invade Poland without worrying about the Soviet Union stopping him.

> **Non-aggression** Agreeing not to attack each other.
>
> **Comintern** The international organisation set up to spread communism around the world.

> **Revision task**
>
> Draw a timeline from 1933 to 1939 and record on it all the main events mentioned in Chapter 2.7 on Nazi foreign policy in the 1930s. Make a list of any connections you can find between agreements made with other countries and Germany's aggressive actions towards other countries.
>
> TESTED

The outbreak of the Second World War in Europe

On 1 September 1939, German troops invaded Poland. The British and French governments gave Hitler an ultimatum demanding the withdrawal of all troops from Poland. Hitler did not reply and on 3 September, Britain and France declared war on Germany.

> **Exam tip**
>
> Make an initial judgement about the accuracy of the interpretation. Use your knowledge to build up a case to support the interpretation. Suggest other interpretations and use your knowledge to build up a case to support other interpretations. Conclude with a reasoned judgement upon the interpretation.

Exam practice

Study the interpretation below and then answer the question that follows.

> Hitler's main aim in foreign policy was to unite all German speaking people in a single country.
>
> Josh Brooman, a historian, writing in a school history textbook, *Hitler's Germany, 1933–1945*, published in 1987

To what extent do you agree with this interpretation?

Section 3 The development of the USA, 1929–2000

1 Economic downturn and recovery

Key question

How was the USA affected by the Great Depression between 1929 and 1945?

The impact of the Wall Street Crash and the Depression

In October 1929, the panic selling of shares on Wall Street led to a loss of confidence in the financial markets. Share prices crashed, causing the collapse of the US stock market. The event became known as the **Wall Street Crash** and it was to lead to the **Great Depression**.

Rising unemployment
- Factories, banks and businesses collapsed.
- Mid 1929 unemployment = 1.5 million
  1930 = 5 million
  1931 = 9 million
  1932 = 13 million.

Depression in the cities
- By 1933 one-third of the workforce in the cities was unemployed.
- Many could not pay their rent and became homeless, forced to live in shanty towns called **Hoovervilles.**

Impact of the Wall Street Crash

Family life
- There was no system of social security so many were forced to rely on charity and handouts.
- There was a sharp rise in suicides, a fall in the number of marriages and a fall in the birth rate.

Depression in the countryside
- Many farmers were unable to sell their produce and became bankrupt.
- Many were evicted and became **hobos** searching for work.
- A drought in 1931 caused the soil in Oklahoma, Colorado, New Mexico and Kansas to turn to dust.
- Dust storms affected 20 million hectares creating a 'dust bowl'.

Wall Street Crash The collapse of the American stock market in October 1929.

Great Depression The economic and social slump which followed the Wall Street Crash.

Hobo An unemployed wanderer searching for work.

Republican attempts to deal with the Depression

REVISED

Herbert Hoover was a Republican who became president in 1928. He was criticised for doing too little to help those affected by the Depression:

- He believed in **balancing the budget** and refused to borrow money to help create jobs.
- He believed in **rugged individualism**.
- In May–June 1932, the **Bonus Army** of unemployed war veterans marched on Washington to demand the early payment of war bonuses which were due to be paid in 1945. They set up a huge **Hooverville** outside the White House. Hoover sent in troops to remove them and burn down the shanty town.

This created an image of a president who did not care. It gave rise to a popular slogan: 'In Hoover we trusted, now we are busted'.

However, in 1932 Hoover did attempt to introduce measures to relieve the crisis.

- Reconstruction Finance Corporation (February 1932) – this gave two billion dollars of federal aid to ailing banks, insurance companies and railways.
- Emergency Relief Act (July 1932) – this gave $300 million to state governments to help the unemployed.
- Home Loan Bank Act (July 1932) – 12 regional banks were set up to stimulate house building and home ownership.

These measures had little time to work before a presidential election was held in November 1932.

> **Balancing the budget** Making sure the government does not spend more money than it gets from taxes.
>
> **Rugged individualism** The idea that individuals were responsible for their own lives and should not expect help from the government.
>
> **Bonus Army** First World War veterans who gathered in Washington in 1932 to demand cash payment of war bonuses.
>
> **Hoovervilles** Shanty towns built on the edges of cities by the unemployed during the Great Depression: named after President Hoover.

The 1932 presidential election

The two candidates fighting the presidential election in November 1932 were the Republican Herbert Hoover, who was attempting to be re-elected, and the Democrat Franklin Delano Roosevelt (FDR). Roosevelt won a landslide victory, securing 42 of the 48 states.

Republican candidate: Herbert Hoover	Democrat candidate: Franklin Delano Roosevelt
Hoover was unpopular because… • Republicans were blamed for the Depression • Hoover was criticised for the harsh treatment of the Bonus Army • relief schemes were too small and too late • Hoover seemed to offer nothing new.	Roosevelt was increasingly popular because… • the Democrats offered a more caring image • he had overcome personal hardship: he suffered from polio – he was a fighter • he kept his message simple • he promised the American people a 'New Deal'.

Revision task

TESTED

1 Using your knowledge of this topic, explain the impact of the Great Depression on:
   - unemployment
   - city dwellers
   - farmers.
2 Give three reasons why Hoover lost and three reasons why Roosevelt won the 1932 presidential election.

President Roosevelt and the New Deal

When he took office as president in January 1933, Roosevelt introduced a change of policy known as the **New Deal**. It was based upon the 'three R's' – Relief, Recovery and Reform. In his first hundred days (9 March–16 June 1933) he introduced a large number of government programmes aimed at restoring the shattered economy. In so doing he created the **Alphabet Agencies**.

> **New Deal** Policies introduced by President Roosevelt to deal with the effects of the Great Depression.
>
> **Alphabet Agencies** Nickname given to the group of organisations set up as part of the New Deal.

The First New Deal

Legislation/Agency	Problem	Solution/Action taken
Emergency Banking Act (EBA)	Americans had little confidence in the banks; many banks had gone bankrupt	The government closed all banks for ten days; Roosevelt reassured the American people that their money was safe; the government officially backed 5,000 banks which helped to restore confidence.
Federal Emergency Relief Administration (FERA)	Poverty and unemployment	This provided $500 million for emergency relief to help the poor and homeless, e.g. providing food and clothing.
Civilian Conservation Corps (CCC)	Unemployment among young people	This provided six months of work for men aged between 18 and 25 in conservation projects such as planting trees to stop soil erosion; by 1940 over 2 million men had been given work in the CCC.
Public Works Administration (PWA)	Unemployment	The government spent $3,300 million on public works projects for the unemployed – slum clearance; building schools; roads; hospitals.
Agricultural Adjustment Administration (AAA)	Rural poverty, low crop prices	This was intended to help farmers increase their profits; subsidies were paid to farmers to destroy their crops and slaughter animals in an effort to push up prices; by 1936, farm incomes were one and a half times higher than in 1933.
National Industrial Recovery Act (NIRA)	Poor economic condition of the USA	This led to the setting up of the National Recovery Administration (NRA) to encourage employers to improve conditions; it introduced codes of practice for minimum wages, hours and conditions; companies complying with the code could display the Blue Eagle symbol.
Tennessee Valley Authority (TVA)	Agricultural over-production; regular flooding in the Tennessee Valley	A huge public works programme was set up to build 21 dams to irrigate the land and generate hydroelectric power; farmers were given loans and training in soil conservation.

In January 1935, Roosevelt introduced a Second New Deal which targeted the rights of workers, the poor and the unemployed.

Exam practice answers at **www.hoddereducation.co.uk/myrevisionnotesdownloads**

The Second New Deal

Legislation/Agency	Problem	Solution/Action taken
Works Progress Administration (WPA)	Unemployment	This oversaw job creation schemes – putting people to work building roads, schools, hospitals, airports, harbours.
National Labour Relations Act (the Wagner Act)	Workers' rights	This gave workers the legal right to join trade unions; it stopped employers sacking union members; it set up the National Labour Relations Board which protected workers against unfair practices.
Fair Labour Standards Act	Fair play for workers	This tightened up laws against child labour and minimum wages; 300,000 workers secured higher wages as a result and 1 million had a shorter working week.
Social Security Act	Poverty	This set up a national system of social security, providing pensions for the over 65s and aid to the disabled, widows and orphans, as well as unemployment benefits.

Revision task

TESTED ☐

For each of the following Alphabet Agencies, write out its full name and describe what it did to help tackle the problems caused by the Great Depression: CCC, AAA, TVA, EBA, PWA.

Successes of the New Deal

The New Deal helped to restore confidence and faith in government; it stimulated the economy and put the country back on its feet.

- America avoided the swing to communism and fascism that overtook Europe.
- Millions of jobs were created through the Alphabet Agencies – 4 million people were employed on public works schemes created by the PWA and WPA; 2.5 million were employed in the CCC.
- The TVA improved the lives of 7 million people.
- The income of farmers doubled between 1932 and 1939 as a result of the AAA.
- The New Deal stabilised the US banking system and restored confidence to the markets.
- Workers were protected by codes of practice and trade unions were allowed.
- It created a semi-welfare state, providing pensions for the elderly and widows and state help for the sick, disabled and unemployed.

Criticisms of the New Deal

1 Some believed the New Deal did not go far enough

- The New Deal agencies discriminated against black people; they either got no work or received lower wages than white workers.
- Huey Long, Governor of Louisiana, criticised Roosevelt for not sharing out the nation's wealth fairly and proposed his own 'Share Our Wealth' campaign.
- Father Charles Coughlin criticised the New Deal for not doing enough to help the needy; his weekly radio broadcasts attracted over 40 million listeners.
- Dr Frances Townsend argued that Roosevelt had not done enough to help old people and proposed a pension of $200 a month for everyone over 60.

2 Some believed that the New Deal undermined important American values, principles and laws

- Some felt that the federal government now interfered too much in the affairs of the American people; the New Deal went against the belief in rugged individualism.
- It was argued that the new social welfare measures encouraged people to live off the state.
- Republicans were highly critical, claiming that Roosevelt was changing the accepted role of government in the USA.
- Many viewed trade unions as un-American as they were seen to take away the right of choice from workers.
- Some conservative Democrats were critical, believing that too much power was given to trade unions.
- In 1935, the Supreme Court ruled that the NRA was unconstitutional, and in 1936 it declared the AAA unconstitutional, claiming that Roosevelt had used federal powers which the constitution had not given him.

3 Later historical reflections concluded ...

- The Alphabet Agencies were short-term solutions that provided cheap labour and did not solve the underlying economic problems.
- Unemployment did fall but it was America's entry into the Second World War in 1941 that ultimately lifted the country out of the Depression.

Revision task

TESTED ☐

1 Which do you think are the three most important successes of the New Deal?
2 Which are the three strongest criticisms?

Exam practice

Describe the impact of the Wall Street Crash upon the US economy.

Exam tip

Make sure you only include information which is directly relevant. It is a good idea to start your answer using the words of the question. For example, 'The Wall Street Crash brought about dramatic change ...' Try to include specific factual detail such as dates, events, names of key people. Aim to write a good sized paragraph, covering at least three key features/points.

2 The economic impact of the Second World War and post-war developments

Key question

How had the economy of the USA changed by the 1960s?

Why did America benefit economically from the Second World War?

REVISED

War had broken out in Europe in 1939 but America did not enter the conflict until after the Japanese bombing of Pearl Harbor in December 1941.

Increased role of the federal government
- The War Production Board (WPB) was set up in 1942.
- It organised and provided for the needs of war.
- By 1945 industrial production had doubled.

Why did America benefit economically from WW2?

Internal migration
- Between 1941 and 1945 over 27 million Americans migrated, mainly in search of better jobs.

Wartime production
- Traditional industries such as coal, iron, steel and oil greatly expanded.
- Arms production rapidly increased.
- By 1944 the USA was producing half the weapons in the world.

End to unemployment
- Conscription meant that more workers were needed and this put an end to unemployment.
- In 1939 unemployment stood at 9.5 million; this had fallen to 670,000 by 1944.

US industry after the Second World War boomed because:
- millions of US citizens who purchased **war bonds** cashed them in
- Americans wanted to leave rationing behind and buy consumer goods
- the automobile industry increased sales again
- there was a surge in house building stimulated by low interest loans for returning servicemen.

By the end of the 1940s, the USA produced one-half of the world's manufactured goods: 57 per cent of steel, 62 per cent of oil and 80 per cent of cars.

Following the death of President Roosevelt in April 1945, the new president, Harry S Truman, introduced a programme of economic development and social welfare which became known as the **Fair Deal**. The policy was continued by his successor, President Dwight Eisenhower, and it led to the prosperity of the 1950s.

War bonds Ordinary people bought these to finance the military during the war and would be paid back when the war was over.

Fair Deal The domestic policies of President Truman, 1945–53.

US Presidents, 1933–61

Roosevelt	1933 – 1945
Truman	1945 – 1953
Eisenhower	1953 – 1961

Revision task

TESTED

Explain why the USA benefitted economically from the Second World War.

Consumerism and suburbanisation

REVISED

Post-war America was an affluent society getting richer because:

- Americans spent money saved during the war on consumer goods, especially televisions and cars
- **hire purchase**, known as consumer credit, increased
- better working practices meant that consumer goods could be produced more cheaply, which kept down prices
- the growth in population also provided a greater demand for goods
- the ongoing **Cold War** (see chapter 3.6) meant that US industry kept turning out new weapons, boosting industries such as steel, coal and electronics.

> **Hire purchase** Paying for goods in instalments over a fixed period of time.
>
> **Cold War** Conflict between the USA and the USSR without direct fighting between 1947 and 1991.

In 1960, the standard of living of the average American was three times that of the average Briton. They were encouraged to spend, and shopping became a popular recreational activity. In new homes, all the modern conveniences were expected and became necessities not luxuries. Vast supermarkets, new freeways (motorways), large cars with fins and chrome, and television games were all, it was claimed, symbols of a flourishing economy and a free society.

During the 1950s many middle-class families moved away from the centre of cities to new homes in the suburbs. Here they could live the 'American Dream' of owning their own home furnished with the latest 'must have' household appliances.

Revision task

How did the following factors make America richer after the Second World War?

- money saved during the war
- hire purchase
- population growth

TESTED

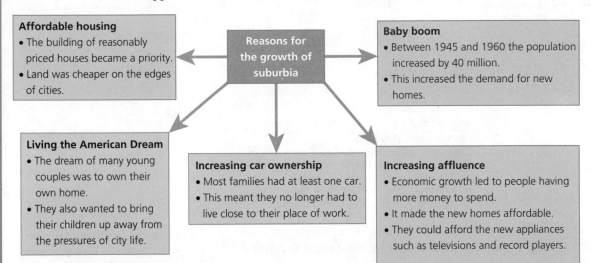

Affordable housing
- The building of reasonably priced houses became a priority.
- Land was cheaper on the edges of cities.

Reasons for the growth of suburbia

Baby boom
- Between 1945 and 1960 the population increased by 40 million.
- This increased the demand for new homes.

Living the American Dream
- The dream of many young couples was to own their own home.
- They also wanted to bring their children up away from the pressures of city life.

Increasing car ownership
- Most families had at least one car.
- This meant they no longer had to live close to their place of work.

Increasing affluence
- Economic growth led to people having more money to spend.
- It made the new homes affordable.
- They could afford the new appliances such as televisions and record players.

Revision task

TESTED

Write a paragraph to describe the key features of life in suburbia in 1950s America.

'Poverty amidst plenty'

REVISED

While the 1950s was a time of growing prosperity from which many Americans benefited, it was not a time of **affluence** for all.

> **Affluence** A time of increasing wealth and prosperity.

Exam practice answers at **www.hoddereducation.co.uk/myrevisionnotesdownloads**

The affluent society	The 'other' America
• By 1960, the standard of living of the average American was three times that of the average Briton. • By 1960, 25 per cent of Americans lived in **suburbia**. • Television sets, record players, swimming pools and at least one car became status symbols, the 'must have' items.	• By 1959, 29 per cent of the population (50 million) lived below the poverty line. • Included among the poor were the 'hillbillies' of the Appalachian mountains; Hispanic workers in the west; black people in the city **ghettos** in the north. • Poor Americans found it hard to afford the rising cost of healthcare (there was no national health service).

Exam practice

The lives of many Americans changed between 1945 and the late 1960s due to the influence of developments such as:
- post-war affluence
- consumerism
- suburbanisation.

Arrange the developments in order of their significance in changing the lives of many Americans between 1945 and the late 1960s. Explain your choices.

Suburbia The residential area on the outskirts of a city.

Ghetto Part of a city inhabited by a minority because of social and economic pressure.

Exam tip

You need to decide in which order to write about the three factors – there is no correct order as it is the quality of the justification of your choice that is most important. You need to demonstrate good subject knowledge by providing specific detail upon each factor. You must fully explain the significance of each factor, using your knowledge to set them within their historical context. Aim to provide a clear, well-supported justification for your reasoning.

3 The issue of civil rights, 1941–1970

Key question

Why was it difficult for black Americans to gain equal rights between 1941 and 1970?

The contribution of black Americans to the war effort

REVISED

On the front line

Following America's entry into the war in 1941, many black Americans enlisted. They had to fight for their country in **segregated** units. In the army there were black-only units which formed the **Jim Crow** Army.
- Before 1944, black soldiers were not allowed into combat in the marines – they were used only to transport supplies or as cooks and labourers.
- The navy would only accept blacks as mess men (working in the canteens).

Segregation Keeping a group separate from the rest of society, usually on the basis of race or religion.

'Jim Crow' laws Laws which introduced segregation and discrimination against black Americans in the southern states.

- The US air force would not accept black pilots until the formation of an African American 332nd Fighter Group known as the Tuskegee airmen; by the end of the war there were 1,000 black pilots.
- The 761st Tank Battalion, nicknamed the 'Black panthers', saw action in the Battle of the Bulge in France and Belgium in 1944.

In 1948, as a direct consequence of the contributions of black Americans to the war effort, President Truman banned 'separate but equal' recruiting, training and service in the army, air force, navy and Marine Corps.

Contribution to the war effort on the Home Front

Black workers made an important contribution to the war effort at home.

- In 1941, fearing race riots, President Roosevelt set up a Fair Employment Practices Committee which banned discrimination against black Americans in those factories used by the government in the production of war goods.
- This was an important victory in the campaign for equality.
- By 1944, nearly 2 million black people were working in war factories.
- Black Americans began a 'Double V' campaign – victory over fascism abroad and victory over discrimination at home.
- Membership of the **NAACP** rose from 50,000 to 450,000 during the war.

> **NAACP** Organisation set up in 1909 to campaign for civil rights.
>
> **Lynching** Illegal execution by a mob, often by hanging.

The impact of the war on the civil rights issue

In 1946, as part of his 'Fair Deal' programme, President Truman set up a civil rights committee. This proposed an anti-**lynching** bill and the abolition of the requirement that black Americans had to prove they had paid tax in order to be able to vote. Due to opposition, Truman was unable to implement these recommendations. However, Truman's support for civil rights gave encouragement to the NAACP which began to challenge the segregation laws in the courts in the 1950s.

The struggle for equal education

REVISED

There was considerable progress in the campaign for improved civil rights during the 1950s and 1960s, particularly in the attempts to remove segregation from education.

Brown v. Topeka Board of Education, 1954

- In 1952, 20 US states had segregated public schools.
- Linda Brown had to walk 20 blocks to her school in Topeka, Kansas, even though there was a school for white pupils just a few blocks from her home.
- In 1952, her father, Oliver Brown, with the help of the NAACP, took the Board of Education to court.
- After losing the case in the state courts, the NAACP took the case to the Supreme Court.
- In May 1954, the Supreme Court ruled that racial segregation in public schools went against the US constitution.
- However, the Supreme Court had no power to impose its decision and many southern states continued to ignore the ruling.

Little Rock Central High School, Arkansas, 1957

- In September 1957, nine African-American students led by Elizabeth Eckford attempted to enter the white-only Central High School in Little Rock.
- The Governor of Arkansas, Orval Faubus, surrounded the school with National Guardsmen to prevent the nine students from entering.
- President Eisenhower responded by sending 1,000 federal troops of the 101st Airborne Division to protect the students for the rest of the school year.
- Eight of the nine students graduated at the end of the year.
- Little Rock is important because it showed that the president could and would enforce court orders with federal troops and it brought publicity to the injustices of segregation.
- However, by 1964 fewer than 2 per cent of African-American children attended multi-racial schools in the southern states.

James Meredith and Mississippi University, 1962

- In June 1962, the Supreme Court upheld a federal court decision to force Mississippi University to accept the black student James Meredith.
- When Meredith arrived to register for admission he was prevented from doing so by the Governor of Mississippi.
- Riots broke out and President Kennedy sent in 2,000 troops to restore order.
- 300 soldiers had to remain on the university campus to protect Meredith until he graduated with his degree three years later.

The struggle for equality in public transport

REVISED

Progress in the campaign for improved civil rights in this period also focused around public transport.

The Montgomery bus boycott, 1955–56

This took place in Montgomery, Alabama, and is considered to mark the beginning of the civil rights movement. In Montgomery a local law stated that African-Americans had to sit on the back seats of buses and had to give up those seats if white people wanted them.

- On 1 December 1955, Rosa Parks, an NAACP activist, refused to give up her seat and was arrested and convicted of breaking the bus laws.
- Local civil rights activists set up the Montgomery Improvement Association (MIA), led by the Reverend Dr Martin Luther King, a young Baptist minister. The group organised a boycott: they deliberately stopped using the buses, arranging private transport for people.
- Civil rights lawyers fought Rosa Parks' case in court and in December 1956 the Supreme Court declared Montgomery's bus laws illegal. The bus company gave in.
- This was the beginning of non-violent mass protests by the civil rights movement.

The 'freedom rides', 1961

Segregation still existed on interstate buses and in May 1961 members of the Congress of Racial Equality (**CORE**) began a form of direct protest in the southern states known as the **freedom rides**.

CORE (Congress of Racial Equality) Founded in 1942 to campaign for black civil rights.

Freedom rides Campaigners rode on interstate buses to see if segregation on buses had been ended.

- They deliberately rode on buses run by companies that were ignoring laws banning segregation. The first freedom rides began at Washington DC on 4 May 1961 with the plan of travelling down to New Orleans – once they reached the southern states the riders met with a hostile reception.
- At Anniston, Alabama, a bus was attacked and burnt. In Montgomery, white racists beat up several freedom riders. At Birmingham there was no police protection for the freedom riders and they were attacked by an angry mob. In Jackson, Mississippi, 27 freedom riders were jailed for 67 days for sitting in the whites–only section of the bus station.
- The freedom riders continued, against much violence, throughout the summer. By September, 70,000 students had taken part and 3,600 had been arrested.
- The Attorney General Robert Kennedy was able to get the Interstate Commerce Committee to end segregation in all bus and rail stations and airports.

Revision task

TESTED

Explain how each of the following protest strategies helped in the campaign to achieve civil rights:
- bus boycotts
- freedom rides.

The roles of Martin Luther King and Malcolm X

REVISED

The dominant figure in the campaign for civil rights was the Reverend Dr Martin Luther King, Minister of the Dexter Avenue Baptist Church in Montgomery, Alabama.

The role and significance of Martin Luther King

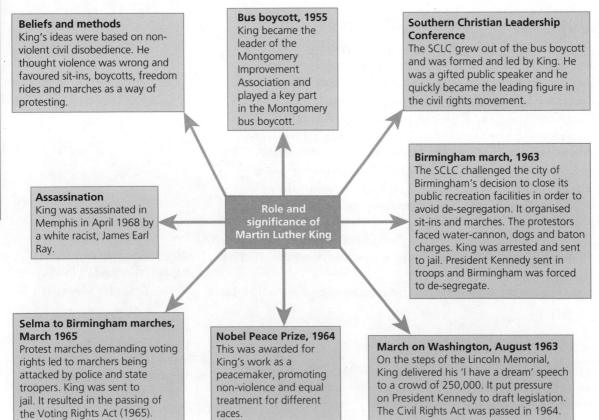

Beliefs and methods
King's ideas were based on non-violent civil disobedience. He thought violence was wrong and favoured sit-ins, boycotts, freedom rides and marches as a way of protesting.

Bus boycott, 1955
King became the leader of the Montgomery Improvement Association and played a key part in the Montgomery bus boycott.

Southern Christian Leadership Conference
The SCLC grew out of the bus boycott and was formed and led by King. He was a gifted public speaker and he quickly became the leading figure in the civil rights movement.

Assassination
King was assassinated in Memphis in April 1968 by a white racist, James Earl Ray.

Role and significance of Martin Luther King

Birmingham march, 1963
The SCLC challenged the city of Birmingham's decision to close its public recreation facilities in order to avoid de-segregation. It organised sit-ins and marches. The protestors faced water-cannon, dogs and baton charges. King was arrested and sent to jail. President Kennedy sent in troops and Birmingham was forced to de-segregate.

Selma to Birmingham marches, March 1965
Protest marches demanding voting rights led to marchers being attacked by police and state troopers. King was sent to jail. It resulted in the passing of the Voting Rights Act (1965).

Nobel Peace Prize, 1964
This was awarded for King's work as a peacemaker, promoting non-violence and equal treatment for different races.

March on Washington, August 1963
On the steps of the Lincoln Memorial, King delivered his 'I have a dream' speech to a crowd of 250,000. It put pressure on President Kennedy to draft legislation. The Civil Rights Act was passed in 1964.

The role and significance of Malcolm X

- Malcolm Little was the son of an African-American Baptist preacher who was murdered by white supremacists.
- In 1952, he joined the Nation of Islam and changed his surname to 'X'.
- He rejected King's peaceful methods and believed violence could be justified to secure a separate black nation.
- He was a good public speaker who attracted support from young black Americans.
- In 1964, he left the Nation of Islam and formed the Muslim Mosque Inc and the black nationalist Organisation of Afro-American Unity.
- He encouraged the self-esteem of black Americans and his views and ideas became the foundation for the radical movements Black Power and the Black Panthers.
- He was shot dead by three members of the Nation of Islam in February 1965.

Stokely Carmichael, the Black Power Movement and the Black Panthers

- The Black Power movement emerged out of the anger and frustration expressed by young black Americans over high unemployment and poverty; its leading spokesperson was Stokely Carmichael.
- In 1966, Carmichael became chairman of the SNCC (Student Non-violent Coordinating Committee).
- He wanted blacks to have pride in their heritage and adopted the slogan 'Black is beautiful'.
- In 1968, Carmichael joined the Black Panthers, a party formed in 1966 by Bobby Seale and Huey Newton; its members wore uniforms and were prepared to use force to achieve their aim of a socialist society.
- In the 1968 Mexico City Olympics, two black athletes, Tommie Smith and John Carlos, both members of the Black Panthers, used their medal ceremony to wear a single black glove and to give the clenched fist salute — it gave the movement international publicity.

> ### Key facts
>
> There are lots of different civil rights organisations with acronyms. This can be confusing. Make sure you know the difference between them.
>
> | Organisation | Date founded | Short for |
> |---|---|---|
> | NAACP | 1909 | National Association for the Advancement of Colored People |
> | CORE | 1942 | Congress of Racial Equality |
> | SCLC | 1957 | Southern Christian Leaders Conference |
> | SNCC | 1960 | Student Non-violent Coordinating Committee |

> ### Revision task
>
> For each of the following individuals, list their aims and beliefs, the methods they used to achieve equal rights for black Americans and their importance in the campaign:
> - Martin Luther King
> - Malcolm X
> - Stokely Carmichael.
>
> TESTED

Civil rights legislation

During the 1960s, legislation appeared which attempted to remove discrimination and secure civil rights.

Civil Rights Act, 1964	• Racial discrimination banned in employment • Black students given equal rights to enter all public places and bodies receiving government money, including schools • Equal Employment Opportunities Commission set up to investigate complaints of discrimination
Voting Rights Act, 1965	• Stopped racial discrimination over the right to vote • Ended literacy tests
Supreme Court ruling, 1967	• Supreme Court ruled that state laws banning interracial marriages were unconstitutional
Fair Housing Act, 1968	• Made racial discrimination illegal in the property market

Exam practice

How important was the issue of education in the struggle for civil rights in the USA between 1941 and 1970?

[In your answer you should discuss the importance of education alongside other factors in order to reach a judgement.]

Exam tip

The question requires you to evaluate the importance or success of a particular event, movement or individual. You must aim to analyse and evaluate the importance or significance of the factor named in the question. You need to support your argument with specific factual detail. You need to consider a counter-argument by considering the importance or significance of other factors. You must end with a reasoned and well-supported judgement

4 Political change, 1960–2000

Key question

What were the main political developments in the USA between 1960 and 2000?

The domestic policies of President Kennedy

In November 1960, John F. Kennedy, a Democrat, was elected president. He introduced a programme of reform called the **New Frontier** which aimed to tackle three focus areas: poverty, inequality and deprivation.

New Frontier The reform policies of President Kennedy in the early 1960s.

The New Frontier

Civil Rights	Kennedy appointed Thurgood Marshall as America's first black federal judge; he sent troops to ensure that James Meredith could be the first black student at Mississippi University; he introduced a Civil Rights Bill.
Economy	Kennedy introduced a $900 million public works programme to build roads and public buildings; he increased spending on defence and space technology which created jobs; he cut taxes to encourage people to buy goods.
Social Reform	Kennedy proposed introducing Medicare – a cheap system of state health insurance; the Social Security Act 1962 gave financial help to the elderly and unemployed; the Area Redevelopment Act 1961 gave loans and grants to states with long-term unemployment; the Housing Act 1961 gave cheap loans for redevelopment of inner cities.

However, Kennedy faced opposition in Congress to his ideas and many of his bills were rejected. He was assassinated in November 1963 and so was unable to complete his reform programme.

The domestic policies of Johnson

REVISED

Johnson's **Great Society** declared war on poverty, aiming to make America a country with high living standards and a sense of community.

> **Great Society** The reform programme of President Johnson in the 1960s.

The Great Society

Civil Rights	The Civil Rights Act 1964 banned discrimination and set up the Equal Opportunities Commission; the Voting Rights Act 1965 ensured fair voting procedures; in 1967 the ban on mixed marriages was lifted.
Economy	Johnson cut taxes to encourage people to spend, help businesses grow and create jobs; he improved the railways and highways; he gave federal funds to help depressed areas such as the Appalachians.
Social Reform	The Medical Care Act 1965 provided Medicare (for the old) and Medicaid (for the poor); the Elementary and Secondary Education Act 1965 provided the first ever federal funding for state education; the Model Cities Act 1966 targeted urban renewal and slum clearance; the minimum wage was increased; funding was provided for education and community projects in inner cities.

Like Kennedy, Johnson faced powerful opposition in Congress to his reform measures. However, following Kennedy's assassination the American people were more sympathetic to the reforms he had wanted for the USA, and Johnson was an experienced politician able to win support for such measures.

Revision task

TESTED

Copy and complete the table below to show how Presidents Kennedy and Johnson attempted to deal with the three key issues of poverty, inequality and deprivation.

	What the New Frontier did to tackle this issue	What the Great Society did to tackle this issue
Poverty		
Inequality		
Deprivation		

Nixon and the Watergate Scandal

REVISED

In 1968, Richard Nixon, a Republican, was elected president and was re-elected in 1972. He promised to end America's involvement in the Vietnam War and to cut federal government expenditure.

In August 1974 Nixon was forced to resign as president because of the Watergate scandal which had begun in 1972.

- In 1972, Nixon set up CREEP – Committee to Re-elect the President – giving permission to use any tactics.
- On 17 June 1972, five members of CREEP were arrested for breaking into the Watergate offices of the Democratic Party.
- Nixon ordered a cover-up and denied any knowledge of the incident and went on to win a landslide re-election victory.
- In January 1973, the Watergate burglars went on trial and were all convicted. Nixon again denied any cover-up.
- On 30 April 1973, Nixon's top advisers Bob Haldeman and John Ehrlichman resigned.
- On 25 June 1973, Nixon's sacked lawyer, John Dean, testified to the Senate Watergate Committee that there had been a cover-up directed by Nixon.
- It was revealed that all the president's conversations had been taped but Nixon refused to hand over the tapes.
- On 21 November 1973, the tapes were handed over but some were missing or contained gaps.
- On 30 April 1974, Nixon was forced to hand over all the tapes unedited which showed that he had repeatedly lied throughout the investigation.
- On 27 July 1974, Congress decided to impeach Nixon.
- On 8 August 1974, Nixon resigned to avoid **impeachment**.
- On 6 September 1974, President Gerald Ford pardoned Nixon for his part in the scandal.

Impeachment To bring the US president to trial for treason.

Effects of the Watergate scandal

- It showed the strength of the US Constitution – the system of checks and balances had brought down a corrupt president.
- It resulted in a reduction in the powers of government: setting limits on election contributions; curbing what the president could/could not spend money on; controlling the President's ability to declare war.
- It undermined people's confidence in politics and politicians.
- It destroyed Nixon's reputation, giving rise to the nickname 'Tricky Dicky'.
- It damaged America's reputation abroad. The USSR said it was an example of a corrupt capitalist system.

US Presidents, 1961–89	
Kennedy	1961 – 63
Johnson	1963 – 69
Nixon	1969 – 74
Ford	1974 – 77
Carter	1977 – 81
Reagan	1981 – 89

Revision task

TESTED

Make a copy of the following table. Use your knowledge of the Watergate scandal to complete each section.

Key events of the Watergate break-in and trial	Reasons for Nixon's resignation	Key effects of the Watergate scandal

Exam practice answers at **www.hoddereducation.co.uk/myrevisionnotesdownloads**

The policies of Ronald Reagan

REVISED

- In 1980, Reagan defeated Jimmy Carter to become president. He inherited severe economic problems – high inflation (15 per cent); rising unemployment (7.5 per cent); high **budget deficit**; world recession.
- Reagan introduced a series of economic reforms which obtained the nickname **Reaganomics**.
- He slashed income tax (cutting taxes by $33 billion, the largest tax cut in US history), hoping to encourage people to spend and thereby create jobs.
- He slashed welfare programmes by $20 billion a year for three years, returning to the ideal of 'rugged individualism'.
- He cut taxes at a time when government expenditure increased (especially on the space programme) and this caused the **national debt** to grow.
- 1987 saw the worst stock market crash since 1929 and the USA began to edge into recession.

> **Budget deficit** When a government spends more money than it receives through taxes and has to borrow.
>
> **Reaganomics** The economic policies of President Reagan in the 1980s.
>
> **National debt** Money owed by the government.

How did America change under Presidents Bush Senior and Clinton?

REVISED

The policies of George Bush Snr

President Bush Snr continued with Reagan's domestic polices but he faced severe economic problems.
- The budget deficit had trebled in size between 1980 and 1990.
- Bush was forced to go back on election promises and increase indirect taxes and impose new taxes on the wealthy.
- The budget deficit continued to grow – in 1992 it was calculated that 14 per cent of all Americans lived in poverty.
- Bush did pass two important acts in 1990 – a Disability Act which forbade discrimination based on disability and a Clear Air Act.
- There were serious race riots in 1992 in Los Angeles, Atlanta, Birmingham, Seattle and Chicago.

US Presidents, 1989–2001	
Bush	1989 – 93
Clinton	1993 – 2001

The policies of Bill Clinton

Unlike Reagan and Bush Snr, Clinton was a Democrat who promised more direct action from the federal government to tackle the country's economic problems. There were three key features to his domestic policies:
- Abandon Reaganomics – he increased federal government spending, increased taxes and reduced the national debt – policies which helped to bring sustained economic growth.
- Welfare reforms – in 1996 he introduced a minimum hourly wage; his Health Security Bill which aimed to set up a system of universal health insurance was rejected by Congress.
- Scandals – an investigation into the Whitewater scandal of 1996 revealed that Clinton had been having an affair with Monica Lewinsky, a former member of the White House staff. He was threatened with impeachment.

Exam tip

You should aim to produce a well-supported judgement upon the extent of change. You need to identify and discuss a number of factors to support your argument. You must demonstrate good understanding of the topics under discussion. Good factual detail will help to provide context. End with a concluding sentence which directly addresses the question.

Exam practice

How far did President Reagan's reform policies deal with the social and economic problems facing America during the late 1980s?

Revision task

Make a copy of the following table. Use your knowledge of the domestic policies of Presidents Reagan, Bush Snr and Clinton to complete each section.

	Response of President Reagan to:	Response of President George Bush Snr to:	Response of President Clinton to:
Taxation			
Government expenditure			
Welfare programmes			

5 Social Change, 1950–2000

Key question

How did American society change between 1950 and 2000?

Changes in music

There were major changes to US society in the second half of the twentieth century, partly resulting from the impact of the cinema, television, music and developments in information technology.

Music

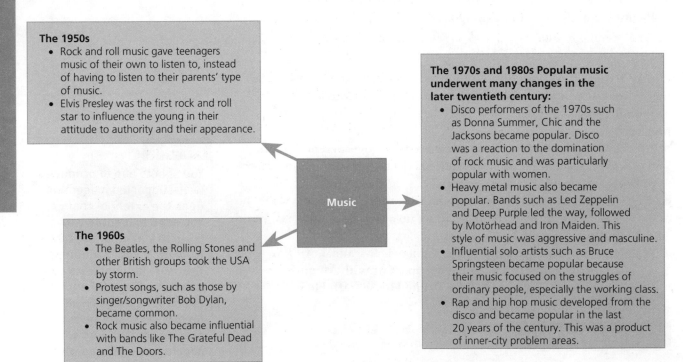

The 1950s
- Rock and roll music gave teenagers music of their own to listen to, instead of having to listen to their parents' type of music.
- Elvis Presley was the first rock and roll star to influence the young in their attitude to authority and their appearance.

The 1960s
- The Beatles, the Rolling Stones and other British groups took the USA by storm.
- Protest songs, such as those by singer/songwriter Bob Dylan, became common.
- Rock music also became influential with bands like The Grateful Dead and The Doors.

Music

The 1970s and 1980s Popular music underwent many changes in the later twentieth century:
- Disco performers of the 1970s such as Donna Summer, Chic and the Jacksons became popular. Disco was a reaction to the domination of rock music and was particularly popular with women.
- Heavy metal music also became popular. Bands such as Led Zeppelin and Deep Purple led the way, followed by Motörhead and Iron Maiden. This style of music was aggressive and masculine.
- Influential solo artists such as Bruce Springsteen became popular because their music focused on the struggles of ordinary people, especially the working class.
- Rap and hip hop music developed from the disco and became popular in the last 20 years of the century. This was a product of inner-city problem areas.

Changes in media and entertainment

The cinema and movie stars

After its significant popularity in the inter-war period, the cinema lost some its appeal from the 1950s onwards, mostly due to the rise in television ownership. However, there were some notable achievements for the cinema.

Key developments in the cinema since 1950

Technology

- Drive-in cinema became popular in the 1950s and 1960s due to the increase in car ownership. Some people criticised drive-ins as 'passion pits'.
- The Multiplex cinema first opened in 1963 in Ward Parkway Center, Kansas City, and quickly spread across America.
- Video recorders (VCRs) appeared in the 1980s and encouraged the hire of films for home viewing; DVDs appeared in the late 1990s.

Content of films

- The anti-hero emerged in the 1950s as young people looked to Hollywood for examples of rebellious anti-heroes – James Dean, Marlon Brando and Marilyn Monroe became huge stars.
- Method actors became very popular during the 1980s: Harrison Ford, Tom Cruise, Meg Ryan and Jack Nicholson among others.
- High-paid movie stars who attracted a cult following became a common feature during the 1990s. These included Arnold Schwarzenegger, Eddie Murphy, Robin Williams, Julia Roberts and Demi Moore.
- Blockbuster films came to dominate the movie business from the 1970s onwards – *Jaws* (1975), *Star Wars* (1977), *ET* (1982), *Indiana Jones* films.
- Technological developments with special effects and advanced digital imagery led to the attraction of films like *Ghostbusters* (1984) and *The Terminator* (1984).

The influence of television

Television quickly established itself as an important feature in American society.

- The number of televisions increased from 7,000 in 1946 to 50 million in 1960 and by 1970, 96 per cent of US households had at least one television.
- TV personalities became household names, such as Lucille Ball who appeared in the popular comedy *I Love Lucy*.
- During the 1950s and 1960s, the 'Western' genre became very popular, especially series programmes such as *The Lone Ranger*, *Bonanza* and *Gunsmoke*.
- By the 1980s, soap operas had taken centre stage, the most popular being *Dallas* (1978–91), *Dynasty* (1981–89) and *Beverly Hills 90210* (1990–2000).
- Chat shows came to attract large audiences, especially the *Oprah Winfrey Show* (1986–2011) and the *Jerry Springer Show* (1991–present).

Developments in information technology

Technological advances in information technology helped cause a massive growth in the use and sale of personal computers.

- In 1975, Bill Gates set up his company Microsoft and in 1985 he launched Microsoft Windows.

- In 1976, Steve Jobs set up his company Apple Computer Inc and soon launched the Macintosh computer.
- The late 1990s saw the development and growth of the internet.
- Since the 1980s, the development of computer-generated games has had a significant impact upon the younger generation – in the 1980s Nintendo introduced the NES game console which was followed by others such as Sega Mega Drive, Sony PlayStation and in 2001, the Microsoft Xbox.
- Recent developments such as email, social networking and text-based discussion forums have helped transform US society.

Changes in literature

REVISED

The quest for the 'great American novel' led to the publication of some of the most popular works in American literature, including:
- *To Kill a Mockingbird* by Harper Lee (1960) – focused on issues of racial inequality and rape
- *The Catcher in the Rye* by J.D. Salinger (1951) – commented on the apparent madness of American society, especially teenagers
- *Rabbit, Run* by John Updike (1960) – focused on changes in middle-class American society.

Another major theme in the development of American literature in the years after the Second World War was counterculture which challenged the traditional conservatism of American society.
- The 'Beat Generation' were a group of novelists and poets who led the way in rebelling against conservative values, like Allen Ginsberg' poem *Howl* (1956) and Jack Kerouac's *On the Road* (1957).
- William S. Burroughs' *Naked Lunch* (1959) and Hunter S. *Thompson's Fear and Loathing in Las Vegas* (1971) dealt with the controversial subject of hard drugs.
- Betty Friedan's *The Feminine Mystique* (1963) challenged the traditional role of women in American society.
- African-American authors focused on racial inequality in American society, like Ralph Ellison's whose *Invisible Man* (1952) highlighted racial tension in the North and Richard Wright's *Black Boy* (1971) drew on the author's own experiences of segregated education in the South.

> ### Revision task
>
> For each factor give three examples of how developments in that aspect of popular culture have impacted upon American society:
> - developments in the cinema
> - the influence of television
> - developments in information technology.
>
> TESTED

Changes in American youth culture

REVISED

One of the greatest social changes in the USA in the 1950s and 1960s was the emergence of a distinct youth culture.

The 1950s – emergence of the teenager and teenage rebellion

- The teenager of the 1950s had more money and free time than ever before.
- Many seemed to want to rebel, especially against whatever their parents believed in.
- Some rebellious teens wore distinctive clothes, formed gangs, cruised in cars, drank heavily and attacked property; those who dropped out of conventional society became known as **beatniks**.
- Many teenagers were influenced by youth films of the 1950s such as *Rebel Without a Cause*, which made a cult hero of James Dean who played a young man who rebelled against his parents and got into trouble with the police for drunken behaviour.

> **Beatniks** Anti-conformist youths of the 1950s.

- Stars like Elvis Presley and Little Richard became heroes to a new youth culture. Many parents disliked Presley's energetic dancing and upfront sexuality.

The 1960s – the hippy movement

- During the 1960s, many young people rejected their parents' lifestyles and values.
- Some young people dropped out of society and became hippies – they wore ethnic style clothes, grew their hair long, took drugs like marijuana and LSD recreationally, followed mystical religions and engaged in 'free love'.
- **Hippies** opposed the Vietnam War, wore flowers in their hair as a symbol of peace, and the slogan 'Make love, not war' became common.
- They settled in communes and San Francisco became the hippy capital of America.

> **Hippy** An individual who rejects conventional social standards in favour of universal love and fellowship; the hippy movement developed in the USA in the mid-1960s.

Revision task

TESTED

Use the information in this section to help you describe the key characteristics of each of the following periods.
- 1950s: teenage rebellion
- 1960s: hippy movement.

Student protest and its impact

REVISED

During the 1960s students became heavily involved in various protest movements.

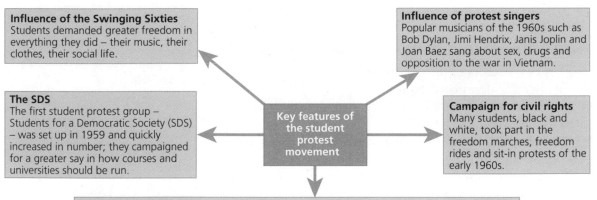

Influence of the Swinging Sixties
Students demanded greater freedom in everything they did – their music, their clothes, their social life.

Influence of protest singers
Popular musicians of the 1960s such as Bob Dylan, Jimi Hendrix, Janis Joplin and Joan Baez sang about sex, drugs and opposition to the war in Vietnam.

The SDS
The first student protest group – Students for a Democratic Society (SDS) – was set up in 1959 and quickly increased in number; they campaigned for a greater say in how courses and universities should be run.

Key features of the student protest movement

Campaign for civil rights
Many students, black and white, took part in the freedom marches, freedom rides and sit-in protests of the early 1960s.

Anti-war protests
- Many students protested against the 'draft system' which called them up to fight in Vietnam.
- Anti-war protests reached a peak during 1968–70; in 1969 700,000 people marched in Washington DC against the war, with students burning their draft cards and the US flag.
- Student protests at Kent State University in May 1970 resulted in National Guardsmen shooting dead four student protestors.

The changing role of women

REVISED

The impact of the Second World War

- The Second World War increased employment opportunities for women: 6 million women entered factories in traditional 'male' jobs as machinists and toolmakers; 300,000 joined the armed forces.
- After the war the majority of women gave up their wartime jobs and returned to their roles as mothers and wives, or to their traditional 'female' jobs in teaching, nursing and secretarial work.

The 1950s

- The media exerted influence in encouraging women to adopt their traditional family role.
- Boredom with the domestic routine and increased freedom due to labour-saving devices encouraged some women to seek paid employment, although the choice of career was very limited.

The growth of the feminist movement – the 1960s and 1970s

- In 1950, women made up 29 per cent of the workforce; by 1960 this had risen to 50 per cent.
- A government report published in 1963 revealed that women earned only 50–60 per cent of the wages of men who did the same job; it showed that 95 per cent of company managers were men and only 7 per cent of all doctors and 4 per cent of all lawyers were women.
- In 1963, Betty Friedan published *The Feminine Mystique* which ridiculed the common belief that women were only suited to low-paid jobs and called for progress in female employment opportunities.
- In 1966, Friedan and others set up the National Organisation for Women (NOW) which demanded equal rights for women and challenged discrimination in the courts; by the early 1970s it had 40,000 members.
- More radical than NOW was the Women's Liberation Movement which became more active in challenging discrimination; it attracted publicity through **feminists** burning their bras in public and in 1965 they picketed the Miss America beauty contest.
- Changes in the law helped to secure more equality:
  - the Civil Rights Act (1964) banned discrimination due to gender
  - in 1973 abortion was legalised, giving women more freedom of choice.

> **Feminist** A person who believes in equal social, economic and political rights for women.

The growth of the feminist movement – 1980 to 2000

- During the last two decades of the twentieth century, women broke into traditionally male-dominated careers:
  - in 1981, Sandra Day O'Connor became the first woman to be appointed to the US Supreme Court
  - in 1983, Dr Sally Ride became the first American woman to enter space on the shuttle Challenger.
- By 1995, 70 per cent of women of working age were in employment, compared with only 38 per cent in 1955.
- However, many of these jobs were in traditional female occupations and by 1998 women's earnings were about 75 per cent of those of men.

Revision task
TESTED ☐

How did these factors help changes women's lives in the USA?
- *The Feminine Mystique*.
- The National Organisation for Women.
- The Civil Rights Act.

Exam practice

How far did developments in music change the lives of young people in America during the 1950s and 1960s?

> **Exam tip**
>
> You should aim to produce a well-supported judgement upon the extent of change. You need to identify and discuss a number of factors to support your argument. You must demonstrate good understanding of the topics under discussion. Good factual detail will help to provide context. End with a concluding sentence which directly addresses the question.

Exam practice answers at **www.hoddereducation.co.uk/myrevisionnotesdownloads**

6 Cold War rivalry

The Truman Doctrine and containment of communism

REVISED

Despite their political and economic differences, the USA and USSR had worked together during the Second World War to fight a common enemy, Germany. Once Germany was defeated in May 1945, relations between the two **superpowers** began to deteriorate. The result was the development of a '**cold war**' which was to last from 1945 to 1991.

The USA believed in **capitalism** and feared the spread of **Communism**.

- By May 1945, Soviet forces occupied large parts of Eastern Europe – Stalin did not intend to withdraw his troops and imposed communist-style governments upon six **satellite states** (Poland, Romania, Bulgaria, Czechoslovakia, Hungary and East Germany).
- President Truman distrusted Stalin and only informed him about America's development of an atomic bomb eleven days before it was dropped; he also made it clear that the secrets were not to be shared.
- When the leaders of the **Big Three** met at Potsdam in late July 1945, relations were strained; while they agreed that Germany was to be divided and Berlin likewise, Stalin was in no mood to allow the holding of free elections in his zones.
- In March 1946, in a speech at Fulton, Missouri, Churchill spoke of an '**iron curtain**' which had descended between the Soviet-controlled Eastern Europe and the free democratic states of Western Europe. It was a division that was to last until the early 1990s.
- In March 1947, President Truman offered help to any government threatened by 'internal or external forces' in the hope of preventing any further spread of communism. Truman's speech marked a turning point in US foreign policy – the USA was now going to be proactive in enforcing the policy of **containment**.

The Marshall Plan (1947)

Truman backed up his policy of containment with economic aid to Europe. US Secretary of State, George C. Marshall, offered over $13 billion in aid to countries recovering from the effects of war. Truman believed that countries with a strong economy would be able to repel communism. Stalin refused to allow Soviet satellite states to accept **Marshall Aid**. By 1953 the USA had provided $17 billion in Marshall Aid.

The Domino Theory

Containment was based on the 'Domino Theory', the belief that if one country fell to communism this would trigger the fall of its neighbouring countries. America's policy was to ensure that the most unstable domino did not fall.

The Berlin Crisis, 1948–49

REVISED

The main flashpoints of the Cold War in Europe concerned attempts by the West to contain the threatened spread of communism.

- After the Second World War, Germany was split into four zones, each one occupied by an Allied power (USA, USSR, Britain and France).

Superpowers The term used to describe the USA and USSR which were so powerful in military and economic terms that they had left all other countries behind.

Cold War State of hostility between the USA and USSR and their allies, without actual fighting.

Capitalism The belief that individuals should be free to make as much money as they can.

Communism The belief that the state should make sure that everyone is equal.

Satellite states Countries under the domination of a foreign power.

Big Three The leaders of the three most powerful Allied powers: USA, USSR and Great Britain.

Iron curtain Term used by Winston Churchill to describe the imaginary barrier between East and West Europe.

Containment Using US influence and military resources to prevent the expansion of communism into non-communist countries.

Marshall Aid US programme of financial and economic aid given to Europe after the end of the Second World War.

Berlin, deep in the Soviet zone, was divided in the same way (see the map below).

- By June 1948, the American, British and French zones had merged together and a new currency had been introduced in an attempt to make West Germany economically prosperous.
- Stalin became increasingly worried that West Berlin would become a wealthy capitalist base within communist Eastern Europe.
- On 24 June 1948, Soviet troops cut off all links (road, rail and canal) between West Berlin and West Germany.
- Stalin hoped the West would be forced to give up their sectors but Truman was determined to follow his policy of containment.
- The West organised an airlift to fly in supplies to West Berlin – the airlift lasted until May 1949 when Stalin gave in and re-opened all routes to West Berlin.
- Truman saw this flashpoint as a success for his policy of containment.

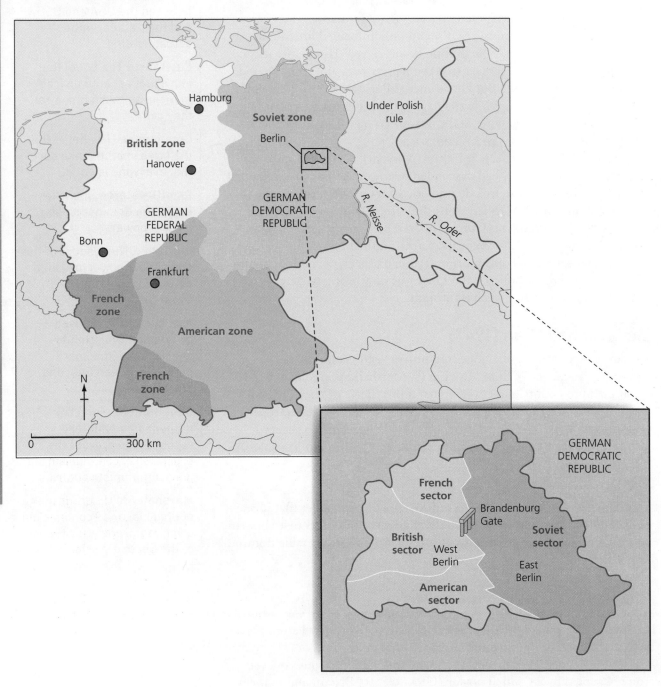

The USA joins NATO, 1949

The Berlin crisis had convinced Truman of the need to contain the spread of communism and for this reason the USA joined with 11 other western powers to form the North Atlantic Treaty Organisation (NATO) in April 1949. Although a defensive alliance, its main purpose was to prevent Soviet expansion. It was the first time in its history that the USA had joined a peacetime alliance. By 1955, the USSR had set up its own rival organisation – the **Warsaw Pact**.

> **Warsaw Pact** A military treaty and association, formed in 1955, of the USSR and its European satellite states.

Revision task

TESTED ☐

Use the information in this section to describe America's response to the Berlin blockade.

The Cuban Missile Crisis

REVISED ☐

Causes

- In January 1959, the US-backed Cuban dictator Batista was overthrown by a left-wing rebel force led by Fidel Castro.
- Castro ejected all US businesses and investment; the USA retaliated by refusing to buy Cuba's biggest export – sugar; the USSR offered to buy the sugar instead.
- Castro now strengthened his relations with the USSR; the threat of a communist country just 90 miles off the Florida coast worried the new US President John F. Kennedy.
- In April 1961, Kennedy supported a landing of Cuban **exiles** at the Bay of Pigs in Cuba, which was intended to overthrow Castro; it was a disaster and a great humiliation for the US president.
- The Soviet leader, Khrushchev, was concerned about the proximity of US missile bases in Italy and Turkey and wanted to establish Soviet bases in Cuba to balance things out; Castro agreed to his request.

> **Exile** A person banished from his or her country of birth.

Key events

On 14 October, an American U2 spy plane took photographs of Soviet missile launch sites being constructed on Cuba; Kennedy was faced with several choices:

- do nothing
- ask the UN for help
- invade Cuba
- attack the Soviet Union
- blockade Cuba using the US navy.

Kennedy decided upon the blockade:

20 October	Kennedy imposed a naval blockade around Cuba.
23 October	Khrushchev sent a letter to Kennedy insisting Soviet ships would cross into the blockade zone.
25 October	Kennedy wrote to Khrushchev asking him to withdraw Soviet missiles from Cuba.
26 October	Khrushchev replied saying he would remove the missiles if the USA lifted its blockade and agreed not to invade Cuba.
27 October	Khrushchev sent a second letter adding that the USA must remove its missiles from Turkey – Kennedy agreed to the first letter in public but the second in private.
28 October	Khrushchev agreed to remove Soviet missiles from Cuba.

Consequences

- Kennedy appeared to have won as Khrushchev had backed down.
- Both Kennedy and Khrushchev were accused of **brinkmanship** – pushing the world to the brink of a nuclear war.
- It was realised that this was too dangerous a game to play and a telephone hotline was installed between the White House and **Kremlin** to ease communication.
- In 1963 a Test Ban Treaty was signed, banning nuclear weapons tests in the atmosphere, under the sea or in space.

> **Brinkmanship** The policy of pushing a dangerous situation to the brink of disaster.
>
> **Kremlin** A complex of buildings in central Moscow which forms the headquarters of the government of the USSR.

Revision task   TESTED ☐

Make a timeline of the Cuban Missile Crisis beginning in 1959 and ending in 1963.

US involvement in Vietnam   REVISED ☐

The USA became involved in the war in Vietnam for a number of reasons:
- Vietnam had been a French colony but the French had withdrawn following defeat against Vietnamese forces in 1954.
- Vietnam became divided along the 17th parallel – North Vietnam fell under communist control under the leadership of Ho Chi Minh, South Vietnam was led by the non-communist leader Ngo Dinh Diem.
- In 1963, Diem was overthrown and it was feared the communists would take over the south.
- The US policy of containment meant America had given support to Diem, and the Domino Theory caused America to believe that if South Vietnam became communist then so would neighbouring Laos and Cambodia.
- The Gulf of Tonkin incident – in August 1964, the US destroyer Maddox was fired on by a North Vietnamese patrol boat; President Johnson used this as an excuse to send troops to aid South Vietnam.

US methods of warfare in Vietnam

- Operation Rolling Thunder – an intense bombing campaign of North Vietnam which lasted from 1965 to 1968 with the aim of destroying **Vietcong** supply routes to the south.
- Chemical warfare – weapons such as Agent Orange, a chemical defoliant used to destroy the jungle, and napalm, a type of burning jelly, were used.
- High tech war – the USA used the latest technology: B52 bombers, helicopters, rocket launchers.
- Increasing troop numbers – in 1964 there were 180,000 US troops in South Vietnam; by 1968 the number had risen to 540,000.
- 'Search and destroy' – the USA used helicopters to drop troops near villages suspected of assisting the Vietcong; the villages were searched and then set alight which made the US forces unpopular.

> **Vietcong** A communist guerrilla force that attempted to overthrow the South Vietnam government.

Exam practice answers at **www.hoddereducation.co.uk/myrevisionnotesdownloads**

Reasons for US defeat in Vietnam

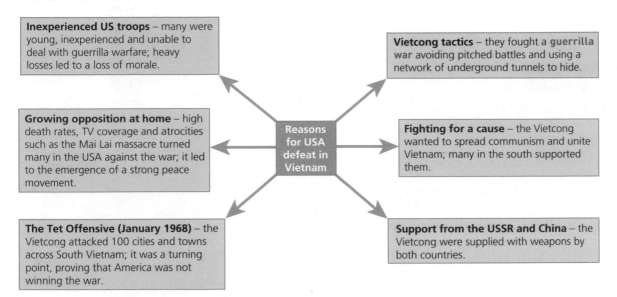

Inexperienced US troops – many were young, inexperienced and unable to deal with guerrilla warfare; heavy losses led to a loss of morale.

Vietcong tactics – they fought a **guerrilla war** avoiding pitched battles and using a network of underground tunnels to hide.

Growing opposition at home – high death rates, TV coverage and atrocities such as the Mai Lai massacre turned many in the USA against the war; it led to the emergence of a strong peace movement.

Reasons for USA defeat in Vietnam

Fighting for a cause – the Vietcong wanted to spread communism and unite Vietnam; many in the south supported them.

The Tet Offensive (January 1968) – the Vietcong attacked 100 cities and towns across South Vietnam; it was a turning point, proving that America was not winning the war.

Support from the USSR and China – the Vietcong were supplied with weapons by both countries.

US withdrawal from Vietnam and its consequences

- Upon entering office in 1969, President Nixon began a policy of **Vietnamisation** and commenced peace talks.
- In 1973, a ceasefire was signed in Paris, followed by a peace treaty, by which time all US troops had left Vietnam.
- North Vietnam was allowed to keep all the land it had captured in South Vietnam.
- By 1975, communist forces had over-run South Vietnam and in 1976 Vietnam was reunited under the leadership of Ho Chi Minh.
- The USA had failed to stop the spread of communism in South East Asia and Laos and Cambodia soon turned communist – the Domino Theory had proved partially true.

> **Guerrilla war** Fighting in small groups against conventional forces, using such methods as sabotage and sudden ambush.
>
> **Vietnamisation** US policy of transferring the fighting of the war in Vietnam from American forces to those of South Vietnam.

Revision task

TESTED ☐

Copy and complete the table below. Use the information in this section to evaluate America's performance in the war in Vietnam. In each column, aim to identify four factors.

Reasons for US involvement	Methods used by the US forces to fight the war	Reasons for US withdrawal

Exam practice

Relations between the USA and USSR deteriorated between 1945 and 1963 due to events such as:
- the Truman Doctrine
- the Berlin Blockade and airlift
- the Cuban Missile Crisis.

Arrange the developments in order of their significance in bringing about a deterioration in relations between the USA and USSR during this period. Explain your choices.

Exam tip

You need to decide in which order to write about the three factors – there is no correct order as it is the quality of the justification of your choice that is most important. You need to demonstrate good subject knowledge by providing specific detail about each factor. You must fully explain the significance of each factor, using your knowledge to set them within their historical context. Aim to provide a clear, well-supported justification for your reasoning.

7 The search for world peace since 1970

Key question

What has been the USA's role in the search for peace since 1970?

Détente and attempts to limit arms

The term **détente** is used to describe periods of thaw in cold war relations, primarily between 1971 and 1979. A second period of détente emerged after Mikhail Gorbachev became Soviet leader in 1985.

Reasons for détente

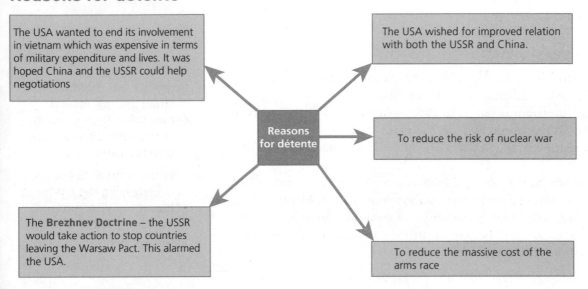

The USA wanted to end its involvement in vietnam which was expensive in terms of military expenditure and lives. It was hoped China and the USSR could help negotiations

The USA wished for improved relation with both the USSR and China.

Reasons for détente

To reduce the risk of nuclear war

The **Brezhnev Doctrine** – the USSR would take action to stop countries leaving the Warsaw Pact. This alarmed the USA.

To reduce the massive cost of the arms race

Détente with USSR – SALT I

- In 1972, President Nixon visited Moscow to improve relations between the USA and USSR.
- Strategic Arms Limitation Talks (SALT) had started in 1969 and this led to the signing of the SALT I agreement in 1972.
- The treaty limited the number of intercontinental missiles (ICBMs) and anti–ballistic missiles (ABMs), and both powers agreed not to test ICBMs and submarine-launched missiles.
- SALT I was important because it was the first agreement between the superpowers to successfully limit the number of nuclear weapons they held.

> **Détente** An attempt to reduce the tension between the USA and USSR.
>
> **Brezhnev Doctrine** A policy launched in 1968 which called for the use of Warsaw Pact forces to intervene if any Eastern bloc country attempted to rebel against the communist system.

The Helsinki Agreements, 1975

In 1975, the USA and USSR, along with 33 other nations, made declarations about international issues:

- security – the USA recognised the frontiers of Eastern Europe; the USSR accepted the existence of West Germany

- human rights – each signatory agreed to respect basic human rights including the freedoms of thought, speech, religion and unlawful arrest
- co-operation – agreements to work towards closer economic, scientific and cultural links.

This new co-operation was shown in 1975 with the docking of the American Apollo and Soviet Soyuz spacecraft in space.

The USA's changing relations with China and the USSR

REVISED

Several reasons account for improved relations between the USA and China.

- Relations between the USSR and China were strained and Nixon hoped to exploit this split; at the same time China desired more friendly relations with the USA; Nixon also hoped better relations with China would help him to negotiate an end to the war against North Vietnam.
- '**Ping-pong diplomacy**' – the Chinese table-tennis team invited the US team to Peking and the visit in 1971 proved successful and set the scene for improved relations between the countries; in April 1971 the USA lifted its 21-year-old trade embargo with China.
- In February 1972, Nixon became the first US president to visit China – one consequence was improved trading links.
- China was allowed to take its seat at the United Nations in October 1971.

> **Ping-pong diplomacy** The exchange of table-tennis players between the USA and the People's Republic of China in the early 1970s which helped pave the way for Nixon's visit to China in 1972.

The ending of détente – the Soviet invasion of Afghanistan, 1979

- By June 1979, the USA and USSR were in the final stages of agreeing SALT II which would set further limits on the number of weapons held.
- The US Senate refused to sign up to the SALT II agreement following the Soviet invasion of Afghanistan in December 1979.
- Diplomatic links between the USA and USSR were cut and President Carter stated that the USA would use military force if necessary to defend its interests in the Persian Gulf.
- The US Olympic team boycotted the 1980 Moscow Olympic Games; 61 other nations also boycotted them.
- This marked the end of the first period of détente.

> **Revision task**
>
> Show how America's relationship with the USSR and China changed during the 1970s, by describing how the following events changed relations between the superpowers:
> - Nixon's visit to Moscow
> - SALT I
> - Helsinki Agreements
> - Ping-pong diplomacy
> - invasion of Afghanistan.
>
> TESTED

The end of the Cold War

REVISED

Reagan and the second Cold War

- In January 1981, Reagan replaced Carter as US president and he returned to an aggressive anti-Soviet foreign policy.
- Reagan vastly increased his defence budget and in 1983 US scientists began work on the Strategic Defence Initiative (SDI) or 'Star Wars', developing satellites with lasers that would destroy Soviet missiles in space before they could hit the USA.
- SDI proved a turning point in the Cold War – the USSR, owing to its weakening economy, no longer had the money to fund more defence spending to keep up with the USA.

Reagan and Gorbachev – a return to détente

- In 1985, Gorbachev became the new leader of the USSR and he started a process of reform which included more friendly relations with the USA.
- In November 1985, Reagan and Gorbachev met in Geneva and agreed to speed up arms reduction talks (the Geneva Accord).
- A second meeting was held in Reykjavik in 1986 but negotiations on limitations were slow.
- In December 1987, a third meeting in Washington led to the signing of the Intermediate Nuclear Forces Treaty (INF) by which both leaders agreed to destroy all medium- and short-range weapons in Europe within three years.
- In 1989, the new US president, George Bush Snr, and Gorbachev met at Malta and announced an end to the Cold War.
- At Washington in 1990, Bush Snr and Gorbachev discussed Strategic Arms Limitation (START) and signed the Treaty for the Reduction and Limitation of Strategic Arms (START I) in July 1991.

The ending of the Cold War

- The reform policies of Gorbachev resulted in the Soviet grip over Eastern Europe loosening.
- In 1989, Gorbachev told the leaders of the six satellite states that Soviet troops would no longer be able to defend them and that members of the Warsaw Pact could make changes to their countries without outside interference.
- Reform quickly spread across the satellite states and the USSR did nothing to stop it.
- **Regime change** was sparked by the fall of the Berlin Wall in November 1989 and, by the end of 1990, communist governments had been swept from power in East Germany, Poland, Hungary, Czechoslovakia, Romania and Bulgaria, to be replaced by democratically elected governments.
- These events weakened the USSR and in 1990 the Baltic states of Estonia, Latvia and Lithuania declared themselves independent; in 1991 Gorbachev resigned as leader and the USSR split up into a commonwealth of independent states.
- Europe was no longer divided between communism and capitalism – the Cold War had ended.

> **Regime change** Changing the government of a country.

Revision task

Explain how these events helped to end the Cold War:
- Strategic Defence Initiative (SDI)
- Intermediate Nuclear Forces Treaty (INF)
- Withdrawal of Soviet troops from Eastern Europe.

TESTED

US involvement in Iran, Iraq and the Gulf War

During the 1980s and 1990s the US became increasingly involved in the Middle East.

Iran

- In January 1979, the Shah of Iran, who had received US backing, was forced to abdicate.
- Iran now fell under the control of a **fundamentalist** religious leader, the Ayatollah Khomeini, who denounced the USA as the 'Great Satan'.
- In November 1979 the US embassy in Tehran was stormed by Iranian students and 66 Americans were taken hostage; they were held for 444 days.
- President Carter authorised a rescue mission in April 1980 but it failed and it served to worsen relations between the USA and Iran.

The Gulf War (1990–91)

- In August 1990, troops from Iraq invaded and captured neighbouring Kuwait.
- Saddam Hussein, the leader of Iraq, saw Kuwait as a rich prize which would help to lessen his country's economic debts.
- The USA wanted to protect its economic interests, especially its oil supplies from this region.
- The United Nations imposed **sanctions** on Iraq. The USA, Britain and other states sent forces to protect Saudi Arabia and its oil reserves (Operation Desert Shield).
- In January 1991, the Allies launched an air assault against Iraq (Operation Desert Storm) and in February, land forces began the liberation of Kuwait (Operation Desert Sabre).
- Saddam was allowed to withdraw with much of his army intact.
- With the defeat of Saddam, President Bush Snr's reputation stood high; America had successfully restored order to the oil-producing states of the Middle East.

Exam practice

Explain why relations between the USA and China changed after 1970.

Revision task

Draw a timeline to record the key events in American foreign policy between 1980 and 2000. Record events showing improved relationships above the dateline and events showing a deterioration in relationships below the line.

TESTED

Fundamentalist A religious extremist

Sanctions A penalty usually adopted by several nations acting together against another nation violating international law.

Exam tip

'Explain why' means to give reasons for something. You need to provide a range of reasons. Each reason needs to be supported with relevant factual detail. Avoid generalised comments. Make sure the information you include is directly relevant, that is, does it answer the question?

Section 4 Changes in crime and punishment

1 Causes of crime

> **Key question**
>
> What have been the main causes of crime over time?

Problems in the medieval era

Most people in medieval times lived in poverty. Their lives were often made worse by:

- famine, for example the Great Famine of 1315–17
- disease, like the Black Death of the 1340s
- high taxation such as the Poll Tax of the late 1370s which led to the 1381 Peasants' Revolt
- warfare, with demands to pay for wars and the destruction caused by them, like the Norman Conquest after 1066 and the Wars of the Roses from 1455 to 1485.

These causes of poverty were constant throughout the medieval period up to the early nineteenth century. Poverty often led to theft of property but also other less common crimes such as revolts and rebellions. As more trade and business began to develop later in the period, merchants and traders used the roads and tracks more often and this encouraged the growth of highway robbery.

Violent crime was also very common because people had easy access to dangerous weapons and farming tools. Twenty per cent of all crimes in the period 1300–1348 were for murder or manslaughter.

How did the causes of crime change in the sixteenth and seventeenth centuries?

In the sixteenth century many people in society were affected by a rise in poverty because:

- the population of England and Wales almost doubled between 1500 and 1600 which meant more demand for food, clothing, housing and work
- rising inflation meant that people's wages were worth less than before
- bad harvests caused a steep rise in the price of food
- many farmers switched to keeping sheep which meant there was less need for labourers
- Henry VIII closed all the monasteries which had taken care of people when they were desperate.

Many left their homes in the countryside to find work in nearby towns, which is known as **vagrancy**. Unable to find work, many vagrants were forced into begging for food and money and often resorted to petty stealing and fraud, especially during the reign of Elizabeth I.

> **Vagrancy** The crime of being a wandering beggar.

Heresy is holding a belief or opinion that is different to accepted religion. It was always regarded as a serious crime in medieval times, but it was rare for people to be accused or convicted of it in Britain. There was an increase in the crime of heresy in the sixteenth century, caused mainly by the Protestant Reformation which spread across Western Europe, including Britain. Later, Tudor monarchs changed the official religion of the country. People who refused to follow the official religion were accused of the medieval crime of heresy. Religion was a fundamental part of people's lives so this change in religion made criminals of people who were worshipping as they always had done.

This kind of heresy was more a crime of **treason**, the crime of betraying one's country, monarch or government. Treason was rare in medieval times because royal and church control over society was strong. Tudor and Stuart monarchs knew there was growing dissatisfaction of the people, caused by poverty, religious change or even a desire for more power. Governments employed agents, spies and informers to keep them informed of any dissatisfaction.

The pressures of industrialisation and urbanisation in the eighteenth and nineteenth centuries

REVISED

Smuggling

Smuggling is the secret trade in goods to avoid paying customs duties. **Smuggling** had never really been seen as a major worry but was turned into a major crime by government policy. The government clamped down hard on smuggling in the eighteenth century because it needed the money for wars, mostly against France. There was no income tax, so the government had to raise money from customs and excise duties on popular imported goods such as chocolate, tea, wine, spirits, salt, leather and soap. Goods such as tea had a 70 per cent tax on them, meaning that people were willing to buy the much cheaper smuggled goods which didn't have the tax on them.

Highway robbery

As with smuggling, **highway robbery** began to rise because of changes in trade and business:

- a general increase in travel as the industrial revolution began to improve trade
- improvements in **turnpike roads** encouraged more people to travel for business
- limited banking facilities meant more money being carried by road to pay for goods and services
- handguns became easier to get hold of.

The most frequent examples of highway robbery occurred on the heaths and commons around London, which was the most prosperous part of the country.

Heresy The crime of holding a belief or opinion that is different to the accepted religion.

Treason The crime of betraying one's country, monarch or government.

Revision task

Why did treason and heresy increase in the sixteenth and seventeenth centuries?

TESTED

Smuggling The secret trade in goods to avoid paying customs duties.

Highway robbery Stopping people as they travel along a road, usually in a coach, and robbing them.

Turnpike roads Roads that had gates (turnpikes) where travellers paid a toll to pass through.

Urbanisation

Urbanisation forced people to move to towns for work. Where there were large numbers of people, there were more opportunities to commit crime. By the nineteenth century crime was increasing because:

- the population of Britain rose from 16 million in 1800, to 42 million in 1900 with most of the increase in town and cities
- of poverty caused by unemployment, for example, after the Napoleonic wars ended in 1815, which led to people committing petty crime
- poor living and working conditions led many people to consider protesting, but agricultural depression also meant protests were seen in rural areas.

Between 1790 and 1850 many ordinary people turned to protest as a means of showing how bad their lives were.

Revision task

Explain why urbanisation led to an increase in crime.

TESTED

Protest	When	Where	Reason for protest
Luddism	1812–1813	Industrial towns in the Midlands and northern England	Weavers protested about machines taking their jobs
Peterloo Massacre	1819	Manchester	A mass meeting to demand electoral reform
Swing Riots	1830–1831	South-east England	Farm labourers protested about machines taking their jobs
Rebecca Riots	1839–1843	South-west Wales	Farmers protested about increased rent and tolls to use roads
Chartism	1839–1848	National	Campaigning for the right to vote for working people and fairer elections

Twentieth century pressures and the impact on the causes of crime

REVISED

Car crime

The 1920s saw the beginnings of mass production in the car industry. By 1930, cars were affordable to many. Driving was popular but dangerous as motorists did not need a licence. After 1935, all drivers had to pass a test, pay road tax, get insurance and maintain a roadworthy car. More cars has also resulted in more car thefts.

Computer crime

The rise of the home computer in the 1980s and the internet in the 1990s has led to an increase in computer related crime from stealing computers and modern mobile devices themselves to internet fraud as well as illegally copying music and films.

Terrorism

There has been an increase in violence to achieve political objectives. For example, the IRA, a nationalist group dedicated to ending British rule in Northern Ireland, carried out a number of attacks in Northern Ireland and in mainland Britain between the 1970s and 1990s. In the twenty-first century, Britain is threatened by global terrorist groups like al-Qaeda and ISIS.

Revision task

How did the following lead to an increase in crime in the twentieth century?
- cars
- computers
- football

TESTED

Football hooliganism

Gang violence at football matches became a problem in the 1970s because rival fans fought each other under the influence of alcohol.

Modern smuggling

Better transport has made smuggling difficult to prevent. Tobacco and alcohol are smuggled into the country in huge quantities because they are cheaper on the continent as taxes are lower.

Drug related crime

The Dangerous Drugs Act of 1920 made possession of certain drugs illegal and various other laws during the century criminalised possession of various drugs, including the Act of 1971 which categorised drugs into Categories A, B and C. Banning possession of certain drugs for recreational purposes has resulted in an increase in the old crime of smuggling, often now described under the term 'trafficking'. Increasing drug addiction has also resulted in higher instances of certain crimes, particularly burglary, mugging and robbery. Rivalry between drug dealers has also resulted in an increase in gun and knife-related attacks.

Gun and knife crime

The rise in juvenile gang culture, particularly in inner city areas, has resulted in a huge increase in gun and knife crime. This has happened because of a lack of opportunity for young people and a breakdown of family values and discipline.

2 Nature of crimes

Key question

How has the nature of criminal activity differed and changed over time?

Common crimes in the medieval era

REVISED

After the Norman Conquest, a criminal was defined as someone who had 'disturbed the king's peace'. Norman laws highlighted offences against authority (crown and church) such as treason, revolt, sheltering criminals, **blasphemy** and heresy. The most common crime was theft. In 1275, King Edward I passed a law that said anyone stealing more than 12d worth of goods could be hanged for their crime. There were some crimes that were particular to the medieval period:

- the Forest Laws which said that trees could no longer be cut down for fuel or for building and anyone caught hunting deer would be punished
- scolding was the use of offensive and abusive speech in public
- treason was defying authority, not just the king but also the husband who was head of the family
- outlaw gangs, made up of criminal already on the run, ambushed travellers and robbed houses
- heresy was spreading false Christian beliefs
- there were several serious rebellions against royal authority during this period. The Peasants' Revolt, 1381, Jack Cade's Revolt, 1450, the Cornish Rebellion, 1497.

Exam practice

Outline how the main causes of crime have changed from c.500 to the present day.

[In your answer you should provide a written narrative discussing the main causes of crime across three historical eras.]

Exam tip

Make sure your answer covers three historical time periods – the medieval, early modern and modern eras. Include specific factual detail such as names, dates, key methods/developments. Start a new paragraph for each time period. Aim to write roughly equal amounts for each time period. Make regular links to the question, evaluating the degree of progress, change or improvement. Check your spelling, punctuation and grammar for accuracy.

Blasphemy Arguing with or insulting a religion.

How did the nature of crime change between the sixteenth and eighteenth centuries?

REVISED

Vagrancy

There was a sharp rise in poverty during the sixteenth century. As a result there was an increase in vagrants wandering from place to place without a settled home or job. Vagabonds were wandering beggars who turned to crime. The rising number of vagabonds, especially during the reign of Elizabeth I, caused people to feel threatened. They used specialist tricks to gain money from people:

- the angler – used a hooked stick to reach through windows and steal goods
- the counterfeit crank – dressed in tatty clothes and pretended to suffer from falling sickness
- the clapper dudgeon – tied arsenic to their skin in order to make it bleed and attract sympathy while begging
- Abraham man – pretended to be mad in order to attract donations through pity.

Tudor governments dealt with the problem of vagrancy by:

- flogging or branding them
- making towns tackle the problem
- making it the duty of each local parish to provide aid for its poor but also punish vagabonds.

Heresy

Religious disputes became more important after the Protestant Reformation, as the official religion of Britain switched between the Roman Catholic and Protestant faiths. People who refused to follow the 'official' religion were accused of heresy, a crime punishable by death.

Changes in religion under the Tudors:

Henry VIII r.1509–1547	Split with the Catholic Church and made himself Head of the Church in England.	Those refusing to accept the split with the Catholic Church were executed.
Edward VI r. 1547–1553	Widened the split with the Catholic Church.	Made laws requiring the people to worship in a more Protestant way.
Mary r. 1553–1558	Wanted to make England a Catholic country again.	Ordered the burning of Protestants for heresy.
Elizabeth I r. 1558–1603	Made compromises towards Catholics but remained firmly Protestant.	Catholics were fined for not attending church. Those plotting to kill the queen were executed for treason.

People who strongly believed in their faith found it hard to accept the swings in religion under the Tudor monarchs. Of those who disagreed:

- some went into exile abroad
- others were willing to die for what they believed in
- others learned to keep quiet and pretended to conform.

Treason

When Henry VIII created himself as Head of the Church in England he issued a Treason Law in 1534 which said that anyone who:

- said or wrote things against the king, his wife or his heirs, or who displayed support for the Pope, was guilty of treason
- said the beliefs of the king went against the teachings of the church, or said that the king was using his power unjustly, was guilty of treason
- kept silent when questioned on what were the rights and authority of the king, was guilty of treason.

During the reign of Elizabeth I, the Treason Law was extended to include anyone who said she was not the rightful queen.

Monarchs in this period were constantly looking out for possible rebellions and plots that might challenge their position. For example:

Event	Main causes	When	Leader
Pilgrimage of Grace	Religion	1536	Robert Aske
Gunpowder Plot	Religion/power	1605	Robert Catesby
Popish Plot	Religion	1678	Titus Oates
Monmouth Rebellion	Religion/power	1685	Duke of Monmouth

One of the most serious acts of treason during this period was the Gunpowder Plot of November 1605, a religiously motivated attempt by a group of Catholic gentlemen to assassinate King James I by blowing up Parliament. Many Catholics were angry that King James had enforced laws against Catholic worship. They disliked the heavy fines imposed on recusants for not attending Church of England services. The plan failed when Guy Fawkes was caught with the gunpowder beneath Parliament.

Revision task

Define:
- vagrancy
- heresy
- treason.

TESTED ☐

Changing crime in the eighteenth century

REVISED ☐

Smuggling

In the eighteenth century, smuggling goods illegally into the country and selling them unofficially on the black market made criminals considerable amounts of money as they were able to sell goods much cheaper than in shops and markets. Gangs employed between 50 and 100 individuals, each performing a specific task:

- venturer (the investor)
- spotsman (responsible for directing the ship to shore)
- lander (arranged the unloading of the smuggled cargo)
- tubsman (carried the goods)
- batsman (protected the tubsman).

The increase in smuggling had been caused by a change in government policy over customs and excise duties. It declined because the government reduced duties to make smuggling unprofitable.

Highway robbery

Highway robbery became more common in the eighteenth century. Robbers who attacked pedestrians were called footpads but there were also mounted highwaymen who held up coaches and riders. These were often armed and worked in pairs. Some of the highway robbers were glamorised by the newspapers and broadsheets, like Dick Turpin. The amount of highway robbery declined as the eighteenth century ended because:

- roads became much busier
- banknotes had to be cashed in and could be traced
- in London, a horse patrol was set up in 1805 to guard the main roads.

How did the Industrial Revolution affect the nature of crime?

REVISED

Industrialisation and urbanisation meant that people moved from close-knit rural communities to overcrowded towns with a lot more opportunities for crime. Certain areas of growing towns and cities became notorious for criminal activities. These were sometimes called rookeries. Examples were St Giles in central London. Certain criminal activities acquired nicknames such as:

- thimble-screwers who stole pocket-watches from their chains
- prop-nailers who stole pins and brooches from women
- drag-sneaks who stole goods or luggage from carts and coaches.

> **Tithe** A tax paid by farmers of one-tenth of their produce/income.

Between 1790 and 1840, poor living and low wages, combined with demands for political reform, resulted in a real threat of revolution. At times, the anger of protesters resulted in outbreaks of violence and criminal activity:

- Luddism 1812–13 – attacks on factory machines in northern England, with handloom weavers protesting over new factory-based machine-woven cloth.
- Swing Riots 1830–31 – agricultural labourers set fire to hayricks and smashed machines; they were angry about their poverty and the introduction of farm machinery.
- Rebecca Riots 1839–43 – gangs of poor farmers disguised as women to hide their identity attacked tollgates in south-west Wales; they were angry about increased rents, **tithe** payments and tolls.

> ## Revision task
>
> Describe these nineteenth century protests:
> - Luddism
> - Swing Riots
> - Rebecca Riots.
>
> TESTED

The growth of crimes in the twentieth and twenty-first century

REVISED

Crime figures have risen sharply since 1900, but much of this increase is associated with the increased reporting and recording of crime, improved policing methods and the improved use of scientific technology to detect crime.

Car crime

The increase in the number of cars on the road led to new laws for regulating motorised transport, such as speed limits (30 m.p.h. on residential roads in 1934, 70 m.p.h. on motorways in 1977), the breathalyser to reduce drink-driving in 1967 and the 2003 law banning use of a mobile phone while driving. Common motoring offences/crimes include:

- dangerous and careless driving; parking violations; speeding; car theft
- driving without a driving licence; no car insurance; no vehicle tax; no MOT
- failing to stop after an accident; failing to report an accident
- driving while being over the legal limit for alcohol
- not wearing a seatbelt.

Computer crime

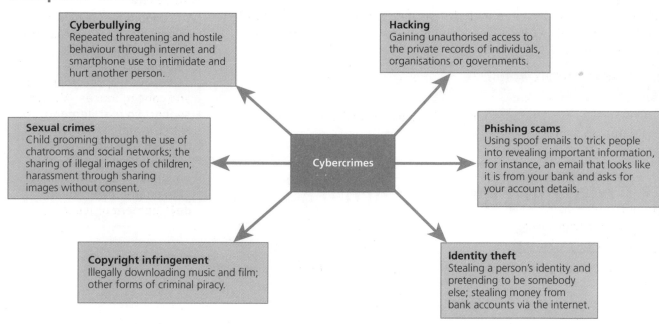

Cyberbullying
Repeated threatening and hostile behaviour through internet and smartphone use to intimidate and hurt another person.

Hacking
Gaining unauthorised access to the private records of individuals, organisations or governments.

Sexual crimes
Child grooming through the use of chatrooms and social networks; the sharing of illegal images of children; harassment through sharing images without consent.

Cybercrimes

Phishing scams
Using spoof emails to trick people into revealing important information, for instance, an email that looks like it is from your bank and asks for your account details.

Copyright infringement
Illegally downloading music and film; other forms of criminal piracy.

Identity theft
Stealing a person's identity and pretending to be somebody else; stealing money from bank accounts via the internet.

Terrorism

Terrorists use a range of methods to push their political demands. These have included hijackings, assassinations, taking hostages, bombings, suicide attacks and arson attacks, such as the IRA's bombing of the Arndale Shopping Centre in Manchester in 1996 or the 7/7 attacks on 7 July 2005 involving a series of co-ordinated suicide bomb attacks on London's public transport network, which were linked to al-Qaeda.

Hate crimes

In 2007, the government introduced a new law covering 'hate crimes'. Hate crimes range from criminal damage and vandalism through to harassment or physical assault. Victims are targeted for their race, sexual orientation, religion or disability. The most common type of hate crime is motivated by racism. In recent years, there has been a growth in religiously motivated hate crimes.

Hooliganism

Hooligans are often members of gangs, like belonging to a tribe, and violence is accepted as the norm. Football hooliganism occurred throughout the twentieth century but became a particular problem from the 1970s. For example, in 1985 fighting between British and Italian fans caused a wall to collapse in the Heysel Stadium in Belgium, killing 38 people.

Drug-related crime

Drug trafficking became more prominent during the late twentieth century. Planes, boats, trucks and people (**mules**) are used by gangs to smuggle illegal drugs into the UK. Drug gangs operate on their own 'turf' and use violence to protect their patch from rival gangs.

Hooligan A person who acts in a violent way and causes damage, often without thinking.

Mule (drug trafficking) A person who agrees to carry illegal drugs into another country in return for payment.

Revision task

Give examples of:
- terrorism
- hooliganism
- hate crimes.

TESTED

Gun and knife crime

As well as being associated with drug gangs, gun and knife crime is often linked to juvenile gangs. Gang members carry knives and sometimes guns as protection.

Exam practice

Explain why opportunities for crime increased by the end of the eighteenth century.

Exam tip

You should aim to give a variety of explained reasons. Try to include specific details such as names, dates, events, developments and consequences. Always support your statements with examples. Remember that you need to provide a judgement, evaluating the importance or significance of the named individual, development or issue.

3 Enforcing law and order

Key question

How has the responsibility of enforcing law and order changed over time?

Communal and family responsibility in Saxon and medieval times

REVISED

The Saxon and medieval system of policing was based on community action:
- adult men were grouped into tens called tithings. If one of them broke a law, the others had to bring him to court
- if a victim raised the '**hue and cry**', everyone who heard it was expected to help catch the criminal
- if local groups did not track down criminals, the sheriff, an agent of the king, would call an armed posse to search for them
- two chief constables were appointed each year to supervise law and order in their area
- the parish constable had to make sure a village responded to crime properly alongside his own full-time work.

Hue and cry Raising the alarm by shouting out when a crime has been committed.

The role of manorial, church and royal courts in the later medieval period

REVISED

There were a number of different court systems in medieval times.
- Manor courts took over the work of the local courts to judge petty crimes that affected the area, including thefts, land disputes, fights and debts. The lord or his steward ran the court with a jury to decide each case. Each manor had its own local laws that had been established over hundreds of years.
- Church courts were for churchmen and were more lenient. They were presided over by the local bishop and never sentenced people to death. They dealt with moral offences including failure to attend church, drunkenness and adultery. If someone was on the run from the law they could claim sanctuary in a church.
- Royal courts heard the most serious criminal cases. Jurors came from the criminal's own area. In 1293, King Edward I made an important change. He ordered that royal judges from London would visit each county two or three times a year to try cases of serious crime from that area. These courts were called the county assizes which lasted until 1971.

Revision task

What were the differences between manor courts, church courts and royal courts?

TESTED

Exam practice answers at **www.hoddereducation.co.uk/myrevisionnotesdownloads**

The growth of civic and parish responsibilities in the sixteenth century

By 1500, the medieval system of policing still worked in rural communities. By the end of the seventeenth century it was more difficult to get this system to work in rapidly growing towns and cities.

All counties in England and Wales still had a system of maintaining law and order headed by Justices of the Peace (JPs) who had to:
- oversee and organise local parish constables and watchmen
- monitor and control beggars and vagrants and administer the new Poor Laws after 1601
- enforce government and local government orders and punish those who disobeyed.

The workload of the JPs grew considerably. They often served their communities for many years, which shows they must have been effective as they had to be elected each year. They were assisted by:
- Parish constables – appointed by JPs, held their unpaid post for a year as well as their day job. Their main role was to keep order in the area and to catch and arrest those who broke the law. The constable could call on the people to give him assistance.
- Watchmen patrolled towns at night. They had the power to challenge strangers and arrest criminals. They were not paid, but all men in the town were expected to carry out this duty on a voluntary basis. There was no uniform, but most carried a bell, a lantern and a weapon for protection.

By the mid-seventeenth century, the city of London was growing so quickly that the old medieval method of using unpaid local people to enforce law and order was not as effective. In 1663, Charles II passed an Act which created a force of paid watchmen to patrol the streets of the growing city. These became known as Charleys. Pay was low and was often done by those that were incapable of finding work elsewhere. They often became objects of ridicule but they were the first law officers paid for by public money.

> ## Revision task
>
> What were the responsibilities of:
> - Justices of the Peace
> - parish constables
> - watchmen?
>
> TESTED

The concept of state police in the nineteenth century

New industrial towns had to have a new system of law enforcement. The idea gradually developed that policing should become the responsibility of government. There was opposition to the idea of a national police force. Some believed that such a force would:
- limit individual freedom and liberty by allowing the government to interfere
- give the police too much power which they could use to limit the rights of individuals
- be very expensive and cause taxes to rise.

The methods introduced by the Fielding brothers and the **Bow Street Runners** were very effective in tackling crime in their area of London. They were among the first to show government how to deal with crime effectively – by using a paid force of police officers. They also developed the idea of 'preventative policing' by attempting to stop crime from being committed rather than dealing with crime after it had been carried out.

> **Bow Street Runners** Part-time paid constables who worked for Bow Street Magistrates Court.

The Metropolitan Police in London was established in 1829. MPs became convinced that an organised police force paid for by government was needed in London. JPs did not like giving up control of constables to Commissioners and at first seemed to take the side of criminals in some court cases. There were even public meetings set up to organise people against the police.

Once the Metropolitan Police had been established and proved effective in London, the government moved to allow other regions of the country to introduce similar forces. A number of Acts were passed to allow this.
- The Municipal Corporations Act of 1835 allowed police forces to be set up in larger borough towns.
- The Rural Police Act of 1839 enabled police forces to be set up in more rural areas of the country.

It was still not compulsory to set up a police force. Only around half the areas decided to set up their own force. Most local authorities claimed they could not afford it.

The County and Borough Police Act in 1856 made it compulsory for a police force to be set up in every county. Setting up a police force in different counties helped to tackle the fear that the government was in control. Within a few years, the old system that operated around JPs and constables was replaced across the country.

The changing nature of policing in the twentieth and twenty-first centuries

REVISED

By the start of the twentieth century the basic role of the police was the maintenance of public order and the prevention of crime. What now changed rapidly were the methods and resources available to the police.

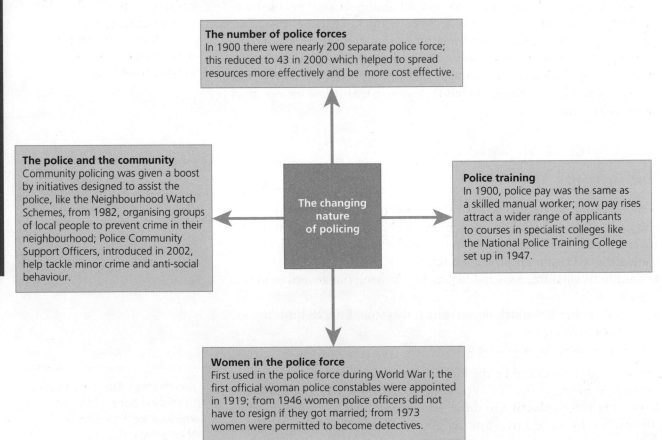

The number of police forces
In 1900 there were nearly 200 separate police force; this reduced to 43 in 2000 which helped to spread resources more effectively and be more cost effective.

The police and the community
Community policing was given a boost by initiatives designed to assist the police, like the Neighbourhood Watch Schemes, from 1982, organising groups of local people to prevent crime in their neighbourhood; Police Community Support Officers, introduced in 2002, help tackle minor crime and anti-social behaviour.

The changing nature of policing

Police training
In 1900, police pay was the same as a skilled manual worker; now pay rises attract a wider range of applicants to courses in specialist colleges like the National Police Training College set up in 1947.

Women in the police force
First used in the police force during World War I; the first official woman police constables were appointed in 1919; from 1946 women police officers did not have to resign if they got married; from 1973 women were permitted to become detectives.

Developments in forensic science

- Fingerprinting – following its first use in 1901, a national register of fingerprints was set up; in 1995 the National Automatic Fingerprint Identification System was introduced.
- Forensic scientists – Scenes of Crime Officers (SOCOs) attend crime scenes to examine and gather forensic evidence; they carry out tests on hair, skin, dust, fibres from clothing and traces of blood to match them to a suspect.
- DNA and **genetic fingerprinting** – since the 1980s, police have increasingly depended on DNA and genetic fingerprinting to help solve crimes and investigate past, unresolved crimes; a DNA National Database was established in 1995.

> **Genetic fingerprinting** The method of matching DNA samples found at a crime scene with a suspect.

> **Revision task**
>
> Make a list of the main developments in policing in the nineteenth and twentieth centuries.
>
> TESTED ☐

Exam practice

Study Sources A and B below and answer the question that follows.

Source A

It is commanded that every man between fifteen and sixty years of age shall keep the watch continually all through the night and if any stranger do pass by them he shall be arrested until morning and if they find cause of suspicion, they shall deliver him to the sheriff. And if they will not obey the arrest, they shall levy hue and cry upon them and follow them with all the town.

> From the Statute of Winchester, a law passed in 1285 by King Edward I to improve methods of catching criminals

Source B

The outdated system of local night-watchmen and parish constables is to be replaced by a centralised and professional police force. I believe it will serve this nation proudly and, indeed, become the envy of the world.

> Robert Peel, the Tory Home Secretary, speaking to the House of Commons on the passing of the Metropolitan Police Act, 1829

Which of the two sources is the more reliable to a historian studying the methods of the enforcing of law and order over time?

[In your answer you should refer to the content and authorship of the sources and use your own knowledge and understanding of the wider historical context.]

(Question from WJEC Eduqas Sample Assessment Materials)

Exam tip

You need to make sure you refer to both the content and the author of each source.

Study the content of Source A and use your knowledge to make a judgement about: the accuracy of what is said or shown in the source; whether the tone of the writing or the style of the picture give a clue as to its reliability. Now study the author of Source A. What information does the attribution give you to make a judgement about reliability? Look at: who wrote/produced it; when it was written/produced; whether the title provides a clue as to its reliability; who the source was aimed at; does the intended audience have an impact upon reliability?

Repeat the same process for Source B.

Conclude with a judgement – which of the two sources is the most reliable and why.

4 Methods of combating crime

Key question

How effective have methods of combating crime been over time?

Communal methods of combatting crime in Saxon and medieval times

REVISED

People in the Saxon and early medieval periods used a system of tithings. This system had several features:

- groups of ten families were entrusted with policing problems like disturbances, fire and wild animals
- their leader was the tithingman who raised the hue and cry to pursue suspected offenders
- ten tithings were grouped into a hundred; the hundredman dealt with more serious crimes.

England was divided up into shires (counties) in the medieval period. The shire reeve (sheriff), a royal official, was responsible for public order in his shire and could raise a posse to capture criminals that had escaped the tithing. Other officials eventually took over some of these jobs.

- In 1326, Justices of the Peace were appointed to assist the sheriffs in controlling the shires. They were usually local landowners who held trials and hearings in manorial and royal courts.
- Parish constables replaced the hundredmen. They had to maintain law and order in communities and report to JPs. The job was unpaid and often time-consuming.
- Watchmen patrolled towns at night and helped protect against robberies, disturbances and fire, reporting directly to the parish constable.

By 1500 this system was fairly consistent all over England and Wales.

> **Revision task**
>
> Make a list of the ways that combatting crime changed in medieval times.
>
> TESTED

The role and effectiveness of JPs and other parish officers

REVISED

The most important law enforcement officer at local level was the Justice of the Peace (JP), who were chosen from local landowners, who commanded obedience through respect not force. Their duties were:

- maintaining law and order – to act as a magistrate and administer justice through the **Petty** and **Quarter Session** courts. They also organised the Parish Constable and the Town Watchman to maintain law and order
- administrating local government – they were responsible for enforcing local laws like licensing and regulating ale houses, checking weights and measures and organising road and bridge repair. They also kept an eye on vagabonds, supervised poor relief and managed **houses of correction**.
- carrying out orders of the Privy Council and Council of the Marches – JPs were expected to ensure that the Acts passed by the Privy Council and the Council of the Marches were enforced and obeyed.

> **Petty Sessions** Local courts at which two or more JPs would sit to deal with minor criminal cases so as not to overwhelm the Quarter Sessions.
>
> **Quarter Sessions** Courts held every three months by JPs.
>
> **House of correction** A prison for beggars who refused to work.

During the Tudor period, the JPs' workload substantially increased, both in the towns, which were expanding, and in the countryside, where they had to deal with the growing problem of vagrancy. They:

- were effective in maintaining law and order at the local level
- performed a vital service in policing and punishing offenders
- were effective in ensuring Acts of Parliament were locally enforced.

The maintenance of law and order depended on community self-policing. The hue and cry still operated. The JP appointed:

- the Parish Constable, from tradesmen or farmers living in the area. They held the unpaid post for one year and were expected to do this job as well as their day job. They did not have a uniform or carry weapons
- the Town Watchman, who patrolled the streets at night and handed over any suspected wrongdoers to the Constable. They did not wear a uniform but carried a bell, a lantern and a staff. They were meant to deter thieves and reassure the townsfolk.

London was rapidly growing. King Charles II created a force of paid nightwatchmen for the capital in 1663, nicknamed the 'Charleys'.

The Constable, Watchman and Charley played an important role in maintaining law and order. However, they were not always the best person to do the job:

- unpaid posts were unpopular among those selected to serve
- few could afford the time to perform their duties properly
- Charleys tended to be old or lazy to perform their duties well.

> **Revision task**
>
> What changed in the way law and order was enforced between medieval times and the end of the seventeenth century? What stayed the same?
>
> TESTED ☐

The establishment and effectiveness of the Bow Street Runners

REVISED ☐

The sharp rise in population levels and the growth of towns and cities during the eighteenth and nineteenth centuries put pressure on the medieval system of using unpaid amateurs to maintain law and order. Some private individuals, known as thief-takers, started acting as unofficial policemen. They captured criminals and claimed the reward money, or negotiated the return of stolen property for a fee. Jonathan Wild (1683–1725), 'Thief-Taker General of Great Britain and Ireland' built up an empire of organised crime; he planned thefts, organised burglaries, and then negotiated the return of the stolen goods. He appeared to 'police' the streets of London.

In 1748, Henry Fielding was appointed Chief Magistrate at Bow Street. In 1751 he published *An Enquiry into the Late Increase of Robbers etc.* He set up a force of six law officers who were paid, full time and well trained. Their motto was 'Quick notice and sudden pursuit'. His brother, John Fielding, continued the work of these 'Runners', enhancing the policing of London's streets:

- In 1763, he secured a government grant of £600 to establish the Bow Street Horse Patrol to deal with highway robbery.
- In 1772, he established a newspaper, *The Quarterly Pursuit*; published four times a year it contained lists of crimes and descriptions of wanted criminals; in 1786 it was renamed *The Public Hue and Cry* and appeared weekly; in the early 1800s it became the *Police Gazette* and it marked the beginnings of a national crime information network.
- In 1792, the Middlesex Justices Act extended the Bow Street scheme by funding seven JPs in other parts of London, each of whom had six

full-time 'Runners' under their command. In 1798, after a campaign by Patrick Colquhoun, the Thames River Police was established. And in 1805, a Horse Patrol of 54 officers armed with swords, truncheons and pistols was set up to patrol the highways around London, nicknamed 'Robin Redbreasts'. By 1829, London had 450 constables and 4,000 watchmen to police a population of 1.5 million. The Runners introduced the idea of 'preventative policing' by attempting to stop crime from being committed, rather than dealing with the consequences of crime.

Peel and the setting up of the Metropolitan Police in 1829

REVISED

In 1829, the Metropolitan Police Act set up a new police force in London under the control of Robert Peel, the Home Secretary. He wanted a force of paid, full-time law officers who would investigate crimes, patrol the streets, prevent crime and apprehend criminals. They were called 'Peelers' or '**Bobbies**' after their founder. The main features of the new force were:

Bobby Nickname for a policeman, after Sir Robert Peel.

- it was run by two Commissioners
- its headquarters were at Scotland Yard in Westminster
- it covered a radius of seven miles, 17 districts each with 144 police constables
- constables had to be able to read and write
- the constable's uniform was a blue jacket, white trousers, a tall white hat; each carried a truncheon and rattle
- constables worked a seven day week, patrolling a set area.

A second Metropolitan Police Act in 1839 extended the area to cover a 15-mile (24 km) radius from Charing Cross. It also saw the River Police and Horse Patrol brought into the Metropolitan Police.

The extension of police forces in the nineteenth centuries

REVISED

Extension of the police force outside London

Municipal Corporations Act (1835)	Allowed borough towns to set up a police force if they wanted to; only a small number had done so by 1837.
Rural Police Act (1839)	Allowed JPs to establish police forces in their county; only a small number had done so by 1856.
County and Borough Police Act (1856)	Made it compulsory for every county to have a police force.

The force developed its own specialist units to help with the detection of crime:

- Detective Branch (1842) – detectives were used to investigate crimes; they dressed in plain clothes. In 1878, this became the Criminal Investigation Department (CID).
- Special Branch (1883) – set up to deal with Irish terrorism, but was expanded to investigating all potential terrorist threats.
- Photography (1850s onwards) – provided visual images of criminals for police forces.
- Fingerprinting (1901) – used to establish unique identity; national register increased the crime detection rate by over 400 per cent.

Developments in policing in the twentieth century

Development of police transport

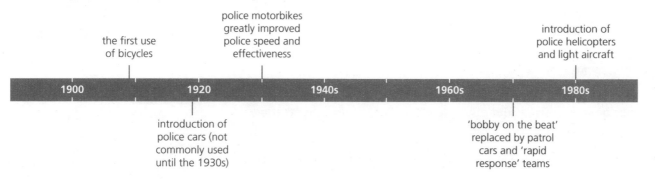

the first use of bicycles

police motorbikes greatly improved police speed and effectiveness

introduction of police helicopters and light aircraft

| 1900 | 1920 | 1940s | 1960s | 1980s |

introduction of police cars (not commonly used until the 1930s)

'bobby on the beat' replaced by patrol cars and 'rapid response' teams

Developments in communications and technology

- Telegraph and radio – first used in 1910; police telephone boxes appeared in the 1920s; the 999 emergency number was available from 1937; two-way radios were used from the 1930s.
- Camera and video technology – in 1901 the first police photographer was employed; police cars and helicopters are now fitted with cameras; the police also make use of **CCTV**.
- Computer technology – the Police National Computer came into use in 1974; it holds databases for fingerprints, **DNA** records, motor vehicle records and missing persons.

CCTV Closed-circuit television used for surveillance.

DNA Present in all living things and provides a unique genetic code or make-up for each individual body.

The specialisation of police services

Specialist unit and year founded	Principal function in the twentieth century
Criminal Investigation Department (CID) (1878)	Plainclothes detectives investigate major crimes such as murders, serious assaults, robberies, fraud and sexual offences.
Flying Squad (1919)	Deals with serious theft; later became the Central Robbery Squad.
Fraud Squad (1946)	Investigates fraud and other economic crimes.
Dog Handling Squad (1946)	Trained officers use dogs to help trace people, property, drugs and explosives.
Anti-Terrorist Branch (1971)	Aims to monitor and prevent terrorist activity.
National Hi-Tech Crime Team (2002)	Deals with serious and organised cybercrime.
Counter Terrorist Command (2006)	Formed from merger of Anti-Terrorist Branch and Special Branch to prevent terrorist-related activity.

Developments in community policing

During the late twentieth century, several initiatives were introduced to help improve police–community relations.

- On the beat – more police officers returned to the beat to provide a visible presence on the streets.
- Neighbourhood Watch Schemes – first introduced in 1982, these have developed into a nationwide membership of 10 million people; they involve organised groups of local people who work with the police to prevent crime in their neighbourhood.

- Police Community Support Officers (PCSOs) – first introduced in 2002, these help deal with anti-social behaviour and minor crime in the hope of making ordinary people feel more secure in their locality.
- Crime Prevention Schemes – these are run by the police and offer advice on personal safety, home and vehicle security and protection against fraud.

Exam practice

Describe the role of a Tudor Justice of the Peace (JP) in combating crime.

(Question from WJEC Eduqas Sample Assessment Materials)

5 Methods of punishment

Key question

How have methods of punishment changed over time?

The harsh nature of punishment in Saxon and medieval times

REVISED

When someone was accused of a crime in Saxon times they faced trial by a jury made up of men from the village. If a local jury could not decide, they turned to trial by ordeal. People believed God would judge guilt or innocence.

- Trial by hot iron – the accused picked up a red-hot weight; if their hand festered they were guilty.
- Trial by hot water – the accused put his hand into boiling water; if their hand festered they were guilty.
- Trial by cold water – the accused was thrown into a pond or river; if they floated they were guilty.
- Trail by blessed bread – if the accused chokes on bread they were given by the priest they were guilty.

The Saxons relied on a system of fines called wergild – compensation paid to the victims of crime or to their families.

Three main types of **corporal punishment** were used in medieval times:

- whipping or **flogging** – used for a variety of offences, like refusing to attend church or stealing goods worth less than a shilling (5p); beggars could be publicly whipped or flogged
- **stocks** and **pillory** – used to punish offenders for minor crimes such as drunkenness, swearing and dishonest trading such as selling underweight goods
- mutilation – punishments for regular offenders, or those committing certain crimes like theft involved physical mutilation – cutting off a hand, an ear or a nose or 'putting out' the eyes. In Tudor times persistent beggars were branded with a hot iron.

Corporal punishment Physical punishment.

Flogging Punishment by beating.

Stocks A wooden frame used as a public punishment with holes for the feet.

Pillory A wooden frame used as a public punishment with holes for the head and hands.

Exam practice answers at **www.hoddereducation.co.uk/myrevisionnotesdownloads**

The use of public punishment up to the nineteenth century

REVISED

Public execution in the sixteenth and seventeenth centuries was a continuation of the punishment administered throughout the medieval period. Crimes punishable by execution included:

● murder, treason, counterfeiting and arson
● some minor crimes like theft of goods valued over a shilling (5p).

During the Tudor period, execution was often the punishment for political and religious crimes.

● Rowland Lee, the President of the Council of Wales and the Marches, had over 5,000 people publicly hanged in an effort to impose law and order between 1534 and 1543.
● Heretics were burned at the stake because it was believed they had rebelled against God, for example Ridley and Latimer, Protestant bishops burned by Mary Tudor.
● Treason was punishable by death, usually by being hung, drawn and quartered. If the person was from a higher social class then they were beheaded. For example, Mary Queen of Scots was found guilty of treason for plotting to kill Queen Elizabeth I and was executed in February 1587.

By 1815, there were 225 **capital crimes** that were punishable by death. The Criminal Code, or 'Bloody' Code as it was more commonly referred to, was criticised for its harshness. Even minor crimes like stealing sheep or rabbits were punishable by death. This meant that juries were often reluctant to convict people as the punishment did not reflect the crime.

> **Capital crime** A crime punishable by the death penalty.

Public executions like those at Tyburn, London, attracted large crowds and were viewed as entertainment but were often the cause of lawlessness. Public execution could make martyrs out of those hanged. A Royal Commission on Capital Punishment was set up in 1864 and recommended an end to public executions. Public executions were stopped in 1868. All hangings had to take place inside prisons.

The use of transportation from the 1770s to the 1860s

REVISED

Transportation was introduced as an alternative to the death penalty. An Act of 1678 allowed **convicts** to be sent to British colonies in North America and the West Indies.

Between 1717 and 1776, over 30,000 prisoners were transported to North America but the outbreak of the American War of Independence ended this. Britain's prisons became overcrowded. **Hulks** were used as emergency prisons. Conditions on board the overcrowded hulks were terrible; at least 25 per cent of the prisoners died from the unclean environment or the outbreaks of violence. Captain Cook's discovery of Australia in 1772 offered an alternative location for convicts.

> **Transportation** Sending convicted criminals overseas for punishment.
>
> **Convict** Someone who is in prison because he or she are guilty of a crime.
>
> **Hulks** Ships used as prisons.

The first fleet of 11 ships carrying 736 convicts arrived at Sydney Cove (Botany Bay) in New South Wales on 26 January 1788. Between 1788 and 1868, 165,000 convicts were transported to Australia – an average of 2,000 convicts a year.

Conditions in the new penal colony were harsh for many convicts. Those who did not conform were sent to the harsher penal settlements like Norfolk Island, working **in chain gangs** at stone-breaking and building roads. Early release was offered as a motive for good behaviour: a conditional pardon could be granted after five years of a sentence, but the person could not return to Britain; a certificate of freedom was granted after the full sentence had been served, allowing the person to return to Britain.

Changing attitudes to punishment, the expense of operating the system and growing resentment from Australia at its use as a dumping ground for criminals resulted in the end of transportation. In 1840, transportation to New South Wales was stopped, in 1852, Tasmania refused to accept any more convicts and Western Australia stopped taking convicts in 1868.

> **Chain gang** A group of prisoners chained together, made to do hard labour.

> **Revision task**
>
> Describe three ways that criminals were punished between 1500 and 1800.
>
> TESTED ☐

The need for prison reform

REVISED ☐

Punishment by imprisonment did not exist in the medieval period. During the Tudor period JPs began to set up houses of correction (**Bridewells**) to reform persistent beggars by putting them to supervised work.

Prison was regarded as a place to hold suspects until they were brought to trial or released. There was no set time for how long suspects could be held. Jailers received no salary and depended on forcing money from prisoners. For many prisoners, conditions were appalling and they were brutally treated. There were 14 prisons in London in the sixteenth century including Newgate (for criminals), The Clink (for religious prisoners) and The King's Bench (for **debtors**).

> **Bridewell** A house of correction, or prison, for persistent beggars.
>
> **Debtor** Someone who owes money to another person.
>
> **Jail fever** Typhus, an infectious disease common in eighteenth-century prisons.
>
> **Solitary confinement** When a prisoner is kept separate from other people.

The dramatic rise in the prison population following the ending of transportation to North America in 1776 caused some people to seek reform of the appalling conditions inside overcrowded prisons. There were several important individuals who campaigned for prison reform.

- In 1776, John Howard, High Sheriff of Bedfordshire, carried out a survey of prisons. He found that prisoners:
  - were forced to stay in prison because they could not pay their fees
  - were not separated by the types of crime they were in prison for;
  - died from disease such as **jail fever**.

  He believed that prisons should reform criminals, clergymen should make regular visits to guide prisoners towards a better life, and prisoners should be kept in **solitary confinement**.

- G.O. Paul had a new jail for the county designed for:
  - security – the building was polygonal (many-sided) to let staff see what was going on, with a 17-foot (5.4 metre) wall around it
  - health – an isolation section checked new prisoners for disease: an exercise yard and good ventilation would keep prisoners healthy
  - separation – there was a jail (for offenders awaiting trial) and a penitentiary (a place for punishment), as well as separate male and female areas.

- Elizabeth Fry was a devout Christian. In 1813, she visited Newgate Prison and was horrified at the conditions, especially for female prisoners. In 1817, she formed the Association for the Improvement of Women Prisoners in Newgate. Female warders, schools for women and their children and work (needlework) for female prisoners were all introduced. She travelled the country and set up Ladies' Prison Committees to carry on her reforms in other prisons. Fry had a big influence on the 1823 Gaols Act, but did not agree with the idea of separation.

A major step in prison reform was the Gaols (pronounced 'jails') Act of 1823. This ordered that JPs visit prisons on a regular basis to inspect conditions, that jailers were to be salaried, prisoners were to follow a reform programme and that all prisoners had to be kept in secure and sanitary accommodation.

Revision task

TESTED

Copy and fill in this table.

Reformer	Contribution to prison reform
John Howard	
G.O. Paul	
Elizabeth Fry	

The silent and separate systems

REVISED

During the Victorian period there were several experiments in prisoners' treatment.

1 The Separate System

Prisoners were:
- kept in individual cells to work, pray and be visited by clergymen
- only left their cells for religious services or exercise; they had to wear masks to take away their identity
- put to work making boots, mats and prison clothes, and sewing mailbags and coal sacks.

By the 1850s, over 50 prisons used the Separate System. The most famous was Pentonville Prison in London, which was built on a radial design with five wings radiating from a central point. Its aim was to give prisoners time to reflect on their mistakes and learn from them.

2 The Silent System

- Prison life was made as unpleasant as possible.
- Prisoners could eat and exercise together.
- Work was boring and pointless as possible, like the **crank**, **shot drill** and the **treadwheel**.

Its aim was to make the prisoners hate the silent system so much they would not re-offend.

Both the separate and silent systems failed to lower the re-offending rate. The high suicide and insanity rates led to further prison reform, which concentrated on harsh punishments; for example, the 1865 Prisons Act imposed strict punishment rather than reform.

> **Crank** Turning a crank handle a set number of times in order to earn food.
>
> **Shot drill** Heavy cannonballs were passed from one to another down a long line of prisoners.
>
> **Treadwheel** A revolving staircase in which prisoners walked for several hours.

Alternative methods used to deal with prisoners in the twentieth century

REVISED

The abolition of corporal and capital punishment in the twentieth century resulted in changes to imprisonment.
- Borstals – set up in 1908 to punish 15- to 21-year-olds. They had very strict rules and were designed for education rather than punishment. Corporal punishment (the **birch**) was abolished in 1962. In 1969, the

> **Birch** A type of cane used for punishment.

minimum age to be sent to Borstal was raised to 17 years. They were abolished in 1982.

- Young Offenders' Institutions – set up in 1988 to reform violent young offenders aged 18 to 21; Secure Training Centres for those up to the age of 17 to prevent re-offending through education and rehabilitation; Juvenile Prisons are for 15- to 18-year-old offenders, focusing on reform.
- Open prisons – started after the Second World War to house non-violent prisoners with a low risk of escaping. Their aim is to resettle prisoners into the community.

Prisons were becoming expensive and overcrowded which made it difficult to reform or rehabilitate offenders. Governments in the later part of the twentieth century have tried different ways to punish offenders without sending them to prison or by reducing their sentence. These include:

- probation– introduced in 1907; the offenders followed a set of orders, kept in touch with their probation officer and reported regularly to the police; from the 1980s they also had to attend courses to discuss issues and get help
- suspended prison sentences – introduced in 1967, the offenders do not go to prison unless they commit another offence during the period of suspension
- parole – introduced in 1967; allowed prisoners to be released before the end of their sentence after their good behaviour in prison; they follow a set of orders like those on probation
- community service – introduced in 1972; offenders do a number of hours of unpaid work to benefit the community, like removing graffiti or rubbish, or doing gardening
- electronic tagging – introduced in the 1990s; offenders are given limits to where and when they can move; they must wear an electronic tag which allows the police to monitor their exact movements.

Revision task

Describe three alternative methods used to deal with prisoners in the twentieth century.

TESTED ☐

Exam practice

Look at the three sources below which show types of punishment over time and answer the question that follows.

Source A

Criminals being punished in the Middle Age

Exam practice answers at **www.hoddereducation.co.uk/myrevisionnotesdownloads**

Source B

A criminal being punished in the seventeenth century

Source C

Criminals being punished in the eighteenth century

Use Sources A, B and C to identify one similarity and one difference in the methods of punishing criminals over time.

(Question from WJEC Eduqas Sample Assessment Materials)

Exam tip

Study the three sources – pick out features that are the same or similar. Pick out points that contrast – which show things that are different. Make sure you refer to both similarity and difference in your answer.

6 Attitudes to crime and punishment

Key question

Why have attitudes to crime and punishment changed over time?

How did the purpose of punishment develop from medieval times?

REVISED

Saxon and medieval punishment had several purposes:

- deterrence – the only way to keep order was to make sure that the people were scared of punishments
- retribution – a kind of revenge as in biblical law ('an eye for an eye')
- keeping order – the authorities were keen to maintain order and avoid unrest.

The Tudor and Stuart period saw little change in how criminals were punished. The increase in the crime rate meant that many more punishments were carried out in public, especially those given to vagabonds who were whipped or flogged through the streets, and to heretics who were burned at the stake.

There would be an element of humiliation for the criminal and the family. For example, those put in the stocks and pillories for drunkenness or swearing were ridiculed by their neighbours and could be pelted with waste and rotten food. Most towns had a gibbet (a wooden post) where the corpses of executed criminals were left as a warning to others.

Public execution continued to be a common feature of punishment in the sixteenth and seventeenth centuries. This was for crimes that the authorities considered to be threatening to the order of society, such as treason, riot, murder, and arson or counterfeiting. Public execution was also used to punish those accused of heresy. The most common form of execution continued to be hanging, which was carried out in public.

Prisons existed during the sixteenth and seventeenth centuries but they were mainly places of detention for holding offenders before other punishments would be carried out. These were often secure rooms or dungeons in castles or fortresses.

The concept of banishment in the eighteenth and twentieth centuries

REVISED

The eighteenth century saw a shift away from brutal punishments to the idea that punishment should fit the seriousness of the crime and that it should aim to help criminals build better lives.

One of the major changes in punishment in the eighteenth century was the introduction of transportation. This was based on the idea of banishing criminals from the country. It was introduced as an alternative to the death penalty. It was first used in 1678 when convicted criminals were sent to work in British colonies in North America and the West Indies. In 1717, an Act laid down a formal system of transportation with

sentences of 7 years, 14 years or life. Convicts would be transported to penal colonies to work. Transportation was introduced for many reasons:
- hanging was the only punishment for crimes like theft, so judges would let offenders off
- building and maintaining enough prisons would be expensive
- workers were needed on the farms and plantations of Britain's overseas empire
- criminals would be reformed by the experience of hard work, which was called the pardon system
- dangerous and undesirable people were removed from the country.

When the American colonies refused to take any more British convicts in 1776, it caused problems as there was no alternative to transportation. One solution was to use hulks, old and rotting ships anchored offshore in rivers as temporary prisons while a new place for transportation was sought. Workers were taken ashore to work but conditions in the hulks were appalling. Captain Cook's discovery of Australia in 1770 provided an alternative destination for transporting convicts. Hulks continued to be used as holding prisons for prisoners awaiting transportation.

The use of prisons to punish and reform in the nineteenth century

The nineteenth century saw the increasing use of prisons because of:
- the gradual abandonment of transportation as Australian penal colonies stopped taking convicts from the 1840s
- the reduction in capital crimes; Home Secretary Sir Robert Peel abolished the death penalty for half of the capital crimes in 1823; only murder and treason were punishable by death by the end of the nineteenth century
- people came to think that punishment should take place inside prisons; 1868 saw an end to public execution
- a belief that most criminals could be reformed given the right punishment, such as the pardon system in transportation.

The pressure to use prison sentences more extensively came from the belief that as well as being used as a deterrent and as retribution, punishment could be focused on rehabilitating (reforming) offenders. Reformer John Howard believed that prisons should be used to reform criminals and that prisoners should be kept mostly in solitary confinement to prevent bad influences. Sir George O. Paul devised a prison which included an exercise yard and had good ventilation, a chapel and workrooms where prisoners were taught to read from religious books.

The 1823 Gaols Act improved security and sanitation and tried to bring some order to the prison system. Two types of prison regimes became common. The basic idea behind each of these was to try and reform the prisoners and encourage them to live better lives. The two methods were the Silent System and the Separate System (see Chapter 4.5).

Neither the Silent System nor the Separate System delivered the results that were expected. The rate of prisoners re-offending did not go down and many prisoners committed suicide or went insane. The government decided to return to deterrence using harsh methods. In 1865, the Penal Servitude Act ruled that all prisoners should experience hard labour (hard, monotonous work), hard fare (eating mainly bread and water) and hard board (sleeping on narrow hard beds).

Revision task

Why were criminals transported in the eighteenth and nineteenth centuries?

TESTED ☐

REVISED ☐

Revision task

Outline how the use of prisons changed in the nineteenth century.

TESTED ☐

Changes in attitudes to punishment in the twentieth century

REVISED

The twentieth century witnessed a debate between contrasting views of punishment:
- Retribution – prisoners should undertake hard labour, be locked up in solitary cells and not have visitors
- Rehabilitation – prisoners should be helped to change their attitudes and behaviour through counselling, education and training.

Dealing with young offenders

Up until the nineteenth century, juveniles were usually treated in the same way as adults. There have been a number of changes to how young offenders are dealt with.
- From the 1850s, Reform Schools were established to separate offenders aged 10–15 from their home environment; in the 1970s they were replaced by Community Homes.
- In 1902, an experimental school to try to reform repeating offenders aged 15–21 was started at Borstal in Kent; focus was on routine, discipline and respecting authority; borstals spread across the UK from 1908; they were abolished in 1982.
- Borstals were replaced by a system of youth custody which was served in Detention Centres or later Young Offenders Institutions. Depending on the seriousness of the offence and their age, young offenders can also be given a custodial sentence at Secure Training Centres or even in Juvenile Prisons.
- As the twenty-first century has dawned, new types of youth punishments have been introduced: ASBOs (Anti-Social Behaviour Orders) were first used in 1999; tagging and curfew orders were introduced in 2003.

The system of dealing with young offenders is still meant to punish by removing liberty, but is also designed to encourage self-respect and self-discipline and develop skills to prepare for employment on release.

Public attitudes turned against inflicting pain as a punishment. Flogging male prisoners was limited in 1914 and was abolished in 1948 (it had been abolished for women in 1820). In 1986 it became illegal to use the cane for punishment in schools.

Abolition of the death sentence

REVISED

Attitudes towards the abolition of capital punishment strengthened during the twentieth century.

Arguments in favour of abolition	Arguments against abolition
<ul><li>An innocent person could be hanged</li><li>It was not a deterrent as most murders happen impulsively</li><li>Even the worst person may be reformed</li><li>The crime rate did not increase in countries which abolished capital punishment</li><li>It can make martyrs of criminals and terrorists</li></ul>	<ul><li>Hanging is the ultimate deterrent</li><li>A dead murderer cannot kill again</li><li>Keeping a murderer in prison is expensive</li><li>It satisfies the victim's family and the public</li></ul>

Attitudes began to shift clearly in the mid twentieth century when there was huge media interest in particular cases which involved use of the death penalty. Each case heightened the call for execution to be abolished as a punishment. The cases involved:

- Timothy Evans (1950) – hanged for murders that he did not commit
- Derek Bentley (1953) – hanged for a murder carried out by his juvenile accomplice
- Ruth Ellis (1955) – hanged for the murder of her lover in circumstances some saw as a 'crime of passion'.

Abolition came as a result of:

- The Homicide Act (1957) – this abolished hanging for all murders except for the murder of a police officer, murder by shooting or murder while resisting arrest
- The Abolition of the Death Penalty Act (1969) – this made all hanging illegal and finally ended capital punishment in the UK.

The last hanging in the UK took place on 13 August 1964.

Attempts to rehabilitate and make restitution

Modern attitudes towards punishment have been more about rehabilitation of offenders and restitution for their crimes.

- Rehabilitation – teaching criminals new skills to prepare them for a return to society, treating their drug or alcohol addiction, providing them with education and counselling.
- Restitution – restorative actions like facing the person who has been wronged, repairing the criminal damage to physical property, or carrying out some form of community service.

Over the previous 60 years various schemes have been introduced to accommodate the process of rehabilitation and restitution.

- Parole was introduced in 1967 as a way to rehabilitate prisoners, releasing them early from prison when they demonstrated that they no longer posed a threat to society.
- Community Orders were introduced in 2003, requiring offenders to attend drug or alcohol treatment programmes, work on community projects, work for charities or repair damage to property and remove graffiti to make offenders understand the effect of their crimes.
- Probation Centres were set up in the 1980s, allowing offenders to discuss issues which result in crime, explore ways to use leisure time in a positive and constructive way and allow probation officers the opportunity to monitor and control the behaviour of offenders.

7 A study of the historic environment connected with changes in crime and punishment in Britain, c.500 to the present day

Please note that you only need to revise this material if you are taking your exam in either 2018 or 2019.

The nominated historic site connected to changes in Crime and punishment in Britain, c.500 to the present day, is the East End of London in the late nineteenth century.

Revision task

Explain why the death penalty was abolished.

TESTED ☐

REVISED ☐

Exam practice

Explain why prisons were reformed in the nineteenth century.

Exam tip

You should aim to give a variety of explained reasons. Try to include specific details such as names, dates, events, developments and consequences. Always support your statements with examples. Remember that you need to provide a judgement, evaluating the importance or significance of the named individual, development or issue.

Key issues

You will need to demonstrate good knowledge and understanding of the key issues of this topic. These are:
- What was life like in the East End of London in the late nineteenth century?
- Why was there so much crime in the East End of London in the late nineteenth century?
- How did policing change in the East End of London in the late nineteenth century?

What was life like in the East End of London in the late nineteenth century?

REVISED

Whitechapel is a district in the East End of London. As the population of London expanded it became an overcrowded slum and a centre for crime. It was the location of the Whitechapel Murders in 1888.

What were living conditions like in the East End?

- In the 1881 census, 1 million people lived in London's East End.
- One-third lived in poverty.
- Houses were divided into apartments so more people could be packed in – cheaper rents but poor conditions.
- The poorest lived in lodging houses, spending one or two nights in a place; beds were used in three eight-hour shifts each day.

Whitechapel was densely populated: 188.6 people lived in each acre. For London as a whole the figure was 45 people per acre. The Booth district of Whitechapel was the eighth most overcrowded in London with 256 people per acre.

- Housing was overcrowded.
- Whole families were crammed into a single room to cook, eat and sleep, sharing beds.
- Rags covered the broken windows in damp, insect-infested rooms which had little ventilation.
- Water came from shared standpipes in the street and sanitation was almost non-existent beyond poorly maintained outside shared lavatories.

The annual death rate in Whitechapel was more than 50 in 1,000. This was double the rest of London. Two out of every ten children died and diseases like tuberculosis, rickets and scarlet fever were very common.

> **Sweatshop** Workshops where people were paid low wages (often only receiving a small sum for each item they finished).
>
> **Workhouse** A building, sometimes like a prison, where people went if they could not afford to feed or house themselves.
>
> **Rookeries** Slum areas of terribly overcrowded and filthy housing.

What opportunities were there for work in the East End?

- Whitechapel residents worked in small, dark, overcrowded and dusty **sweatshops**.
- They were shoe-makers, tailors, labourers in railway construction, slaughterhouse or dock workers.
- Hours were long and wages were low.
- The amount of paid work varied from day to day and many families could not rely on a steady income; without regular pay many turned to crime to avoid the **workhouse**.

Those who were too young, too old or too unwell to work could go to the workhouse. The Whitechapel Workhouse was a last resort. Rules in workhouses were very strict. Families were kept apart. Inmates were expected to earn their bed for the night by doing hard labour.

> ### Revision task
>
> Describe (a) living conditions and (b) working conditions in the East End of London in the late nineteenth century.
>
> TESTED

How did conditions in the East End link to criminal activity?

- Thick fogs caused by moist air from the Thames and coal dust from domestic fireplaces often rolled in.
- The local council showed little interest in lighting streets properly at night until the summer of 1888.
- Poor visibility made it much easier for criminals to go about their business.
- The layout of streets meant criminals could hide from the police in the **rookeries** and use the alleys to watch for victims.

Exam practice answers at **www.hoddereducation.co.uk/myrevisionnotesdownloads**

Why was there so much crime in the East End of London in the late nineteenth century?

There were a number of reasons for the high rate of crime in the East End.

Attacks on Jews
Jewish immigrants spoke **Yiddish** and worked for established Jewish employers in sweatshops. Jewish workers were separate from the wider community and a target for prejudice. There were anti-Semitic attacks on Jews. This created tensions that the police had to spend time dealing with.

'Rookeries' and lodging houses
Narrow streets in rookeries provided places for criminals to operate and hide from the law. Lodging houses attracted criminals, drunkards and prostitutes. Cramped conditions caused tensions and opportunities for petty theft. All the identified victims of Jack the Ripper lived in the heart of the rookery in Spitalfields.

Reasons for the high rate of crime in the East End of London

Criminal gangs
The Bessarabian Tigers and the Odessians demanded protection money from small businesses. People feared speaking out against the gangs. It was difficult for the police to prosecute them.

Prostitution
There were 1,200 prostitutes in Whitechapel. It made women more vulnerable to attack. It was necessary in desperate situations, or when their lives were affected by alcoholism. All of the victims of Jack the Ripper had sold sex in order to pay for lodgings or alcohol, but they had all done other work before they started to work as prostitutes.

Ale-houses and drinking dens
Drinking helped people deal with life in Whitechapel. Drinking made people vulnerable – all the Ripper's victims were probably drunk when attacked. Victims were robbed while drunk. Alcohol caused disagreements to escalate into violence. The high number of pubs in Whitechapel meant alcohol was easily available. They were stop-off points for prostitutes looking for clients and thieves looking for people to steal from.

Was policing ineffective?

- There was a general feeling that crime in London was increasing.
- The reputation of the East End was so bad that policemen would only enter the area in pairs.
- The Metropolitan Police at the time were poorly paid and worked long hours.
- If they were not local, finding their way around the maze-like streets of the East End was difficult.
- Local people were not always keen to co-operate with the police.

There seemed to be a crisis in the police force.

- The detective service had just survived mistaken identity and corruption scandals.
- Two Commissioners had been forced to resign: one after a riot got out of control, the other after accusing the government of being too lenient on protesters.
- The head of the CID (Criminal Investigation Division) had resigned and his replacement was on a holiday in Switzerland.

The *New York Times* newspaper called the London police 'The stupidest detectives in the world'.

> **Yiddish** A language used by Jews in central and eastern Europe.

> ## Revision task
>
> How do the following features explain why there was so much crime in the Whitechapel area in the nineteenth century?
> - Jewish immigrants.
> - Rival gangs.
> - Drinking dens.
> - Rookeries.
> - Problems with policing.
>
> TESTED

How did policing change in the East End of London in the late nineteenth century?

REVISED

The 'beat' constable

- Prevented crime by being an obvious presence.
- Arrested those committing a crime.
- Walked a specific route in a fixed time.
- Was expected to know the pubs, shops, alleyways, yards and squares that led off their beat.
- Sometimes reversed their beat to guard against criminals learning their route.

After a month, a policeman would be moved to another beat to prevent corruption between officers and locals.

What were the Whitechapel murders?

REVISED

Between 31 August and 9 November 1888, five women were murdered in similar and gruesome ways in Whitechapel.

- Mary Nichols (31 August) was found with her throat cut and abdomen cut open.
- Annie Chapman (8 September) was found with her throat cut following strangulation; some intestines had been pulled from her body.
- Elizabeth Stride and Catherine Eddowes (30 September) – Stride's throat was cut but there were no further injuries; Eddowes' face was mutilated and she was disembowelled.
- Mary Kelly (9 November) was found in her room with body parts removed and spread out.

There was a frenzy of coverage in the press, with letters from hoaxers claiming to be the murderer – one signed himself 'Jack the Ripper'. The killer opened the bodies of his victims, taking body parts as 'souvenirs'.

How did the police investigate?

There were no forensic techniques available to help catch the killer. Scientists could not even distinguish different types of blood. Instead they relied on:

- observation – officers made detailed notes about the crime scenes
- autopsy – all the Ripper's victims had autopsies. The police thought that they were looking for a left-handed murderer and the cuts also suggested a measure of skill and basic knowledge of anatomy
- photography – photos were taken of bodies before and after a post-mortem. These were used more to identify the victim rather than to help solve the crime
- sketches – for example, to record Catherine Eddowes' crime scene
- interviews – the police visited houses and businesses in the areas around where the bodies were found and questioned more than 2,000 people
- witness statements – written using only the words of the witness and then read back to them. Errors were corrected by crossing out so that the error should still be seen, after which each page was signed
- following up clues – the police then followed up 300 lines of enquiry and arrested 80 people across London for further investigation and questioning. All these clues and leads came to nothing, but they show how active the police were in tracing them to the end.

The police worked extraordinarily hard and tried a number of ways to capture the killer, though none were successful. There is even evidence that the police improved their use of some techniques as the case went on.

- Plain-clothes and extra officers – 20 more constables to work in plain clothes and 50 constables transferred temporarily to Whitechapel to work on the Ripper case.
- Identity parades – used without success, although they were useful in ruling out suspects such as Jack Pizer or 'Leather Apron', whose nickname was circulated in the press.
- Criminal profiles – this was the first documented use of a criminal profile. These involve using the evidence gathered about the criminal and from the crime scene to work out the type of person that the police should be looking for.

What was the impact of national press coverage?

Newspapers presented the police as utterly useless as they could not catch the Ripper, even though they were making the job of the police even harder.

- Sensational newspaper stories encouraged the 300 hoax letters sent to the press and the police, from men claiming to be the Ripper. These wasted considerable police time.
- Rumours that the newspapers published led to dead ends; suspects like John Pizer ('Leather Apron') went into hiding.
- The press also published unofficial sketches of 'foreign-looking' suspects which increased tensions towards immigrants, especially Jews.
- Journalists had to rely on speaking to people that gathered when the body had been found in order to get a description, so many details and stories weren't true or were exaggerated.
- As newspapers filled with apparent witnesses and descriptions of the murderer it made it seem even more incredible that the police had not caught the killer.

The national press reported the Whitechapel murders in great detail. It revealed the appalling deprivation and poverty of East London slum dwellers. George Bernard Shaw commented that Jack the Ripper had done more to spotlight the terrible conditions in the East End than any social reformer.

Improvements in policing

There were two important advances in policing that came out of this:

- profiling of suspects – to find suspects even when they did not have a description, although criminology did not become a recognised branch of psychiatry until the 1920s
- from the 1890s mug-shots and facial measurements to reconstructed sketches of suspects from descriptions. However, this was not available to the police investigating the Ripper murders.

The idea of using fingerprints had been suggested, but it wasn't until the early years of the twentieth century that they were actually first used in criminal investigations.

Improvements in living conditions

There was now a lot of pressure for the rookeries and lodging houses to be demolished and replaced with better housing.

- The Working Classes Dwellings Act in 1890 placed a new responsibility to house residents who lost their homes to slum clearance programmes.
- The creation of the world's first council housing, the LCC Boundary Estate, which replaced the neglected and crowded streets of the Old Nichol Street Rookery.
- Flower and Dean Street and Dorset Street were demolished and replaced by model dwellings.
- Charitable schemes like the Peabody Trust and the Four Per Cent Industrial Dwellings Company, provided new, cleaner houses for thousands of people

Revision task

How did the Whitechapel murders change policing, and living conditions in the East End of London?

TESTED ☐

How is the East End of London important in showing how crime and punishment changed during the nineteenth century?

The East End of London was very significant in the history of crime and punishment. The criminal activity in the area was a major cause of the spread of new police forces across London from the mid–1850s. The degree of crime in the East End and the amount of attention it got from the press led to improved social conditions. Due to these improvements, the crime rate in areas like the East End of London started to decline by the end of the century.

Exam practice

Describe two main features of the lives of poor people living in the East End of London in the late nineteenth century.

Exam tip

You need to identify and describe two key features. Only include information that is directly relevant. Be specific; avoid generalised comments.

8 A study of the historic environment connected with changes in crime and punishment in Britain, c.500 to the present day

Please note that you only need to revise this material if you are taking your exam in either 2020 or 2021.

The nominated historic site connected to changes in Crime and punishment in Britain, c.500 to the present day, is Botany Bay: the settlement of criminals in New South Wales in the late eighteenth and nineteenth centuries.

Key issues

You will need to demonstrate good knowledge and understanding of the key issues of this topic. These are:
- Why was Botany Bay used as a penal colony?
- What was life like for convicts in Botany Bay?
- How did the treatment of convicts in Botany Bay change over time?

Why was Botany Bay used as a penal colony?

In 1788, the first fleet of 11 ships carrying 736 convicts arrived in Botany Bay. 'Botany Bay' came to include a number of different **penal colonies** in Australia. By the 1830s, 5,000 people a year were sent to penal colonies in Australia.

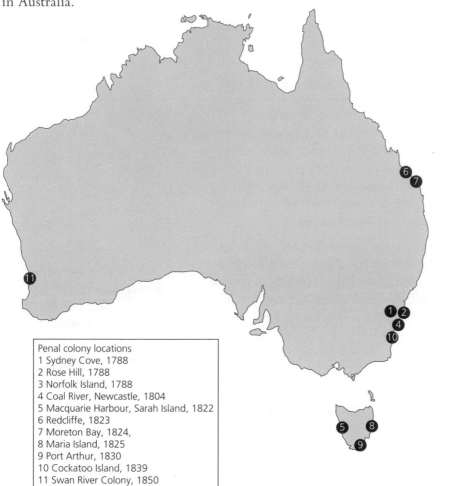

Penal colony locations
1 Sydney Cove, 1788
2 Rose Hill, 1788
3 Norfolk Island, 1788
4 Coal River, Newcastle, 1804
5 Macquarie Harbour, Sarah Island, 1822
6 Redcliffe, 1823
7 Moreton Bay, 1824,
8 Maria Island, 1825
9 Port Arthur, 1830
10 Cockatoo Island, 1839
11 Swan River Colony, 1850

Why were convicts transported to Australia?

Transportation to America had been used as a punishment since the end of the seventeenth century, but in 1776 America declared its independence from Britain. The government needed to find another place to use for transportation. Australia had just been claimed for Britain by Captain Cook.

Transportation was important as:

- Britain did not have enough prisons. 1,000 extra prison places would be needed each year. Most crimes carried the death penalty in the eighteenth century. Judges did not like executing people for minor offences. They tried to imprison people on 'hulks' – old, rotting warships situated on the River Thames. Conditions on the overcrowded and filthy 'hulks' were terrible. Prisoners were kept in irons. Many died of diseases such as dysentery and typhus.
- Convicts could provide the labour needed to build Britain's colony in Australia. The government wanted to re-enforce their claim that Australia was part of the **British Empire**. They hoped to turn it into an important port for trading in the Pacific, as well as for growing flax and timber for the Royal Navy. Convict labour could be used cheaply until immigrant labour arrived to continue what they had started.

> **Penal colony** Settlement used to separate convicted criminals from the general population by placing them in a remote location. countries around the world that were controlled by Britain.
>
> **British Empire** A number of countries around the world that were controlled by Britain.

Convicts were transported to Australia for 7 years, 14 years or a lifetime of hard labour. When their sentence was served, convicts were granted either:

- a conditional pardon which set them free but not to return to Britain
- absolute pardon which gave them the right to return home.

Few convicts returned because they had to pay for their own tickets. Australia offered them opportunities they would not have if they returned home.

What was life like for convicts in Botany Bay?

REVISED

When the 'first fleet' arrived in January 1788, they did not land at Botany Bay because the harbour was not safe enough and there was too little fresh water. They moved further down the coast and landed at Port Jackson (modern Sydney Harbour). Two more convict fleets arrived in 1790 and 1791. The first free settlers arrived in 1793. By the mid-1800s they were also being sent directly to Norfolk Island, Van Diemen's Land (modern-day Tasmania), Port Macquarie and Moreton Bay.

The first colonists had to overcome poisonous and unfamiliar insects and reptiles. Crops did not respond well to the dry conditions. Poor diet led to **scurvy** and virtual starvation. It was only the supply ships from Britain that enabled the colony to continue. However, although farming was tricky, the settlers discovered that the climate was suitable for livestock and especially sheep.

> **Scurvy** A serious and sometimes fatal disease caused by a lack of vitamin C.

How were convicts treated?

- On arrival convicts were registered, asked their place of origin, religion, whether they could read and write and their previous job. They were also physically inspected for any outstanding marks which could be used to identify them should they escape. There were those who, having left a family at home, declared themselves single. It was not unusual for a convict to reinvent a new identity for him/herself.
- After convicts had been formally handed over into the charge of the governor, the prisoners were often segregated, with the most hardened criminals being sent to special prisons or areas. The rest acted as servants to the settlers or carried out hard labour in gangs. They were also assessed to see how healthy they were and what skills they had that could be of use to the colony.
- When the first convicts arrived, work was focused on the basics of survival and shelter: clearing land; cutting trees; forming docks, tracks, bridges and fortifications; and gathering materials for storehouses and workshops, such as logs and rocks.
- Convicts were set fixed amounts of 'public work' each day but could spend the rest of their free time doing paid work for others. This is not as generous as it seems as the money was needed to pay for their accommodation and food. To begin with, they were not closely guarded or confined like they would have been in prison.
- Convicts built their own houses until government buildings like Hyde Park Barracks in Sydney were built. They hunted and fished, gathering vegetables and tea from the bush as the food they were given was not good quality. It was a much better diet than they would have eaten back in Britain and many lived longer because of it. Knives and forks were forbidden so convicts had to eat with their hands.

> **Revision task**
>
> Make a list of the difficulties faced by the early settlers and convicts in Botany Bay.
>
> TESTED

Until 1810, the government handed out civilian clothes to convicts – there was no need for a uniform because nearly everyone in the colony was a convict. As more free settlers moved to Australia and convicts finished their sentences, it was necessary to be able to easily distinguish the convicts. The new uniform consisted of a coarse woollen jacket, a yellow or grey waistcoat, a pair of trousers and long socks, shoes, two cotton or linen shirts, a neckerchief and hat.

Punishment was extremely harsh with floggings and beatings for the most minor offences. By the mid-1830s, only around 6 per cent of the convict population were 'locked up', the majority working for free settlers and the authorities around the nation.

Revision task

Describe what happened to convicts when they arrived in the Botany Bay penal colony.

TESTED ☐

What work did convicts do?

To begin with, all convicts were needed to do the basic building and farming necessary to begin the colony. Later convicts found there was a wider range of work on offer.

- Educated convicts were given the relatively easy work of record-keeping for the convict administration. Those with training in professions like medicine, architecture or building were used to help the colony.
- Those who had little education were used to develop the public facilities of the colonies – roads, causeways, bridges, courthouses and hospitals.
- Convicts who possessed useful skills worked in specialist gangs – boat gangs, shell gangs, shingling gangs and a range of gangs in the lumberyard, dockyard, quarries and gardens.
- Bakers, carpenters, shepherds, etc., were given similar work in Australia.
- Female convicts who had been domestic servants or farm labourers were assigned to households in towns or the countryside.
- Female convicts were useful as wives and mothers. Marriage effectively freed a woman convict.

After the colony was established, convicts still worked for the colonial government but increasingly they were assigned to work for settlers and convicts who had served their sentences. If they were not treated well they could complain to the colonial government who would investigate and punish the settlers if they were found guilty. The non-convict population continued to grow, not only as more and more settlers came to live in Australia but also as convicts completed their sentences and decided to stay.

How were female convicts treated?

Once the colony was established, female convicts who needed additional punishment were imprisoned in 'female factories'. They were prisons and places of work. They were also shelters for female convicts between work assignments and for those who were pregnant or ill. Employers could get a domestic servant there. Settlers could get female farm workers. A free settler or pardoned convict could select a wife from the inmates.

In Parramatta, women were employed in washing, sewing, carding and spinning. Factories were overcrowded, punishment was harsh – cutting hair, iron collars, solitary confinement, reduced rations and hard labour. Their children were sent to orphanages at the age of 4, but they could claim them back when they were released.

How were convicts punished?

If convicts did not follow the rules of the colony they could have their sentences extended or could be sent to work on chain gangs building roads. There were also a series of 'banishment' stations built in remote locations in Port Arthur. They were founded in the 1820s because the British government thought that convict life was not harsh enough. Discipline was severe. If they disobeyed or tried to escape, they were whipped, chained up or even executed.

Convicts were sent to these punishment stations for theft, but also for trying to escape. Some had been re-captured as far away as Britain. Others were sent for mutinous conduct in other colonies or even in the hulks back in Britain. Hard labour such as cutting down trees or mining coal was done in chain gangs. Prisoners were regularly flogged or locked in solitary confinement. If they behaved they were trained to do more skilled work.

'Bolters' tried to escape but few survived very long in the harsh environment of the Australian bushland. They tried to stowaway on ships or wandered back into settlements, starving: 100 lashes was the common sentence for those who attempted escape. Some survived by stealing from settlers and travellers, sometimes even becoming cannibals. Some worked alone, others formed gangs. The authorities tried to hunt them down and bring them back, rewarding Aboriginal peoples for returning convicts to custody.

How did the treatment of convicts in Botany Bay change over time?

REVISED

The penal colony in Australia led to new ideas about prison design and criminal behaviour. Many convicts went on to make good and successful lives as settlers. Some became tradesmen or tried their luck at gold prospecting. Many married and had families.

How did the penal colony experiment with systems of punishment?

From 1840, most new convicts had served part of their sentence in a new British prison like Pentonville. There they were subjected to separate treatment which strictly limited contact between inmates. Separate prisons were also constructed in Australian penal stations like Port Arthur to deal with the behaviour of the 'worst' of the colonial convicts.

They believed corporal punishment only hardened criminals. Extra food was used to reward well-behaved prisoners and reducing rations was a punishment for troublemakers. Prisoners were also hooded and made to stay silent, to allow time for them to reflect on their crimes. Port Arthur was the model for many in the penal reform movement.

How did the treatment of convicts change?

Until the late 1810s, convicts worked under government direction on public works and agriculture. As the colonial population increased in the 1820s and 1830s, discipline was toughened and convicts were isolated from view. Private assignment on distant country estates was the common experience of convicts as settlements spread across the mountains and along the coast. Fewer convicts remained in the towns.

Exam practice answers at **www.hoddereducation.co.uk/myrevisionnotesdownloads**

After 1840, new arrivals were placed in highly regimented probation stations scattered across Australia. Strict routines of work, religious learning and segregation were based on progressive ideas trialled in the new model British prisons. Convicts could only work on private assignment after completing probation.

Why did transportation come to an end?

By the 1830s, people were beginning to criticise the use of transportation as a punishment.

- An enquiry into transportation led by William Molesworth in 1838 reported that transportation should be ended. It compared the lives of convicts to those of slaves.
- Humanitarians argued that conditions on the convict ships and in the penal colony were cruel and inhumane and there were religious objections to the number of children being born outside marriage.
- New model prisons like Pentonville had now been built back in Britain that reflected the idea that punishment should be at least as much psychological as it was physical.
- Transportation had now become more expensive than prison back in Britain.
- Ratepayers complained that they had to support the families of men who were transported.
- Transportation was seen as a 'soft option', as it gave released prisoners the chance to start a new life in Australia.
- Free settlers and businessmen resented having to compete with businesses that could rely on cheap convict labour.
- Australians objected to the 'dumping' of convicts in their country. They wanted Australia to attract entrepreneurs, not the poor.
- The New South Wales gold rush of the 1850s brought thousands of willing migrants to Australia and convict labour was no longer needed.

Transportation to the colony of New South Wales was officially abolished in 1850 and in Van Diemen's Land in 1853. After the 1853 Penal Servitude Act, only long-term transportation was kept. It was finally abolished after another Act in 1857. The last convicts were transported to Western Australia in 1868 when the government stopped funding it.

Exam practice

Explain why the establishment of Botany Bay was a significant change in the punishment of criminals in the late 18th and early 19th centuries.

(Question from WJEC Eduqas Sample Assessment Materials)

Revision task

Explain why transportation came to an end.

TESTED ☐

Exam tip

You should aim to give a variety of explained reasons. Try to include specific details such as names, dates, events, developments and consequences. Always support your statements with examples. Remember that you need to provide a judgement, evaluating the importance or significance of the named individual, development or issue.

Section 5 Changes in health and medicine

1 Causes of illness and disease

Key question

What have been the causes of illness and disease over time?

General causes of illness and disease

REVISED

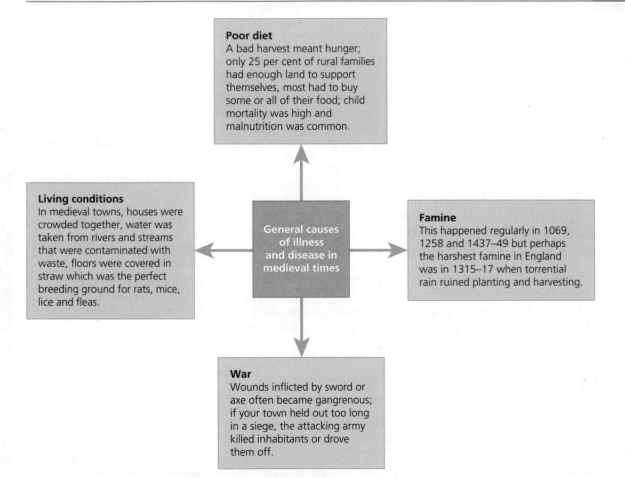

Poor diet
A bad harvest meant hunger; only 25 per cent of rural families had enough land to support themselves, most had to buy some or all of their food; child mortality was high and malnutrition was common.

Living conditions
In medieval towns, houses were crowded together, water was taken from rivers and streams that were contaminated with waste, floors were covered in straw which was the perfect breeding ground for rats, mice, lice and fleas.

General causes of illness and disease in medieval times

Famine
This happened regularly in 1069, 1258 and 1437–49 but perhaps the harshest famine in England was in 1315–17 when torrential rain ruined planting and harvesting.

War
Wounds inflicted by sword or axe often became gangrenous; if your town held out too long in a siege, the attacking army killed inhabitants or drove them off.

Problems in the medieval era

REVISED

Medieval people did not understand the link between disease and germs. Towns remained the breeding grounds for infection and vermin and this resulted in further outbreaks of plague after 1348, one of the last being the Great Plague of London in 1665. There were two types of plague and each spread in different ways.

- Bubonic plague was spread by fleas from black rats. Swellings called buboes appeared in the armpits and the groin, followed by fever, headache and boils all over the body; death occurred within a few days.

- Pneumonic plague was spread by people breathing or coughing germs onto one another; the disease attacked the lungs, causing breathing problems and coughing up blood; death occurred quite quickly.

The Black Death entered Britain in July 1348 through the port of Melcombe on the south coast. By the end of 1349 it had spread across England, Wales and Scotland. Up to 40 per cent of the UK population was killed by the disease. In 1665, around 100,000 people died of the plague in London. That was nearly 25 per cent of the population. Other places were affected too, for example Eyam in Derbyshire (see Chapter 5.7). Most doctors fled, fearing for their lives. Wealthy people fled the city for their country houses until the plague left, but in many cases that just spread the plague to new places.

Revision task

Give three reasons to explain why the Black Death spread so quickly.

TESTED

The effects of industrialisation and the incidence of cholera and typhoid in the nineteenth century

REVISED

The Industrial Revolution resulted in the spread of factories and the growth of industrial towns and cities such as Glasgow, Manchester, Birmingham and Sheffield. Factories needed housing to be built for workers.

Revision task

How did industrialisation lead to an increase in disease?

TESTED

Population	1801	1851	1901
Manchester	75,000	303,000	645,000

Public health problems in industrial towns

- Squalid living conditions meant that outbreaks of disease were common.
- **Tenements** were overcrowded, large families lived in cramped conditions.
- Sewage contaminated drinking water, which led to outbreaks of **cholera** and **typhoid**; people did not know infected water spread cholera germs.

Tenement A large building divided into separate flats.

Cholera An acute intestinal infection which causes severe diarrhoea and stomach cramps, caused by contaminated water or food.

Typhoid A serious infectious disease that produces fever and diarrhoea, caused by dirty water or food.

The spread of bacterial and viral diseases in the twentieth century

REVISED

In the twentieth century, both bacterial and viral diseases continued to spread.

Case study 1: Spanish Flu, 1918–19

In 1918, a **pandemic** spread around the world. Up to 40 million people died from this strain of bird flu. It infected 20 per cent of the world's population. Troop movements at the end of the First World War helped transmit the disease as returning troops spread the disease to the civilian population. Seven million deaths were reported in Spain, so the disease was called Spanish Flu. It could kill a person in a day. Symptoms were headaches, sore throat and loss of appetite. Hospitals could not cope. It killed 280,000 people in the UK.

Pandemic A disease that spreads across a wide geographical area.

Case study 2: The HIV/AIDS threat

In 1981, the first cases of **AIDS** were reported in the USA. The AIDS virus is spread through the blood or body fluids of infected people – via sexual contact or by sharing injection needles with an infected person. In an AIDS sufferer the virus called **HIV** destroys the body's immune system, reducing its defences against attack; the victim does not die of AIDS but of other infections that their body can no longer fight. By 2000 an estimated 30 million people were infected with AIDS, the worst affected area being Africa which accounted for 63 per cent of all those infected. By 2000 over 8 million people had died because of AIDS.

AIDS Acquired Immune Deficiency Syndrome.

HIV Human Immunodeficiency Virus.

Revision task

Explain why Spanish Flu and HIV were dangerous diseases in the twentieth century.

TESTED ☐

Exam practice

Look at the three sources below which show the treatment of illness over time. Use Sources A, B and C to identify one similarity and one difference in the treatment of illness over time.

Source A

Treatment of illness in medieval times

Source B

Treatment of illness in the twentieth century

Exam practice answers at **www.hoddereducation.co.uk/myrevisionnotesdownloads**

Source C

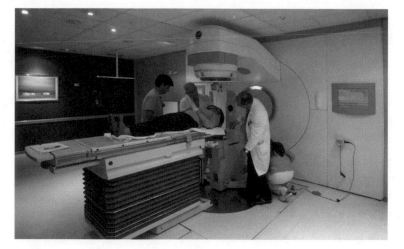

Treatment of illness in the twenty-first century

Exam tip

Study the three sources and pick out features that are the same or similar. Pick out points that contrast – which show things that are different. Make sure you refer to both similarity and difference in your answer.

2 Attempts to prevent illness and disease

Key question

How effective were attempts to prevent illness and disease over time?

Early methods of prevention and disease

REVISED

Medieval people did not understand disease, which is why the ways they tried to limit the spread of the Black Death were often ineffective.

- Travellers had to spend up to a month outside town walls in **quarantine**.
- Infected families were boarded up inside their homes.
- Beggars were paid to take the dead to mass burial pits outside the town walls.
- Some held scented flowers to their noses or held their heads over buckets of dung to avoid bad air (**miasma**).
- Some took potions like **theriac**, believing they would kill off the plague.
- Doctors wore gowns and hoods, with a beak stuffed with herbs or sponges soaked in vinegar.
- **Flagellants** whipped themselves so that God would not punish them with plague.
- Others disinfected their house with herbs and burned the clothes of victims.

Alchemy came to Europe in the late Middle Ages when ancient writings were translated into Latin. It was a mixture of science, philosophy and **mysticism**.

Quarantine Isolation of a person who may be carrying an infectious disease.

Miasma The 'bad air' they believed carried disease.

Theriac An ointment or potion used to treat a poison.

Flagellant A person who whips himself as part of a religious penance.

Alchemy A type of chemistry in the Middle Ages that aimed to find a way to change ordinary metals into gold and a medicine to cure any disease.

Mysticism The belief that there is a hidden meaning to life.

Alchemists tried to use alchemy to make:
● ordinary metal turn into gold
● an 'elixir of life' to make a person immortal or forever youthful.

Elixir A liquid with magical power that would prolong life indefinitely.

In their experiments, alchemists developed new equipment and technology for extracting chemicals, refining liquids and mixing potions. They:
● produced hydrochloric acid, nitric acid, potash and sodium carbonate
● identified the elements arsenic, antimony and bismuth.

By these means they laid the foundation for the development of chemistry as a scientific discipline.

Physicians trained at a university medical school in Italy or Paris and used a variety of methods when treating a patient, including urine chart and 'zodiac man' charts (see page 149). Very few knew much about preventing disease, because they did not know about the causes of disease.

As there were very few qualified doctors in medieval England, most people depended on the local 'wise woman' or soothsayer who had built up knowledge of sickness and disease over several generations and each would have their own favourite methods. They would collect plants and herbs, special stones, anything that might help, and carry this about with them in a willow basket. They would make special charms to protect against evil. Mother Shipton became famous as a fifteenth century soothsayer.

Revision task

Write a brief explanation of each of the following terms:
● Alchemist
● Physician
● Soothsayer.

TESTED ☐

The application of science to the prevention of disease in the late eighteenth and nineteenth centuries

REVISED ☐

During the eighteenth century, modern science began to develop through detailed observation, experimentation and measurement helped by the development of the microscope from its origins in 1590. As part of their training, doctors had to carry out dissections, use microscopes and think scientifically. As a result, the ideas in the medical books of the ancient writers, such as the Theory of the Four Humours (see page 149), were proved wrong or new discoveries were made, such as William Withering's use of the foxglove plant (Digitalis purpura) to treat heart disease.

Smallpox and inoculation

Smallpox was spread by coughing, sneezing and personal contact with an infected person. The disease had a high death rate and there was no cure. Those who survived were often left deaf, blind, brain damaged, physically disabled and disfigured by pock marks. During the eighteenth century, two methods of preventing smallpox were developed – **inoculation** and **vaccination**.

Inoculation involved spreading matter from a smallpox scab onto an open cut on a healthy person's skin, giving them a mild dose of the disease and so protecting them from the full effects of smallpox. Inoculation became popular but it was not completely safe. Some patients died because they contracted a fatal form of the disease.

Inoculation To put a low dose of a disease into the body to help it fight against a more serious attack of the disease.

Vaccination Injecting a harmless form of a disease into a person or animal to prevent them from getting that disease.

Revision task

What is the difference between inoculation and vaccination?

TESTED ☐

Smallpox and vaccination

A safer method of preventing the smallpox disease was developed by Edward Jenner (1749–1823). He experimented to try to find out why milkmaids who had suffered from cowpox never caught smallpox. In 1796 he injected a small boy, James Phipps, with the pus from the sores of a milkmaid with cowpox. Phipps developed cowpox. When he recovered he was given a dose of smallpox but did not develop smallpox. Jenner had found a way of making people immune from a deadly infectious disease without the risks of inoculation; he called this method vaccination (after the Latin word *vacca*, meaning cow).

Since 1977 there have been no recorded cases of smallpox. In 1979, the World Health Organisation (WHO) declared smallpox extinct. In the twentieth century, what were once endemic diseases and childhood killers such as diphtheria (1940), polio (from 1955), whooping cough (1956) and measles (from 1963), have almost been eliminated through vaccination programmes.

The discovery of antibodies and developments in the field of bacteriology

In the nineteenth century, Robert Koch (see page 151) began to identify the specific bacteria that caused specific diseases. This new science was called **bacteriology**. Koch also realised that **antibodies** could help to destroy bacteria and build an immunity against the disease. However, each antibody worked specifically on only one bacteria. If you could introduce a weakened form of the disease into the body when the deadly version of the disease attacked, the body would be able to resist.

Revision task

Why was Edward Jenner an important individual in the development of vaccination?

TESTED ☐

REVISED ☐

Bacteriology The study of bacteria and how to deal with them.

Antibody A natural defence mechanism of the body against germs.

Exam practice

Study the sources below and then answer the question that follows.

Source A

Case 17 James Phipps. I selected a healthy boy, about eight years old. The matter was taken from the [cowpox] sore on the hand of Sarah Nelmes and it was inserted on 14 May 1796 into the boy by two cuts each about half an inch long. On the seventh day he complained of uneasiness, on the ninth he became a little chilly, lost his appetite and had a slight headache and spent the night with some degree of restlessness, but on the following day he was perfectly well. In order to ascertain that the boy was secure from the contagion of the smallpox, he was inoculated with smallpox matter, but no disease followed.

Extract from Dr Edward Jenner's book *An Enquiry into the causes and effects of Variola Vaccinae, known by the name of Cowpox*, which was published in 1798

Source B

Which of the two sources is the more reliable to a historian studying the development of vaccination during the late eighteenth and early nineteenth centuries?

[In your answer you should refer to the content and authorship of the sources and use your own knowledge and understanding of the wider historical context.]

The Cow-Pock — or — the Wonderful Effects of the New Inoculation!

A cartoon drawn by James Gillray which was given the title *The Cowpox – or – the Wonderful Effects of the New Inoculation*. It was published in 1802 and shows people's panic over the new process of vaccination

Exam tip

You need to make sure you refer to both the content and the author of each source.

Study the content of Source A and use your knowledge to make a judgement about: the accuracy of what is said or shown in the source; whether the tone of the writing or the style of the picture give a clue as to its reliability. Now study the author of Source A. What information does the attribution give you to make a judgement about reliability? Look at: who wrote/produced it; when it was written/produced; whether the title provides a clue as to its reliability; who the source was aimed at; does the intended audience have an impact upon reliability.

Repeat the same process for Source B.

Conclude with a judgement – which of the two sources is the most reliable and why?

3 Attempts to treat and cure illness and disease

Key question

How have attempts to treat illness and disease changed over time?

Section 5 Changes in health and medicine

Traditional treatments and remedies common in the medieval era

REVISED

Herbal medicines

Doctors and women healers used herbs to treat everyday illnesses. Herbs were ground with a **pestle and mortar**, liquid was added to make a herbal drink, or the herbs were mixed with plant oil to make an ointment. Books like the *Leech Book of Bald*, an Anglo-Saxon physician in the tenth century, provided many remedies which actually worked. The herb plantain was a common ingredient in the *Leech Book*, being recommended for boils in the ear, dog bites, and other cuts and wounds. The invention of the printing press made it possible for books called **herbals** to be produced, for example William Turner's (c.1510–1568) *A New Herbal* (1551).

Barber surgeons

Barber surgeons were the most common medical practitioners during the Middle Ages, blood-letting, extracting teeth, performing minor surgery, selling medicines and cutting hair. They learnt their trade by being apprenticed to a more experienced colleague. They carried on their trade in a shop open to the street, advertising their services by a red and white pole (white stood for bandages, red for blood). They were limited in what they could do by pain and the danger from blood loss. They had to work quickly, for example, using a hot iron to burn away diseased tissue, seal wounds and stop bleeding.

Blood letting

According to the theory of the **Four Humours** (see page 149), imbalances in the human body caused illnesses. This could only be fixed by blood-letting or purging. Blood-letting was the most common way of treating illness. This was done either by making an incision in a person's vein and draining the blood (a process called 'venesection') or by putting leeches on a person's body and allowing them to suck out the blood. There was also purging which involved pumping a liquid made of herbs, honey and water into the bowels through the rectum, using a tube and a pig's bladder to act as a pump.

James Lister and the use of antiseptics

REVISED

Surgeons needed to work quickly and they operated with few instruments – a sharp knife and a strong saw. Patients suffered extreme pain and the chances of infection were high. During the nineteenth century, two major advances improved surgical methods – the discovery of **anaesthetics** and **antiseptics**.

Pestle and mortar A club-shaped tool (pestle) used for mixing or grinding substances in a bowl (mortar).

Herbals Books describing and listing the medical properties of plants.

Barber surgeons Medieval doctors who performed surgery.

Four Humours Belief that the body was made up of four body fluids and that people became ill when these humours were out of balance.

Anaesthetic A substance or gas that produces unconsciousness before and during surgery.

Antiseptic Chemicals used to destroy bacteria and prevent infection in a wound or cut.

Revision task

Describe the role played by each of the following in the treatment of illness and disease before the eighteenth century:
- herbal remedies
- Barber surgeons
- blood-letting.

TESTED

James Simpson and the development of anaesthetics

James Simpson, Professor of Midwifery at Edinburgh University, carried out experiments using different chemicals before discovering that chloroform could help relieve pain for women during childbirth. He wrote articles about his discovery. Surgeons did not know what dose to give patients and a patient died during an operation in 1848 from an overdose. Its use by Queen Victoria in 1857 as pain relief, during the birth of her eighth child, helped change public opinion. Chloroform improved surgical techniques by allowing operations to proceed with care rather than speed and provided effective pain relief for patients

Joseph Lister and antiseptics

The problem of pain during surgery had been overcome, but the problem of infection remained; for example, almost half of all patients who had leg amputations died from blood poisoning. Joseph Lister worked as Professor of Surgery at several universities. He believed in the 'germ theory' put forward by Pasteur (see page 151) and began experiments to prevent patients from dying from blood poisoning after an operation. Lister used carbolic acid to wash his hands and all his instruments before an operation, to soak bandages before applying them to wounds, to soak silk threads in it before tying up wounds. He reduced the infection rate by doing this. He invented a spray machine so that carbolic acid could be sprayed over a patient's wound during an operation. He published his findings in 1867.

Lister's methods marked a turning point in surgery. The discovery that a bacterium caused septicaemia (blood poisoning) in 1878 helped the acceptance of Lister's ideas. By the 1890s Lister's methods were widely adopted:
- operating theatres were cleaned
- surgical instruments were steam-sterilised
- sterilised rubber gloves were first used.

Revision task

List four reasons to support the view that Joseph Lister deserves to be regarded as 'the father of antiseptic surgery'.

Twentieth century developments

Marie Curie

Marie Curie and her husband were the first to discover and isolate radium and polonium. These radioactive elements played a key role in destroying tissue, opening up a way of treating cancer. Her 1911 Nobel Prize was for discovering a means to measure radiation. She also played a leading role in developing mobile X-ray units during the First World War, which could be used nearer the front line and thus making diagnosis and treatment of injured soldiers quicker and easier. She died in 1934 from diseases brought on by excessive exposure to radiation.

The roles of Fleming, Florey and Chain in antibiotics

In 1928, Alexander Fleming, Professor of Bacteriology at St Mary's, discovered penicillium notatum, a mould that killed bacteria. In

1929, Fleming published a detailed report on the antibiotic powers of penicillin in fighting infection. It took ten years to find a way to mass produce penicillin. Howard Florey and Ernst Chain were experimental scientists at Oxford University. They perfected a method of mass producing penicillin and by 1941 had produced enough penicillin to begin human trials. The Second World War created a high demand for penicillin to treat infected wounds. By 1944 there was enough penicillin to treat all Allied casualties. In 1945, penicillin became available for civilians, while Fleming, Florey and Chain were awarded the Nobel Prize for Medicine for their research into the **antibiotic** 'wonder drug'.

Barnard and transplant surgery

The first human organ to be transplanted was the kidney in the 1950s because it was the easiest organ to remove. Even if the operation failed, the patient could be kept alive by kidney **dialysis**. The development of a heart-lung machine in 1953, which allowed the heartbeat to be stopped so the surgeon had time to work on the inactive heart and 1960s heart by-pass surgery, taking veins from the legs to sew into the heart muscle to restore its blood supply, both made heart transplants possible.

In 1958, Christiaan Barnard created a heart unit in Cape Town, South Africa. In December 1967 he performed the world's first human heart transplant on Louis Washkansky. He survived the operation but lived for only 18 days, dying of pneumonia. Barnard performed ten heart transplants between 1967 and 1973, but rejection of the transplanted organ remained a problem. The development of **immunosuppressive drugs** solved the problem of transplant rejection.

Modern advances in cancer treatment and surgery

REVISED

Cancer is the uncontrolled growth of cells in a part of the human body. Cancerous growths begin because of a change in the DNA of a cell but scientists have not yet found out what causes this change. Secondary cancers occur when cancer cells split off and move into vital organs like the lungs. Cancer can be treated by several processes:
● radiotherapy – attacking the cancer cells with X-rays
● chemotherapy – using chemicals to attack the cancer
● surgery – to remove the cancerous cells by operation.

The fight against cancer includes encouraging prevention by advising regular check-ups, following a healthy lifestyle and avoiding cancer-causing activities such as smoking.

Heart disease is the most common cause of death in the UK, accounting for one in three deaths. Common causes of heart disease are bad diet, smoking, stress, alcohol abuse, being overweight and viruses. The treatment of heart disease can consist of:
● advice about diet and exercise
● use of drugs to steady the pulse, lower blood pressure or reduce cholesterol levels
● surgery to install a pacemaker to regulate the heart rate; by-pass surgery; the insertion of a **stent** to widen an artery; a heart transplant.

Antibiotics A group of drugs used to treat infections caused by bacteria.

Dialysis The process of cleaning or purifying the blood of a person whose kidneys are not working properly.

Immunosuppressive drug A drug that suppresses the body's immune system in order to limit rejection of a transplanted organ.

Stent Short tube of stainless steel mesh.

In recent years, miniaturisation, fibre-optic cables and the use of computers have enabled surgeons to perform keyhole surgery. It involves using an **endoscope**, which includes all the tools needed to perform operations on knee joints, hernias, the gall bladder and the kidneys. Keyhole surgery avoids large incisions and speeds up the recovery process; often patients do not have to stay in hospital overnight. Recent advances in microsurgery have enabled surgeons to re-join nerves and small blood vessels, enabling limbs such as fingers and hands to be re-attached after being severed and restoring feeling.

> **Endoscope** An instrument used to view the inside of the body.

Revision task

TESTED

1 For each of the following diseases, write out two bullet points explaining how they are currently treated:
   a cancer
   b heart disease.
2 What is microsurgery?

Alternative treatments

REVISED

Some people distrust orthodox medicine and there has been a huge increase in interest in what became known as alternative or holistic medicine. Treatments like **hydrotherapy**, **aromatherapy**, **hypnotherapy** and **acupuncture** became popular. They were based on traditional treatments designed to work in harmony with the body, rather than using chemicals against illness.

> **Hydrotherapy** Using water to treat illness.
>
> **Aromatherapy** Using plant material and oils to treat illness.
>
> **Hypnotherapy** Using hypnosis to help patients deal with medical problems.
>
> **Acupuncture** Using needles stuck in the body to deal with medical problems.

Exam practice

Describe the development of methods used to combat the spread of the plague during the Black Death.

Exam tip

You need to identify and describe at least two key features. Only include information that is directly relevant. Be specific; avoid generalised comments.

4 Advances in medical knowledge

Key question

How much progress has been made in medical knowledge over time?

Common medical ideas of the medieval era

REVISED

In the medieval times, physicians used variety of methods when treating a patient, including alchemy (see page 141) and examining a patient's urine. Urine samples were matched against a colour on a urine chart and a written description for that colour; this helped the physician to make a diagnosis.

Astrology

Medieval physicians also used astrology to help treat patients. They believed the movement of the planets affected people's health. Astrology is the study of the planets and how they might influence people's lives. They consulted a book called the *Valemecum*, which contained the signs of the zodiac and 'zodiac man' charts. By consulting the chart and the position of the stars, they could work out which treatments could be used on certain parts of the body at that time.

The theory of the Four Humours

The theory of the Four Humours was developed by ancient Greek and Roman doctors. It said that the body contained four important liquids, called **humours**. If the humours stayed in balance then a person remained healthy. A person became ill when there was too much of one humour and not enough of another. The body got rid of excess humours through sweat, urine and faeces; when this did not happen enough, illness occurred. Treatment involved getting the humours within the body back into balance and might require removing excess liquid by making the patient bleed or vomit.

> **Humours** Four liquids (phlegm, blood, black bile and yellow bile) in the body, that were related to the four seasons and to the four elements (air, fire, earth and water) and believed to cause illness when they became unbalanced.

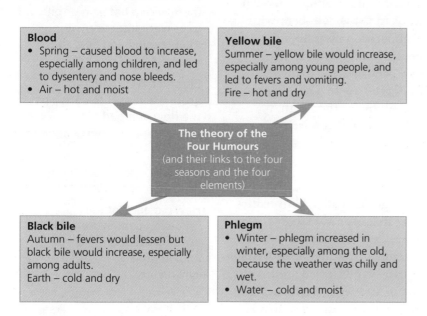

Blood
- Spring – caused blood to increase, especially among children, and led to dysentery and nose bleeds.
- Air – hot and moist

Yellow bile
Summer – yellow bile would increase, especially among young people, and led to fevers and vomiting.
Fire – hot and dry

The theory of the Four Humours (and their links to the four seasons and the four elements)

Black bile
Autumn – fevers would lessen but black bile would increase, especially among adults.
Earth – cold and dry

Phlegm
- Winter – phlegm increased in winter, especially among the old, because the weather was chilly and wet.
- Water – cold and moist

Revision task

TESTED ☐

Copy out the table below and use the information in this section to complete it.

	How physicians used this method to treat patients
Urine chart	
Zodiac chart	
Theory of Four Humours	

The influence of Vesalius, Paré and Harvey on medical knowledge

REVISED

During the sixteenth century there was a rebirth or 'Renaissance' in learning and science. The invention of the mechanical printing press in Germany helped spread new ideas. There were also new scientific inventions like the thermometer and microscope, both of which helped improve medical observation.

Andreas Versalius

Andreas Vesalius was Professor of **Anatomy** at Padua University in Italy. He worked with Renaissance artists dissecting corpses so he could understand human anatomy. In 1543, he published his famous book *The Fabric of the Human Body*, which contained detailed anatomical drawings. His insistence on **dissection** of human, not animal, bodies introduced new scientific methods of enquiry and helped further medical knowledge.

Ambroise Paré

Ambroise Paré was an army surgeon who spent years treating wounded soldiers. Treatment for battlefield wounds was to **cauterise** them with boiling oil and bleeding was stopped after amputation by sealing the arteries with a red-hot iron. Paré experimented and discovered that wounds healed more quickly if covered with bandages and the ends of arteries were tied using silk thread called **ligatures**. In 1562, Paré published his *Five Books of Surgery*. He followed this in 1575 with *The Collected Works of Surgery*, which provided the latest research on amputations, setting fractures and the treatment of wounds.

William Harvey

William Harvey studied medicine in Cambridge and Padua Universities before becoming a doctor and then a lecturer in anatomy. Harvey believed in the importance of observation and experimentation to increase his knowledge. By dissecting live animals to study the movement of the muscles in the heart, Harvey proved that blood flowed around the body and it was carried away from the heart in arteries and returned to the heart in veins; he proved that the heart acted as a pump. In 1628 he published his findings in his book, *An Anatomical Account of the Motion of the Heart and Blood in Animals*.

> **Anatomy** The study of how the human skeleton fits together.
>
> **Dissection** Cutting open and examining the structure of a dead body.
>
> **Cauterise** A method of treating amputated limbs or wounds by burning them with a hot iron or oil to prevent infection, stop the bleeding and seal the wound.
>
> **Ligature** A thread tied around a vessel to constrict the flow of blood.

> **Revision task**
>
> How did each of the following contribute to the advancement of medical knowledge?
> ● Vesalius
> ● Paré
> ● Harvey.
>
> TESTED

Nineteenth-century advances in medical knowledge

REVISED

In the early nineteenth century, doctors believed in the theory of **spontaneous generation** – that poisonous fumes (miasma) given off by decaying material were blown around, causing disease to spread. Improvements in microscopes in the late seventeenth century led to the discovery of **micro-organisms**, but their link to the spread of disease was not made until later in the nineteenth century.

> **Spontaneous generation** The belief that living organisms could arise from non-living matter.

> **Micro-organisms (or microbes)** Tiny single-celled living organisms too small to be seen by the naked eye, such as disease-causing bacteria.

Louis Pasteur and Robert Koch

Pasteur

Louis Pasteur carried out scientific research at several French universities before being appointed Professor of Chemistry at the Sorbonne University in Paris in 1867. His most important research included:

- **pasteurisation** – he discovered that boiling the liquid killed harmful germs. It was soon used to stop milk turning sour, as well as beer, wine and vinegar going bad.
- germ theory – he believed that microbes in the air caused decay so he carried out some experiments. In 1861, Pasteur published his 'germ theory'
- vaccines – in 1879, Pasteur took the germ that caused **chicken cholera** and injected chickens with a weakened form of the disease; it prevented them from catching chicken cholera; he did the same for **anthrax** in 1881 and **rabies** in 1885.

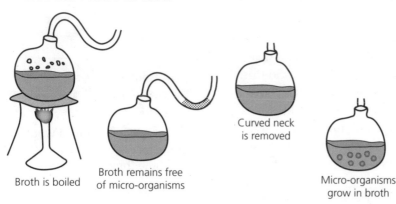

Broth is boiled

Broth remains free of micro-organisms

Curved neck is removed

Micro-organisms grow in broth

> **Pasteurisation** The process of heating liquids to destroy harmful micro-organisms.
>
> **Chicken cholera** An acute infection of the bowels seen in chickens.
>
> **Anthrax** A highly infectious and often fatal disease affecting cattle and sheep.
>
> **Rabies** An acute infectious disease of the nervous system spread by the saliva of infected animals.
>
> **Culture** The experimental growth of micro-organisms in a jelly-like substance.
>
> **Tuberculosis** Often abbreviated to TB, it is a serious infectious disease that affects the lungs.

Koch

Robert Koch was a German doctor who furthered the work of Pasteur. He could link a particular germ or microbe to a particular disease. For example, in 1872 Koch began a study of anthrax and by 1875, by studying the blood of affected and unaffected animals, he had identified the bacterium that caused anthrax. In 1878 he did the same for septicaemia (blood poisoning), staining the microbe purple so it could be seen under a microscope. He also developed a solid **culture** on which to breed colonies of germs and later identified the **tuberculosis** or TB germ and the cholera germ. Koch was a pioneer of the new science of 'bacteriology', proving that a specific germ caused a particular disease. His work caused the German government to set up the Institute of Infectious Diseases in Berlin in 1891. In 1905 he was awarded the Nobel Prize for his research.

> ## Revision task
>
> Test your understanding of this section by writing out brief explanations of each of the following terms:
> - germ theory
> - pasteurisation
> - vaccine
> - bacteriology.
>
> TESTED

The development of scanning techniques in the twentieth century

X-rays

In 1895, Wilhelm Röntgen, Professor of Physics at the University of Würzburg in Germany, discovered **X-rays**. He was experimenting with electro-magnetic cathode rays when he discovered that they would pass through items like paper, wood, rubber and human flesh but not through bone or metal. The first ever X-ray photograph was of the hand of Röntgen's wife, which was published in December 1895. X-rays enabled surgeons to look inside the patient without surgery and marked

> **X-ray** A picture produced by exposing photographic film to X-radiation (made up of X-rays), a form of electro-magnetic radiation; doctors use these images to see the bone structure of parts of the body.

the beginning of non-invasive surgery. X-rays really became important during the First World War, enabling doctors to locate deeply lodged bullets and shrapnel inside the bodies of soldiers.

Ultrasound and MRI scans

The second half of the twentieth century saw the development of a new range of scanning techniques, which transformed doctors' abilities to see inside the body without invasive surgery.

- Ultrasound scanning has developed since the 1950s using high-frequency sound to produce 3D images of the inside of the body.
- First used in 1977, the magnetic resonance imaging (MRI) scanner uses a strong magnetic field and radio waves to create pictures of tissues, organs and features inside the body on a computer.

The discovery of DNA and genetic research in the later twentieth century

REVISED

In the early twentieth century, scientists knew **DNA** existed and that it carried **genetic** information, but they did not know how it did this. It took a series of discoveries over a long period to unravel the genetic secrets of DNA. The Human **Genome** Project was set up to identify the role of each of the 100,000 genes in a human DNA molecule. It was completed in 2003 and provided the complete genetic blueprint of a human being. As a result of the work on DNA, scientists identified that the causes of some illnesses are genetic. Genetic screening and testing has been used for preventing disease. Work continues on gene therapy, using genes from healthy people to cure the sick.

> **DNA** Deoxyribonucleic acid, the molecule that genes are made of.
>
> **Genetics** The study of what genes are, how they work and how they are passed on.
>
> **Genome** Complete set of chromosomes and genes that an individual organism inherits.

Exam practice

Explain why the work of Pasteur and Koch was important in the advancement of medical knowledge during the nineteenth and twentieth centuries.

Exam tip

You should aim to give a variety of explained reasons. Try to include specific details such as names, dates, events, developments and consequences. Always support your statements with examples. Remember that you need to provide a judgement, evaluating the importance or significance of the named individual, development or issue.

Exam practice answers at **www.hoddereducation.co.uk/myrevisionnotesdownloads**

5 Developments in patient care

Key question

How has the care of patients improved over time?

The role of the church and monasteries

REVISED

Medieval monasteries played an important role in caring for the sick. The **infirmary** was a type of hospital ward for sick patients. It was separated from the rest of the monastery to stop infection spreading. In the twelfth century, the Christian Church began setting up hospitals which were run by monks and nuns. They were called 'hospitals' because they offered 'hospitality' by providing shelter to travellers and pilgrims, or a place for the poor and elderly to stay, or a place for lepers to shut themselves away. Only a small number of these hospitals actually cared for the sick. There were no doctors within these hospitals; monks would pray for the souls of the patients while the nuns looked after the welfare of the patients and administered herbal remedies.

> **Infirmary** A hospital or place where sick people are cared for.
>
> **Philanthropist** A person who gives money to help improve the lives of others.

The roles of voluntary charities in patient care after the mid-sixteenth century

REVISED

When Henry VIII ordered the dissolution of the monasteries in the 1530s, it resulted in the closure of many hospitals. Some hospitals were taken on by voluntary charities. In some areas, town or city councils stepped in to take over. For example, in London five major hospitals were endowed with royal funds during the mid-sixteenth century to care for the sick and poor of the capital, such as St. Bartholomew's Hospital serving the poor of the area of West Smithfield and St. Mary Bethleham which concentrated upon looking after the mentally insane.

As the new industrial towns expanded in the eighteenth century there was demand for increased hospital provision. Part of that demand was met through financial donations from new wealthy industrialists. One of these early **philanthropists** was Thomas Guy, a wealthy printer and bookseller who financed the establishment of Guys Hospital in 1724. Eleven new hospitals were founded in London during this period and a further 46 across the country in the growing industrial towns and cities, including Westminster Hospital in London, Addenbrooke's Hospital in Cambridge and the Royal Infirmary Hospitals in Edinburgh and Manchester.

Science and the development of endowed hospitals in the late eighteenth century

The establishment of endowed hospitals marked a turning point in the development of the hospital. They now evolved from being a place to provide basic care of the sick to becoming a centre in which to treat illness and conditions that required surgery. Patients were looked after by nursing helpers who ensured that the patients were washed, kept warm and fed regularly. Nursing sisters were able to treat ill patients with herbal remedies. Simple surgery such as the removal of bladder stones and the setting of broken bones was carried out by physicians. Another function of the hospital was the dispensing of medicines. Treatment was normally free.

Florence Nightingale and the professionalisation of nursing

The quality of nursing in hospitals was generally poor as they lacked training or medical knowledge. Florence Nightingale (1820–1901) was a pioneer in the way she improved standards in hospitals and patient care. Between 1854 and 1856, Britain fought Russia in the Crimean War; on hearing about the poor treatment of British soldiers in the military hospital at Scutari in the Crimea, Nightingale secured funds from the government to send herself there.

She found that there were 1,700 patients in the field hospital, many of whom were suffering from cholera and typhoid, housed in filthy wards. One of her first tasks was to clean the wards. Patients were given a regular wash, clean clothes and had their bedding changed regularly. To prevent the spread of disease, patients were separated according to their illness. These measures had dramatic results.

The influence of Florence Nightingale

On her return to England in 1856, Florence Nightingale began a campaign to reform army medical services; she called for purpose-built hospitals with trained nurses, clean floors, plenty of light and fresh air and better food. In 1859, Nightingale published her *Notes on Nursing*. *The Times* set up a Florence Nightingale fund, which raised £50,000. In 1860, Nightingale used this money to set up training schools for nurses at St Thomas's Hospital and at King's College Hospital in London; the training was based on her principles of patient care. New hospitals like the Royal Liverpool Infirmary were built to her designs. By 1900, nursing had become recognised as a profession.

The impact of the early twentieth century Liberal reforms

During the nineteenth century, governments had traditionally followed a policy of laissez-faire, believing it was not their job to interfere with people's lives unless they really had to. During the early twentieth century, however, attitudes began to change and the Liberal Governments of 1906–14 broke with the past and introduced a series of welfare reforms designed to help people who fell into difficulty through sickness, old age or unemployment. The reforms tackled such areas as the provision of education, the medical inspection of school pupils, free school meals, workers compensation rights and the provision of old age pensions.

Revision task

Describe the role played in patient care by:
- churches and monasteries in medieval times
- voluntary charities in the 16th and 17th centuries
- endowed hospitals in the 18th century.

Revision task

Make a list of reasons why Florence Nightingale is an important figure in the history of medicine.

Exam practice answers at **www.hoddereducation.co.uk/myrevisionnotesdownloads**

The impact of Liberal welfare reforms

In introducing the 1909 Budget, Lloyd George stated: 'This is a war budget ... to wage implacable warfare against poverty and squalidness.' But did these measures have as much impact as he stated they would? Medical inspections were introduced in 1907, but poor families could not afford to pay for necessary treatment. Pensions were introduced for over 70s (the average age of death was around 50), but only if you had worked all your life and could prove you were not a drunkard. The National Insurance scheme only applied if you paid regular contributions, but part of the cause of poverty was irregular employment. And so on.

Among the most significant was the introduction of the National Insurance Act of 1911, which laid down the first steps towards the creation of a welfare state. Chancellor of the Exchequer Lloyd George proposed an insurance scheme which involved workers and their employers making weekly contributions into a central fund which was used to give workers sickness benefit and free medical care from a panel doctor if they became ill. The scheme was restricted to certain trades and occupations and it did not cover families (wives and children), only the insured husbands. Neither did it cover the unemployed, the elderly, the mentally ill or the chronically ill.

The Beveridge Report (1944) and the provision under the NHS after 1946

REVISED

The Beveridge Report of 1942 identified 'disease' as one of the 'Five Evil Giants' facing British society and suggested that it could be addressed through a free national health service.

- Aneurin Bevan, Labour MP for Ebbw Vale, was appointed Minister of Health in 1945. He argued that everybody had the right to medical treatment according to need; having contributed into a weekly health insurance scheme, everybody should be treated the same – rich or poor.
- Bevan faced opposition to his National Health Service Act 1946 from (a) the authorities and voluntary bodies that ran hospitals and (b) the British Medical Association (**BMA**) who complained that doctors would make less money; he overcame this opposition.
- From 28 July 1948 the NHS offered a range of services and care such as prescriptions, hospital treatment, dentists, opticians, vaccinations, maternity care, district nurses, health visitors and ambulances.

> **BMA** British Medical Association, which represents all doctors.

The demand for health care under the new NHS went well beyond original predictions.

- In 1947, doctors issued 7 million prescriptions per month; by 1951 the figure was 19 million per month.
- By 1949, 8.5 million people had received free dental treatment.

For the first time poorer people now had free access to doctors and medical treatment which previously they could not afford. The NHS has played an important part in prevention as well as cure; it has launched health campaigns to warn of the dangers of smoking, drinking alcohol and the lack of a healthy diet. The NHS has had a huge impact on improving the nation's health.

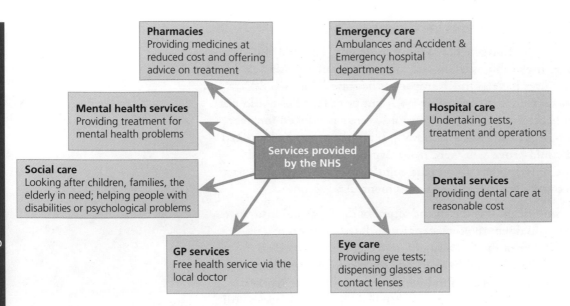

Pharmacies
Providing medicines at reduced cost and offering advice on treatment

Emergency care
Ambulances and Accident & Emergency hospital departments

Mental health services
Providing treatment for mental health problems

Hospital care
Undertaking tests, treatment and operations

Services provided by the NHS

Social care
Looking after children, families, the elderly in need; helping people with disabilities or psychological problems

Dental services
Providing dental care at reasonable cost

GP services
Free health service via the local doctor

Eye care
Providing eye tests; dispensing glasses and contact lenses

Exam practice

Outline how the methods of caring for patients have improved between c.500 and the present day.

Exam tip

Make sure your answer covers three historical time periods – the medieval, early modern and modern eras. Include specific factual detail such as names, dates, key methods/developments. Start a new paragraph for each time period. Aim to write roughly equal amounts for each time period. Make regular links to the question, evaluating the degree of progress, change or improvement. Check your spelling, punctuation and grammar for accuracy.

Revision task

1 Give three reasons why the National Health Service Act was passed in 1946.
2 Describe five services provided by the NHS today.

TESTED

6 Developments in public health and welfare

Key question

How effective were attempts to improve public health and welfare over time?

Public health and hygiene from the medieval period to the sixteenth and seventeenth centuries

REVISED

In medieval times, mortality rates were higher in the towns and cities than in the countryside. People lived closer together, alongside their animals and their filth (see Chapter 5.1). There were several attempts to improve public health in the sixteenth century:

● Henry VII passed a law forbidding slaughterhouses within cities or towns.
● Henry VIII passed an Act of Parliament giving towns and cities the power to impose a tax in order to build sewers.

Exam practice answers at **www.hoddereducation.co.uk/myrevisionnotesdownloads**

Towns and cities were growing so fast it was impossible to keep them clean. London was not a healthy place to live. There were outbreaks of the plague in 1563 (when 17,000 people were said to have died in London), 1575, 1584, 1589, 1603, 1636, 1647, and of course the biggest outbreak of all in 1665. After the Great Fire of London in 1666, an Act of Parliament was passed to limit fire destruction by making streets wider and by insisting houses were built of stone with tile or slate roofs. Some historians argue that the rebuilding of London after the fire made it a healthier place.

Revision task

Make a list of sixteenth and seventeenth century attempts to improve the health of towns.

TESTED

The impact of industrialisation on public health in the nineteenth century

REVISED

At the start of the nineteenth century, local authorities and central government were not interested in public health. They believed it was not their job to interfere in the building of houses, the planning of towns, the collection of refuse or the provision for piped drinking water or sewage disposal. Serious outbreaks of cholera in 1832 and 1849 forced the government to begin investigating living conditions in the rapidly expanding industrial towns.

The work of Edwin Chadwick

Edwin Chadwick was appointed a **Poor Law** Commissioner in 1832. He witnessed the dreadful living conditions in the industrial towns. He believed in the 'miasma theory' (see page 141) but was convinced that there was a link between poor health and bad living conditions. In 1838, he appointed three doctors to investigate housing conditions in East London. In 1839, the government asked Chadwick to head a Royal Commission to enquire into the living conditions of working people.

Poor Law Laws relating to how local authorities should give welfare support to the poor.

In 1842, Chadwick published his *Report on the Sanitary Conditions of the Labouring Population of Great Britain*. This report recommended Parliament should pass and enforce laws to make drainage and sanitation effective, paying for them from local rates and increases in rents. Local authorities should be made responsible for improving drainage, collecting refuse and improving water supplies. His report shocked people but the government was still not quite ready to act.

The 1848 Public Health Act

A Public Health Act was passed in 1848 which set up a Board of Health run by three commissioners; they had the power to set up local boards of health in areas with high death rates. Towns could volunteer to set up their own local health board; 182 towns had done so by 1854. The cholera epidemic of 1848–49 helped to generate interest in public health reform. However, the Public Health Act of 1848 did not force local authorities to act, it only recommended. Also it had no authority in London. In 1854, the government closed down the Board of Health.

More improvements in public health

There were some improvements in this period:

- In 1859, Joseph Bazalgette (1819–1891) was appointed to oversee the building of London's new sewage system; this dumped the capital's sewage downstream, away from the city.
- Parliament passed a Sanitary Act in 1866, which forced local authorities to construct sewers.
- The Public Health Act of 1875 made it compulsory for local authorities to lay sewers, drains and pavements.
- The Artisans' Dwellings Act of 1875 gave councils the power to take over and clear whole slum districts.

Revision task

TESTED

1 Construct a mind map or spider diagram which identifies the unhealthy living conditions in nineteenth-century industrial towns and cities in Britain.
2 What did Edwin Chadwick do to improve public health?
3 Copy and complete this table for years 1848, 1866 and 1875.

Year	Act of Parliament	What it did to improve public health

Efforts to improve housing and pollution in the twentieth century

REVISED

Various attempts were made during the twentieth century to improve housing conditions in industrial towns and cities.

- In 1918, the Prime Minister, David Lloyd George, promised to clear away slum housing and replace it with 'homes fit for heroes'.
- The Housing Act of 1919 gave grants to local councils to build homes, so estates of council houses were built all over the country.
- There was mass demolition of back-to-back housing in the 1920s, although it continued to exist until the 1960s.
- The Beveridge Report of 1942 identified 'squalor' as one of the 'Five Evil Giants' facing British society that had to be tackled after the war and could be done by building 'more and better homes'.
- After the Second World War there was a housing shortage so grants were given to local councils to build new homes and charge low rents; 1.25 million new homes were built by 1951.
- During the 1960s many inner-city slums were cleared and replaced by high-rise blocks of flats.

By the mid-twentieth century, the air quality in many industrial towns and cities was heavily polluted. London experienced frequent bouts of **smog**. In December 1952 the 'Great Smog' fell over London; it was so thick it stopped trains, cars and public events. Over 4,000 people died of respiratory illness. It resulted in the Clean Air Act, which was passed in 1956 to introduce smokeless zones in cities, encouraging the use of cleaner coals, electricity and gas for heating. It also tried to relocate power stations away from cities.

> **Smog** A mixture of smoke, fog and chemical fumes which occurs in some busy industrial cities.

Revision task

1 What was back-to-back housing?
2 How did the First and Second World Wars help to bring about improvements in housing?
3 How did the Clean Air Act of 1956 improve air quality?

TESTED

Exam practice answers at **www.hoddereducation.co.uk/myrevisionnotesdownloads**

Local and national government attempts to improve public health and welfare in the twenty-first century

In the twenty-first century, governments have put more and more effort into health education to persuade people to live healthier lifestyles. For example, if people stopped smoking this would save the NHS millions of pounds each year. Some people argue it is better to spend money on prevention than having to spend money on curing diseases that could be prevented.

'Walking for health' is a fitness drive to encourage people to take more exercise, to walk 10,000 steps a day, at a moderate to fast pace. 'Be Active' is Birmingham City Council's scheme to provide free leisure services to its residents. A third of the local population have got involved since the project was launched in 2008. For every £1 spent on the scheme, £23 is estimated to have been recouped in health benefits.

The 'Five A Day' campaign is an attempt to get people to eat more fruit and vegetables. It has been proven that eating more fruit and vegetables reduces your risk of heart disease and cancer. *The Eatwell Guide*, issued in March 2016, is typical of National Government campaigns. It depicts a healthy, balanced diet, which includes eating at least five portions of a variety of fruit and vegetables every day.

Exam practice

Explain why it would be so difficult to improve public health in the new industrial cities of the nineteenth century.

Exam tip

You should aim to give a variety of explained reasons. Try to include specific details such as names, dates, events, developments and consequences. Always support your statements with examples. Remember that you need to provide a judgement, evaluating the importance or significance of the named individual, development or issue.

7 A study of the historic environment connected with changes in health and medicine in Britain, c.500 to the present day: The village of Eyam during the Great Plague

Please note that you only need to revise this material if you are taking your exam in either 2018 or 2019.

Key issues

You will need to demonstrate good knowledge and understanding of the key issues of this topic. These are:
- What impact did the arrival of plague in 1665 have on Eyam?
- How did the villagers of Eyam attempt to combat the plague?
- What were the consequences of the plague in Eyam?

What impact did the arrival of plague in 1665 have on Eyam?

The last major **epidemic** of the plague to occur in England was in 1665–66. London was the largest centre of population in the country and plague deaths first began to be reported in the spring of 1665. People who had money, including King Charles II and his family, fled the capital to their estates in the countryside. Poor people had no option but to stay and face the full force of the epidemic. The authorities tried to contain the epidemic but did little to stop the spread of the plague and during the hot weeks of the summer months thousands died. The Great Fire of 1666 helped to cleanse the city of the disease.

> **Epidemic** A rapidly spreading disease.

The Great Plague spread to other urban and rural areas as people moved around. These included the larger settlements of Newcastle and Southampton, as well as small villages such as Eyam. Eyam is a small village in Derbyshire which lies between the larger settlements of Buxton and Chesterfield and is just north of Bakewell in the Peak District. Most of the population were farmers while some were employed in the nearby lead mines. In 1665 the population of Eyam stood at around 800 people.

> The plague reached Eyam in late August 1665 in a parcel of cloth sent from London to the village tailor, Alexander Hadfield.

↓

> Hadfield's assistant George Viccars spread the cloth by the fire to dry. It was infested with rat fleas. He was dead a few days later.

↓

> In two months more people had died than in the previous decade.

↓

> The rich fled the village. About 50 individuals left, including the Sheldons, a gentry family.

↓

> Winter slowed the spread of the disease as the rat population declined.

↓

> The following spring, the rat population increased and there was an increase in the number of humans catching the plague.

↓

> By November 1666 there was only a single plague death recorded.

Causes and treatment of plague

Bubonic plague was spread by fleas from black rats. When a person was infected by being bitten by a flea carrying the plague bacillus germ, large swellings called buboes appeared in the armpits and the groin. This was followed by a high fever and severe headache and soon afterwards by the appearance of boils all over the body. Death occurred within a few days.

Nobody at this time understood the cause of the Great Plague and there were numerous theories:

- it was sent by God as a punishment for being sinful. People sought divine forgiveness through prayer and by repenting their sins in the hope this would spare them from catching the plague
- it was caused by bad air which was often referred to as miasma
- it was spread by cats and dogs.

Medical treatment was quite primitive and tended to rely upon herbal remedies, nostrums and charms:

- carrying sweet smelling flowers or pomanders stuffed with herbs and spices
- smoking tobacco
- windows and doors were closed
- rosemary and incense were burned
- poultices were commonly used to burst the lump or bubo
- taking possets, a mixture of boiled milk, ale and bread.

Revision task

Describe three causes and three treatments of the plague, according to people in the seventeenth century.

TESTED ☐

How did the villagers of Eyam attempt to combat the plague?

REVISED ☐

What is unique about events in Eyam is that the villagers themselves took decisive steps to try to prevent the spread of the disease beyond the immediate village and its neighbouring farms.

The Rev. William Mompesson had worked in the village for a year. His predecessor, the Rev. Thomas Stanley, was a Puritan who had been dismissed from his post for refusing to take the Oath of Conformity and for refusing to use the new Book of Common Prayer. They set up a quarantine zone, a circle half a mile from the village centre, to confine the disease to Eyam and stop it spreading to neighbouring towns, villages and farms.

Villagers were banned from leaving and travellers could not enter. There were notices and boundary stones to mark the border. No one tried to break the quarantine line, even as the infection peaked during the summer of 1666. Some of the villagers wanted to go to the nearby city of Sheffield but Mompesson persuaded them not to. Their sacrifice probably saved many lives in the towns of northern England.

Villagers agreed a three-point plan:

1 Plague victims were buried as quickly as possible near to their homes rather than in the village cemetery to reduce the risk of the disease spreading from corpses awaiting burial.
2 The church was locked until the epidemic was over; all religious services were held in the open air to avoid the risk of the disease spreading.
3 The quarantine (see above).

Villagers were supplied with food and other essentials from surrounding villages. The boundary stones served as dropping off points for supplies of food, medicine and other goods. To pay for the supplies, the villagers left money in water troughs filled with vinegar to kill off the disease. The disease did not spread beyond Eyam to the neighbouring villages of Bakewell, Fulwood and beyond.

Had villagers been allowed to leave, their lives may well have been saved, but they would have risked spreading the disease to neighbouring settlements, a risk they chose to avoid. The plague killed 260 inhabitants out of a population of 800. The percentage of the population of Eyam that died was exceptionally higher than the percentage of those who died of plague in London in 1665: 76 families were affected by the plague, some paying a very heavy price.

What were the consequences of the plague in Eyam?

REVISED

By Christmas of 1666, the plague had died out and life slowly began to return to normal. The village had lost one-third of its inhabitants. When the quarantine was lifted, those who had originally fled began to return home. In an attempt to prevent further outbreaks of the plague a 'great burning' was organised. There was a belief that these items held the plague 'seeds' and therefore had to be destroyed.

Quarantine had proved to be effective as there were no deaths outside the parish and nowhere else in Derbyshire was afflicted by the plague. However, the visit of the Great Plague did have a long-term demographic effect:

- a sharp fall in population immediately after 1666, followed by a sharp rise between 1667 and 1670 due to the return of people who had fled the village in 1665–66
- the mortality rate in Eyam in 1665–66 was extremely high. It had a ratio of epidemic to average burials of 10.2
- the number of baptisms entered a period of sharp decline after 1666 as there were few adults of child-bearing age
- farms were left empty, key businesses and trades were left unfilled; some of the vacancies took many years to fill.

> **Revision task**
>
> Make a list of ways in which the villagers of Eyam tried to stop the plague from spreading.
>
> TESTED

The quarantine is a unique example of community action by a few people to save the greater number of people in an area. In the longer term, doctors and medical staff were able to learn from actions taken at Eyam.

- Doctors realised that the use of an enforced quarantine zone could prevent the spread of disease; farmers still use this to limit the spread of diseases such as foot and mouth.
- By the nineteenth century, patients in hospitals with infectious diseases were isolated in particular wards, as is done today to contain norovirus.
- Doctors also became aware that the risk of contamination could be limited by paying for food by dropping coins into pots of vinegar or water to prevent spreading infection.
- Quick disposal of infected bodies limited the risk of spreading the disease, as has been done in Africa to deal with the Ebola epidemic recently.
- At Eyam, contaminated items were burned which eventually led to the sterilisation of equipment and medical clothing.

Revision task

Make a list of the ways that Eyam was affected by the plague.

TESTED ☐

Exam practice

Describe two main consequences of the visit of the Great Plague to Eyam in 1665–66.

Exam tip

You need to identify and describe two key features. Only include information that is directly relevant. Be specific; avoid generalised comments.

8 A study of the historic environment connected with changes in health and medicine in Britain, c.500 to the present day: The British sector of the Western Front, 1914–1918 and the treatment and care of the wounded

Please note that you only need to revise this material if you are taking your exam in 2020 or 2021.

Key issues

You will need to demonstrate good knowledge and understanding of the key issues of this topic. These are:
- What caused the wounds to British soldiers fighting on the Western Front?
- How were wounded British soldiers on the Western Front treated?
- How did medical treatment change as a result of the treatment of British soldiers on the Western Front?

What caused the wounds to British soldiers fighting on the Western Front?

REVISED

In the late summer of 1914, war broke out in Europe and spread to become a World War. It caused death and injury to armed personnel on a scale never seen before in human history.

● Conventional warfare – before 1914, field guns were used to weaken and tear holes in the enemy lines. The infantry, assisted by the cavalry, then moved forward to attack.

● Trench warfare – by the end of 1914, both sides were forced to dig in and oppose each other across a narrow stretch of No Man's land, with each side attempting to wear down the other.

The Western Front stretched from the English Channel coast on Belgium to the French border with Switzerland, a distance of around 430 miles (700 kilometres) where the Allied armies of Britain, France and Belgium (together with the USA from 1917) faced the Kaiser's army of Imperial Germany.

Trenches were dug very quickly as temporary shelter for the troops. As the war dragged, trenches became more permanent.

The front line-the firing line-the trench neareast the enemy.

Traverses protected soldiers from shell blasts and stopped the enemy moving quickly along trenches.

Command trench 10 to 20 metres behind the firing line.

Communication trenches linked the firing line with the command support and reserve trench.

The support line-200 to 500 metres behind the firing line.

The reserve line troops who could mount a counter- attack if the enemy entered the front line.

Latrines behind the trenches or at the end of the communication trench.

A section of the french system on the Western Front.

Exam practice answers at **www.hoddereducation.co.uk/myrevisionnotesdownloads**

Trenches were very difficult to capture since the trench system consisted of at least three lines of defence. They were connected to each other by communication trenches. Trenches were usually zig-zagged so that if the enemy captured a section they could not fire down its length or if a shell landed in the trench it would not blow away all the soldiers right down the trench line. Barbed wire, artillery and machine guns made it extremely difficult for the enemy to break through the trench system and any attack would result in high numbers of dead and injured soldiers.

Generals on both sides hoped to wear down the enemy with regular attacks across No Man's Land. Casualties were very high because:
- machine guns could mow down charging soldiers
- gas was first used in 1915
- artillery could kill and injure hundreds of soldiers during a bombardment
- barbed wire, lack of cover and shell craters, often filled with water, made soldiers easy targets for enemy snipers and machine gunners.

The effect of weapons used in the First World War

During the course of the war over 22 million men were wounded, either physically or psychologically. Medical services found themselves facing casualties with severe wounds and injuries received from a variety of weapons:
- Rifles – these fired bullets with a pointed tip, designed to go deeper into the body from a longer distance, breaking major bones and piercing vital organs.
- Machine guns – these were capable of firing up to 500 rounds per minute and they could have a devastating impact against advancing soldiers attempting to cross No Man's land.
- Artillery – the British developed the howitzer guns which could fire powerful shells a distance of over 12 miles; such shells were the cause of over half of all injuries sustained by soldiers at the front; jagged fragments of the iron casing and the steel balls inside could tear off a limb and shatter bones.
- Gas – first used by the German Army in April 1915, chlorine gas caused choking due to the gas stripping away the linings of the lungs, causing the victims to drown from water produced in their own lungs; phosgene gas caused spasms and vomiting followed by their lungs filling up with a yellow liquid; mustard gas burned the skin and eyes.

Illness and disease on the Western Front

Soldiers also experienced outbreaks of illness and disease at the front:
- Bullet and shell fragments carried other material such as pieces of muddy clothing and soil deep into the body which often led to infection like gangrene, causing wounds to swell up.
- Trench fever (pyrexia) was spread by lice which lived in the seams of clothing and in blankets and caused headaches, shivering and pains in the bones and joints which could last for days, making soldiers unfit to fight.
- Trench foot was a fungal infection caused by constant immersion of feet in water, leaving them numb, swollen, blistered and turning them blue from the restriction of blood flow; it could lead to gangrene and even amputation.

- Frostbite, which was caused by exposure to extreme cold, damaged the skin and sometimes muscle tissue. It cut off circulation, usually to the hands and feet, causing fingers, toes and sometimes feet to have to be amputated.
- Body lice, which lived in the uniforms of soldiers and on the skin, lived off the blood of their hosts and their bites caused intense itching which could lead to blisters, which could become infected.

Beyond the wounds and illness there was psychological damage. Many soldiers suffered from 'shell shock' – anxiety, nervous tics and severe nightmares. Initial treatment was to keep the men at the front and give them rest, food and talks to calm them down. If the condition showed no signs of improvement they were sent to hospital.

Revision task

Make a list of the dangers and problems facing soldiers in the trenches on the Western Front.

TESTED ☐

How were wounded British soldiers on the Western Front treated?

REVISED ☐

Stretcher bearers recovered men from the battlefield and carried them, often under fire, to the nearest trench's Regimental Aid Post to receive emergency treatment with bandages and morphine.

Casualty Clearing Stations were based in either wooden huts or tents with operating theatres, mobile X-ray machines and a ward to accommodate around 50 men; they divided the wounded into three groups: 1) less severely wounded, to be put on trains and sent to a base hospital; 2) those in need of a life-saving operation such as an amputation of a badly damaged limb or the cleaning and sewing up of wounds; 3) those beyond medical help who were sent to the 'moribund ward' to be made comfortable in their final hours.

How wounded British soldiers were treated on the Western Front.

Dressing Stations behind the front lines operated a system of triage which involved making an initial assessment of the wounded, sorting them into groups depending upon the severity of the wound; serious cases were passed on to Casualty Clearing Stations by motorised or horse-drawn ambulances.

Base hospitals were a civilian hospital or a converted building near railways so patients could be moved quickly; they contained operating theatres, X-ray machines and laboratories for the identification of infections; from here those patients who had a wound which was not severe but bad enough to get them sent back home to Blighty (England) for further treatment and recovery were put on hospital trains heading for the port, or were sent to a recovery ward before being sent back to the front.

All medical personnel in 1914 belonged to the RAMC – Royal Army Medical Corps. It consisted of all ranks ranging from doctors to ambulance drivers and stretcher bearers.

At the start of the war the only nurses allowed to treat soldiers were the well-trained Queen Alexandra's nurses. By 1918 they had been joined by volunteer nurses who belonged to the VAD (Voluntary Aid Detachment) and were mainly middle- and upper-class women who had never previously had a job but who now felt the need to nurse the wounded at the front.

How did medical treatment change as a result of the treatment of British soldiers on the Western Front?

The war saw the development of new types of weapons which caused death and injury on a scale not seen in any previous wars. This demanded changes in the way medical staff dealt with and treated soldiers wounded and injured during battle.

- Many soldiers in the trenches died from **typhus** or **tetanus**; from 1915 troops were vaccinated against typhus and tetanus and this reduced the death rate; vaccination became routine in the post-war years.
- Many wounded soldiers had limbs amputated to stop the spread of gangrene; there were considerable advances in the development of artificial limbs and moving joints.
- Some soldiers experienced terrible wounds caused by bullet and shell damage, especially to the face; Harold Gillies, a British army surgeon, developed plastic surgery at the Queen's Hospital in Kent to treat facial injuries by rebuilding noses with bits of bone taken from a rib, or grafting skin from one part of the body to another.
- The huge number of head and brain injuries pushed surgeons to develop surgical techniques, particularly brain surgery helped by blood transfusions and X-rays to locate metal fragments located inside the head; American surgeon Harvey Cushing invented a surgical magnet to extract bullets from head wounds.

> **Revision task**
>
> Make a simple timeline to show the different stages in treating the wounded on the Western Front.
>
> TESTED

REVISED

> **Typhus** A disease transferred by bites from infected fleas (also known as 'jail fever').
>
> **Tetanus** A disease that infects open wounds (also known as 'lock jaw').

> **Revision task**
>
> How did these First World War developments improve medicine?
> - the Thomas splint
> - aseptic surgery
> - blood transfusions
>
> TESTED

The First World War was a catalyst for medical improvement:

- Thomas Splint – an invention in 1916 by the Welsh surgeon Hugh Owen Thomas had a dramatic impact, causing the death rate from leg fractures to reduce from 80 to 20 per cent; the 'Thomas splint' was designed to stabilise the fracture, putting the leg lengthways to stop the bones grinding against each other which reduced blood loss, infection and amputations; its basic design is still in use today.

- Aseptic surgery – surgeons used chemicals such as carbolic acid and hydrogen peroxide to kill bacteria already in wounds; by cutting away infected tissue and soaking the wound with saline solution, infections were reduced.

- Blood transfusions – in 1900, Karl Landsteiner discovered that blood could be grouped into four types and that each patient needs blood from someone of the same blood group and that only some blood groups could be mixed together safely; blood transfusions were given on the Western Front, especially at Casualty Clearing Stations; Richard Lewisohn discovered that sodium citrate could be added to blood to stop it clotting; Geoffrey Keynes developed a portable refrigeration machine that could store blood to enable transfusions to be carried out more easily.

- Portable X-Rays – X-rays could help to save lives by allowing for the speedy location of bullets, shrapnel and tiny fragments of metal in the body of wounded soldier, enabling surgeons to locate them; Marie Currie gave up her work to develop a portable X-ray machine; by 1916 most Casualty Clearing Stations and hospitals had X-ray equipment and they became standard equipment in post-war hospitals.

Exam practice

Explain how the environment of the Western Front during the First World War was significant in bringing about change in the methods used to combat illness and disease during the twentieth century.

Exam tip

You should aim to give a variety of explained reasons. Try to include specific details such as names, dates, events, developments and consequences. Always support your statements with examples. Remember that you need to provide a judgement, evaluating the importance or significance of the named individual, development or issue.